# Hallowed walls

# Hallowed walls
## church architecture of Upper Canada

By Marion MacRae in continuing
consultation with Anthony Adamson
who wrote the Postlude and made
the drawings. Photographs, except
where noted, by Page Toles.

Clarke, Irwin & Company Limited, Toronto, Vancouver

© 1975 by Clarke, Irwin & Company Limited
ISBN 0-7720-1029-4

1  2  3  4  5  RCS  79  78  77  76  75
Printed in Canada

In memory of
Hazel Ross Carlyle MacRae

# *Prelude*

While the field survey of pre-Confederation domestic architecture in Ontario (which produced *The Ancestral Roof*) was under way, it became all too evident that the churches of that period were also endangered. The team, after pausing briefly to catch up with their own lives, therefore undertook a similar survey of Ontario's early places of worship.

The land now called Ontario has harboured the idea of worship almost as long as any place in the world. Pictographs, earth-sculptures and place names like Manitoulin chart the passage of early Ontarian belief. Seventeenth-century missions passed like shadows over the land; a few places of worship remain from the eighteenth century, but the story of such buildings in Ontario is largely a nineteenth-century one.

The northern drainage basin of the Great Lakes and the Upper St. Lawrence, spasmodically occupied by a shifting Amerindian population for centuries, did not begin to be surveyed systematically for settlement until after 1783. The destitute displaced North Americans who came into the area after the American Revolution, and the hopeful hordes of Europeans who followed, required the sustaining force of strong religious conviction if they were to survive the long years of toil, privation and epidemic implicit in a pioneer existence. They had such faith and they built for it, places of worship which were temples of the spirit, social centres of the growing communities and, all too frequently, the only buildings in which they could afford the luxury of beautiful space. It would be an irreparable mistake to let buildings which played so vital a role in the social history of the province disappear without record or comment.

Many people have done much to record and preserve the stories of individual churches through the publication of monographs or by inclusion in county or community histories. But there has not yet been a book on the churches of Ontario, although several have been written on the churches of Quebec.

The present study was carried out over a period of six years. It began with intensive field research in which existing structures were examined and recorded and local documentation and oral tradition checked. Public collections and church archives were searched for further material on surviving buildings and in the interests of both continuity and comparison, for the evidence provided by buildings which had been destroyed.

The field of study had to be extended to the parent countries from which Ontario's early settlers came, in order to trace the origins of vernacular style and lingering archaic liturgical practices which affected church planning. Churches and customs of worship were considered in Quebec, the Maritimes, the United Kingdom, the

United States, the Republic of Ireland, the Netherlands, Switzerland, Denmark, Norway and Sweden, as well as temples and religious sites in the Valley of Mexico and Yucatan.

Although neither of the collaborators aspires to nicety of discernment in matters theological, a working knowledge of the belief, dogma and practice of the major faiths prevalent in nineteenth-century Ontario had to be acquired. For only thus could the architectural aspirations of the clergy and their congregations be understood and the problems confronting the architects and builders of the time realized.

Throughout the ten chapters which constitute the bulk of this work, each religious group was considered to be correct, infallible, and irrefutable in belief and practice while its buildings were being discussed. When the work of another group came under review, it in turn was similarly treated.

All major religious denominations which were present in pre-Confederation Ontario and which still possess places of worship from that period were studied. The reader is, however, respectfully asked to remember that it was the inhospitable nature of the Precambrian Shield which dictated that the majority of churches built in Ontario before 1880 are to be found in the southern part of the province.

The reader is also asked to bear in mind that few churches were completed within a single year and that the dates available may refer to the year of planning, of the laying of the cornerstone or of the dedication; and that churches which have been altered many times may be discussed under the period of major alteration.

Every effort has been made to identify the designers, builders and craftsmen who produced the churches of Upper Canada and Canada West. Their names, and as much pertinent information as possible about them, have been inserted into the text or the captions of relevant photographs and drawings. Unfortunately, many of the craftsmen seem to have left no recoverable information for posterity; consequently some attributions have been made which appear reasonable on the basis of structural or stylistic evidence. However, if evidence to the contrary exists, it is to be hoped that those in possession of it will make it available, either through publication or by depositing the documents in the Public Archives of Ontario. This is particularly desirable when the manuscript material consists of architects' and builders' drawings, plans and office journals or account books.

The co-authors and the photographer wish to thank all those clergymen, churchwardens, secretaries, caretakers and parishioners who have unlocked church doors, carried step-ladders, located electrical outlets, and borne cheerfully with structural and local archival research.

Anthony Adamson and I are indebted to the archivists and librarians in charge of public collections and those who have denominational documents in their keeping. Of the many persons to whose knowledge and kindness we are so deeply indebted special thanks are due to Margaret Angus, Reverend R.E. Brossel, Elizabeth Cook, William Dendy, R. Alan Douglas, Reverend E.J. Lajeunesse, Reverend Glenn Lucas, Reverend Douglas S. MacKay, Dorothy McClure, Mrs. I.C. MacNaughton, Shirley Moriss, Reverend Bryen Price, Anthony Rees, Douglas Scott Richardson, B. Napier Simpson, Jr., Peter John Stokes, Allan Sudden, Reverend Stanley Vance, Margaret Van Every, Arthur Wallace, and Ian E. Wilson.

Sustaining support of a more material nature has been thankfully received from several sources. We are indebted to Proteus Limited for indemnifying the major costs of the field survey, the photography and the drawings. I am most grateful to the Ontario College of Art for granting me leave of absence in the 1972-73 academic year in which to complete the research and, in consultation with my colleague, to write the bulk of the manuscript. I am infinitely indebted to the Canada Council for a major grant under the Canadian Horizons Program which sustained life during that time.

MARION MACRAE

*Toronto*
*1 July 1975*

# Contents

# I
# *Amerindian*

*And some there be which have no memorial.*
*Ecclesiasticus* XLV: *9*

The earliest structure in Ontario known to have been designed for purposes of worship is an earth sculpture. That venerable monument, a serpent mound, lies curled in gentle undulations on a bluff above the calm waters of Rice Lake. It has lain there, flecked in endless renewal by the light and shade of seventeen centuries. The pines and oaks decayed and grew again. The Serpent, as became a powerful water-god, was made of sterner stuff; he endured, though the repeated assaults of pioneer agriculture wrought havoc with his head and tail (I-1). This was doubly tragic, for the Serpent Mound was built by very early Amerindian farmers. Planters from the south, they brought corn, squash and tobacco with them. And when the gardens were growing well, they built, from the familiar earth, an effigy of their principal deity.

The Rice Lake Serpent Mound was a vernacular expression, the most northerly example of the remarkable religious architecture of pre-Columbian America. The nearest monument of consequence, at the time, was the Great Serpent Mound on the Ohio (I-2), but spectacular serpent temple sites lay far to the south, increasing in brilliance from the lower Mississippi to the valley of Mexico.

The Aztecs of Mexico called the great serpent Quetzalcoatl; the Maya knew him as Kukulcan—names which were still in use when the Spanish reached Middle America. The Ontarian Serpent cannot be presented formally to his admirers because his name has been forgotten. His authority was challenged and his name suppressed some time during the thirteenth century—long before Europeans arrived on the scene. (Both French and English were far away and typically employed when the Great Serpent lost his hold on the Great Lakes region. The French were embarking on their last Crusade; the English were assembling for their first parliament.)

The rule of the Great Serpent was disputed by Iroquoian Amerindians, the Ho-de-no-sau-nee, the People of the Longhouse, who believed that an abstract supreme spirit, the Giver of Power, controlled the universe, with all its attendant lesser spirits. In pursuance of their belief, the Longhouse People demoted the Great Serpent to demon status before destroying him. It was in this guise that the Serpent entered the legends of the Algonkians. Among them he became a malevolent water-spirit, pursued from refuge to refuge by opposing thunder-spirits who splintered with lightning every tree he hid beneath. In desperation the Serpent crawled into the Niagara River, and was promptly pushed over the Falls. Driven deeper and ever deeper into the rock at its base, he lashed the river into a whirling cauldron in his death-struggle.

The Ho-de-no-sau-nee were not given to grandiose architectural enterprises. They cleared land for gardens and established

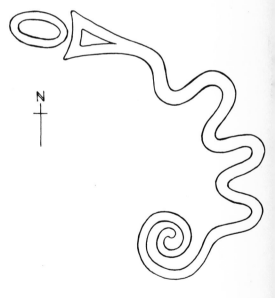

*I-2: The Great Serpent Mound, Marietta, Ohio (above) and the lesser Serpent Mound, Rice Lake, Ontario (I-1 opposite), two durable reminders of human need for structured worship.*

villages of communal longhouses grouped about a somewhat larger councilhouse, which often was simply the longhouse of the chief sachem, or civil leader. As a people they were divided into a number of distinct nations which, in historic times, occupied well-defined territories spreading over vast tracts of the Eastern Woodlands—an estimated sixty thousand people in over two million square miles. They were a vigorous, imaginative people who shared a common agricultural economy, a common language, and a complex neo-monotheistic religious philosophy expressed in satisfying ritual. Their social organization was based on a matrilineal clan system within a tribal and national framework.

Unfortunately the Ho-de-no-sau-nee were not exempt from that pitfall of all tribal systems, the blood feud, and by the middle of the fifteenth century the Iroquoian peoples were following a warpath of revenge towards racial suicide. Then, about 1450, Deganawidah, a prophet-statesman of the Hurons, called a halt to the disastrous progress. Deganawidah envisioned a confederation, the League of the Great Tree of Peace, in which all Iroquoian people would be united around a central council. The vision of Deganawidah was codified and implemented by a great Mohawk thinker, the legendary Hiawatha. Unfortunately for the peace of the St. Lawrence and the Great Lakes, the Hurons did not see fit to join the league. Initially only the Mohawks, Oneidas, Onondagas, Cayugas, and Senecas became members. They were later joined by the Tuscororas from the Allegheny area. But the Hurons continued to stand aloof, eventually forming, with the Tobacco and Neutral peoples, an alliance of their own, the Wendet.

The subsequent role—brilliant, tragic, always difficult—played by the League of the Great Tree of Peace in the political and military history of North America has been examined in a considerable body of literature. It is pertinent here only in so far as it

*I-3: Iroquoian longhouse as described by Champlain.*

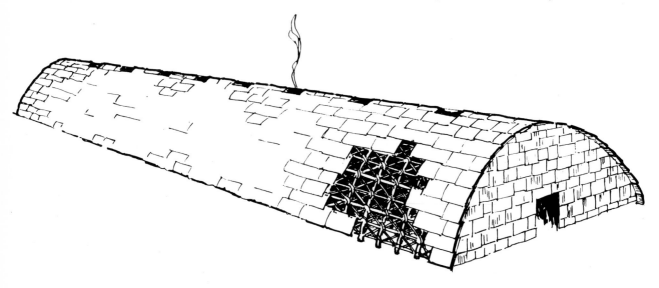

affected the social and religious life of all the Longhouse peoples and the consequent development and location of their places of worship.

According to the French explorer, Samuel de Champlain, a typical Huron longhouse was one hundred and eighty feet long and thirty-six feet wide (I-3). It was, he said, like an arbour covered with bark. There were platforms along both sides of a wide central aisle, down the length of which were spaced some twelve fires, with corresponding smoke holes in the roof above them. The structure itself was built up on a skeletal framework of parabolic arches made from light poles lashed together. The cladding was composed of overlapping sheets of thick elm bark. The description applied equally well to the longhouses of the League tribes.

Each village had a council longhouse which was used at regular intervals for religious festivals. In it the wide platforms were often replaced by more adaptable forms of seating of a less permanent character.

Each day of every festival began with a devotional service of thanksgiving in the council longhouse, during which a litany of thanks to the spirits of all created beings was recited. It reached its crescendo in thanks and praise to the Giver of Power, for continual guidance and blessing. Special religious ceremonies peculiar to the day and/or the season were enacted, followed by a feast for all. The secondary session in the afternoon was usually less formal in character.

Religious festivals came under the surveillance of Faith Keepers—selected persons with a rigorous training in memorizing and declamation, whose duty it was to recite the prayers and beliefs to the people at the morning services. Children received their names before the assembled company at either the Midwinter festival or the Green Corn festival of late summer. One day of the Midwinter festival bore a name which could be literally translated as "the boiling of the babies." This caused some confusion in the minds of some early French explorers who did not comprehend that the term "boiling" referred to the food prepared for the sponsors of the infants.

French explorers had stumbled on Canada lying innocently athwart their path when they were looking for something else. By 1639 it had been well established that there was great deal of it and that they could not get around it by sea. With a practical shrug they had settled down to trade where they could and colonize where they must.

Hard on the heels of the hearty, hedonistic traders came a company of vastly different Frenchmen. Brave, devout and intolerant, as only the truly idealistic can be, the Society of Jesus marched in to win Huronia for their God. For ten years they preached and prayed and exhorted, with some success and many

*I-4: Section through Iroquoian longhouse showing storage and sleeping platform.*

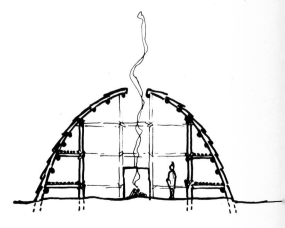

reversals. They set up a number of resident missions (I-5), and of these Fort Ste Marie on the Isiaragui (the Wye River, near the present town of Midland) was the centre and the chief. It was of some size, for at its peak it had a population of at least sixty Frenchmen and several hundred Hurons. The ceremonial religious needs of the community demanded both a church for public worship and a chapel private to the Jesuit priesthood.

The dimensions of the mission buildings reported to the General of the Order in Rome at the time have since been verified by archaeological examination of the site. The church was seventy feet long, twenty-seven feet wide, and had an entrance doorway six feet in width. The chapel was thirty-one feet by forty-eight feet. Both buildings were framed of heavy upright cedar posts. The walls between them were made from double rows of planked timber packed with clay and fieldstone. The roofs were shingled in Iroquoian style with lapped elm bark.

Fort Ste Marie was planned by Father Lalemant. The church and chapel were built under his direction according to the designs of the resident master-builder, Charles Boivin, who had come to New France from Rouen before 1635. Boivin was resident builder at Fort Ste Marie for nine years, and went with the fathers to Christian Island when Ste Marie had to be dismantled. In the decade following his work in Huronia, Charles Boivin designed a church at Trois Rivières and a chapel for the Ursulines. During his first year at Ste Marie he had as his assistant Guillaume Couture. Couture too had been trained in Rouen where his father was a cabinet-maker. The church and chapel which they produced must have been gracefully proportioned and enriched with some ornament.

The church and chapel have been restored in accordance with the twentieth-century concept of rustic simplicity (I-6) which seems to be strangely puritan even for so remote an outpost of the Jesuits, the order which built the first truly Baroque churches of Counter-Reformation Europe. Especially so as it was recorded in the *Jesuit Relations* that the fathers had a painting of the Crucifixion in their chapel and a statue of the Blessed Virgin that was pronounced beautiful by a sophisticated French visitor. The tabernacle on their altar was adorned with seven angels and in front of it stood an elaborate reliquary cross. Their credenza was supplied with Venetian glass cruets. All these precious objects were bundled up and removed to Christian Island and thence to Quebec in the eventual withdrawal. Only broken glass from the

*I-5: Ste Marie aux Hurons,*
*a brave attempt to bridge*
*mutual misunderstanding.*

chapel windows, embedded in the rubble, was left to hint at former graciousness.

For ten years Ste Marie had been poised, a tiny island France, on the great bay of Lake Huron. When it finally succumbed, it fell victim not to the League tribes (who merely seized the opportunity to mop up the rear-guard) but to political manoeuvering and social change. Huronia was already dwindling from a populous trading area to a frightened fringe when Ste Marie was built. The Jesuits who toiled earnestly and selflessly to bring salvation and healing, as they knew them, to the Indians, came into a situation hopelessly beyond their power to remedy. Every boat which preceded them from Europe had unintentionally brought in germs of diseases new to North America—measles, smallpox, tuberculosis and the common cold. Years before, Samuel de Champlain had fired the imagination of the Jesuits with tales of thirty thousand Hurons waiting to be saved. Three hundred accompanied the retreating priests from Christian Island to Quebec.

Another small remnant of the great Huron nation, the unconverted, melted away into the forest. Some of them journeyed westward with the fragments of the Neutral and Tobacco people

*I-6: The reconstructed chapel, a cautious pine platitude super-imposed on the old footings.*

to become historically confused as the Wyandots. Others at last went to shelter under the Pine Tree of Peace, becoming in name, as in language, Iroquois. And so, for another century The People scattered over the Great Lakes region worshipped the Giver of Power in the Old Way.

The years that lay between 1649 and 1784 were crowded with the tumultuous genesis of Canada and the United States. Europeans immigrating to North America in search of freedom of thought, of worship, of government, brought all their hereditary feuds with them. They squabbled up and down the fair new land, snatching time to implore the Deity to espouse their several causes and to confound their enemies—who were, presumably, His worshippers also. Generous piety did not, of course, vanish from the earth. It contrived to be exercised sporadically, in the gaps—as it were—between the territorial struggles, the wars, the rebellions, and the revolutions.

No church or garrison chapel from this period has survived in Ontario. The citizens of Kingston petitioned in vain in 1826 to retain the early buildings in their city; the fragments of St. François and Fort Frontenac were obliterated, as were those of Fort Rouillé at the Toronto Carrying-Place and the installations at Matchedache.

The signatories of the Treaty of Paris bisected North America horizontally in 1783. The warm, arable southern portion was retained by the triumphant Thirteen Colonies – the new United States. The colder northern half was conceded to the British who were at that time far more interested in the fate of India. The British Governor-in-Chief at Quebec, Frederick Haldimand, a trilingual Swiss, was left to cope with the unhappy flotsam of war as best he might. After a vast deal of correspondence—of frantic requests and slow, stately replies – it was decided to settle a large number of the displaced loyal colonists and Indians up-river from Montreal and thence along the northern shores of the Great Lakes to the Detroit River.

As they moved into their new land, both groups tended to settle in denominational clusters, drawn together by the simple need to worship in a familiar pattern. They congregated about a clergyman or, since clergymen were very rare phenomena, around a nucleus of thoughtful, reverent laymen. To live at all was to struggle against every conceivable obstacle, but mere existence was not enough. Somehow that extra ounce of energy had to be found. The will to work beyond exhaustion, the determination to keep the mind and soul alive, could only be buttressed by a strong faith.

For a time that faith was matched by a vast tolerance. Adam delved and Eve span on the narrow margin of security provided by mutual, unquestioning assistance. The early denominational clusters were never totally homogeneous, nor did they attempt ex-

*I-7: Mohawk Chapel, Brantford, first phase, 1785.*

clusive settlement, yet for quite a long time they were remarkably harmonious.

The earliest house of worship still standing in Ontario, which was built for the refugees, is St. Paul's Church of England, Brantford (since 1906 a Chapel Royal, Her Majesty's Chapel of the Mohawks). It was framed with exemplary—nay, unexampled —promptitude, by order of Governor Haldimand; when completed for use, in 1785, it was still within the confines of the vast territory of Quebec (I-7).

It was right, just—and unusual—that this structure should have precedence in Upper Canadian church-building. These People of the Longhouse had been twice dispossessed. Encroaching European settlement had earlier forced them from Lake Champlain to the Mohawk; now a conflict of loyalties had separated them from their land and their kindred in the pitiless choice imposed by civil war. The majority of the Seneca had chosen to remain neutral during the Revolution. A portion of each of the other five nations was in agreement with this attitude, and remained on their land in New York. Those members of the League who wished to continue to live under the rule of Great Britain migrated to Canada. Some, who had been converted to Roman Catholicism, joined the old colony of Praying Indians at Caughnawaga near Montreal or its western outpost at St. Regis on the Upper St. Lawrence. The principal band—both the followers of the Old Way and the Anglican converts from Fort Hunter on the Mohawk—moved inland. Some settled on the Bay of Quinte, on land selected by their chief, John Deseryonteo; others travelled on to Niagara, built a village near the fort, and petitioned the Governor for a church and a school. They were sent instead a consignment of prayer books and the unwelcome news that, as the fort had been ceded to the United States, they must move again.

Their leader, Joseph Brant, worked tirelessly until he had secured lands which were comparable to those the band had lost. Furthermore, the lands were on a river whose majestic sweep to Lake Erie was strangely like the course of the familiar Mohawk. French explorers had, in their practical, graphic way, called the waterway the Big River, the Grand, and after an abortive attempt by the first Governor to anglicize it improbably as the Ouse, the Grand it has remained. The band settled along its banks, and at the best fording place established their village. Here was the councilhouse and here would be the church, sited on the water, the first building to be seen on the upstream approach and hence an important landmark on the river.

In 1787, William Claus, Deputy Superintendent of Indian Affairs, reported to his superior, Evan Nepean: "Captain Brant at his Departure from hence requested me to represent to you that as Government was graciously disposed to encourage their Settlements in religious as well as in other Matters he could wish to have in his new church such Ornaments as were over the altar in the Church of Fort Hunter in the Mohawk River sent there by Her Majesty Queen Anne of Glorious Memory by the first Indian Missry part of them was lost or destroyed by the Americans during the rebelln. The ornaments consisted of 2 Tables painted black wrote upon in gold letters The Lord's Prayer, the Creed and Ten Commandmts, a purple altar or pulpit cloath with the usual embroydery in Gold and a Communion Service of solid plate; the two latter Articles were saved by the missionary having them at his house among his Effects. But their having since the peace found two Settlements as above mentioned and his Brant's settlement having no Claim on the ornaments which belonged to Fort Hunter; His church *which was built at the expense of the government* was entirely destitute of Such Ornaments. And therefore would be extremely happy to have it decently ornamented . . . ."

In 1788 Reverend John Stuart of Kingston, formerly missionary at Fort Hunter, reported to the Society for the Propagation of the Gospel, on his return from visiting the Six Nations of the League: "The Mohawk village is pleasantly situated on a small but deep river – the church about sixty feet in length and forty-five in breadth, built with squared logs and boarded on the outside and painted – with a handsome steeple bell, a pulpit, a reading desk and Communion table, with convenient pews. That the church furniture lately given by the government not having arrived (though at the date of Mr. Stuart's letter at Niagara) he took with him the plate and furniture which formerly belonged to their church at Fort Hunter – a small organ was employed in the service."

The service was ordinarily taken by a Mohawk lay-reader, an arrangement which did not commend itself to the congregation, who desired a regular clergyman. Neither the Reverend John Stuart of Kingston nor the Reverend Robert Addison of Niagara was able to convince the S.P.G. by his impassioned representations – and each made many – that distance prohibited them both from taking the services themselves.

Until 1787 it had not been possible for either Stuart or Addison to address an ecclesiastical superior who had any conception of the scale of their difficulties. In that year Charles Inglis, formerly a member of the Board of Governors of Kings College, New York, was consecrated Bishop of Nova Scotia. His diocese was a large one. It extended from St. John's, Newfoundland to the Detroit River and as far to the northward as anyone cared to go. He and Dr. Samuel Seabury, first Bishop of Connecticut (consecrated in Aberdeen in 1784) between them shared responsibility for the Anglican (or Episcopal) communion in the entire North American Continent.

The Mohawks, in the face of repeated disappointment in their efforts to secure a clergyman of their own, kept up their weekly

*I-8: Mohawk Chapel, Brantford, second phase, 1833 – reconstruction based on an early illustration which had been improved for publication by the addition of an unlikely chancel window.*

service of worship. Finally, in 1826, they were assigned a regular missionary, the Reverend Robert Lugger, and in 1829 a resident clergyman, the Reverend Abraham Nelles, who having been brought up among them, spoke their language.

By this time the chapel had been standing for more than forty years. It was sadly in need of renovation. Moreover, land clearance and drainage had altered the course of the river so that the chapel, once sited beautifully to the approaching canoe, now stood with its back to the high road, dismally contemplating a silting swamp. It would not do.

Nelles heartily endorsed the desire of the Mohawks to improve their church. Thus it was that in 1829 the congregation (I-8), reoriented the building, closing up the entrance doorway in one end wall and opening a new one in the other.

Does their early church yet stand, and with it the proud claim to be the oldest in Ontario? Yes indeed. Every living organism renews itself; buildings have to be assisted. The timber framing of the Mohawk church stands where and as it did. The builders of 1829 did not turn the building about; they simply reversed its liturgical direction. The walls of the church have remained constant, and it is possible, on the skeleton of that constant structure, to recreate visually, with archival assistance, the appearance of the chapel of the Mohawks, dedicated to St. Paul, as built to the order of Governor Haldimand by John Smith and John Wilson in 1785.

Wilson and Smith, Loyalists from the Mohawk Valley, had been friends of Brant's for many years. They had accepted his invitation to settle among the Mohawks on the Grand. Their building traditions were those of their native land, and the church which they built was from that memory—a Georgian building of simple elegance, in wood. Its sturdy walls, of timber framing infilled with baulks of squared log, encompassed a floor space some thirty feet by forty-four feet, the time-honoured proportion of the golden mean of antiquity. So well had they disposed the furnishings within the space that the Reverend John Stuart, correctly identifying the ratio, over-estimated the measurements. The walls, weather-boarded and painted externally, had four windows on either side. All window frames had semicircular heads—a Georgian refinement proper to a masonry building and not easily inserted in planked log construction. The steeply-pitched, narrow-eaved roof was crowned with a belfry fashioned with comparable skill. An octagonal drum rose above the shingled roof ridge, the round-arched openings in its side echoing the window pattern. The drum was roofed with a truncated cone surmounted by a small decorative lantern with a diminutive conical roof topped off by a weathervane. There is little evidence existent on the manner in which Smith and Wilson saw fit to adorn the entrance door, but with their known addiction to the

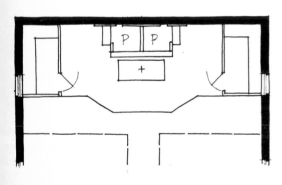

*I-9: Bilingual Georgians. Elevation and plan of altar place, St. Paul's, Brantford, 1787. Altar (+), pulpits (P) for rector and interpreter.*

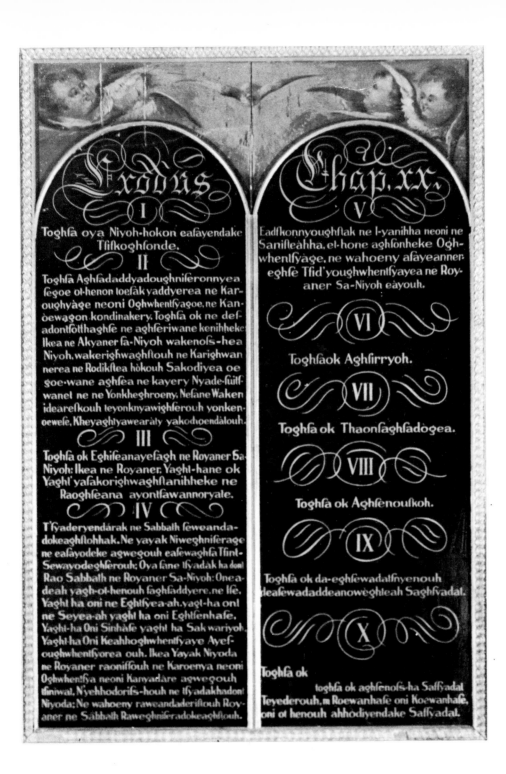

*I-10: The Ten Commandments in
the Mohawk language and the
Anglican liturgical arrangement —
four on one board, six on the other.*

*I-11: The Royal Arms, gift of George III to the Six Nations.*

semicircular arch, it seems likely that they placed one as a transom over it also.

The earliest description of the interior of the Mohawk church appeared in 1846, by which date it had been reoriented, but not—it would appear—redesigned (I-9). James Beaven, D.D., published *Recreations of a Long Vacation, or a Visit to the Indian Missions* in 1846. In it he described the Mohawk church: "At the upper end is a sort of pulpit, divided in the middle, one side for the preacher the other for the interpreter: behind which on the wall are the Creed, the Lord's Prayer and the Commandments in the Mohawk language. In front of it is the Communion Table an arrangement derived from the U.S., a little further down a separate pew for the church wardens. The rest of the church is divided into open seats, one side for men and the other for women."

The Mohawk church was a provincial adaptation, derived by way of the charming Georgian churches of colonial America, of the North European churches of the seventeenth and eighteenth centuries. The auditory, or "preaching" church, was not a mutilated Gothic building, but rather one which had been newly designed to accommodate a new philosophy. And as such it was a reasonable, rather than an emotional composition—its purpose as transparent as the carefully selected glass in its many-paned windows. It was pre-eminently the church of the Word, designed about a single liturgical centre so that all could clearly see and hear. The focal point of such a composition was the pulpit, in close association with the altar table; backed morally and physically by the Decalogue, the Creed and the Lord's Prayer set forth in lettering of unsurpassed elegance and legibility in the vernacular tongue (I-10). Close association of the pulpit, font, and holy table was achieved by architects and master-builders of the eighteenth century in a number of ways, some of which would commend themselves to twentieth-century liturgists although they were anathema to the nineteenth. Beaven's description indicated that one of the more moderate solutions was used in St. Paul's —the placing of the altar table in front of the pulpit-reading desk.

In the last quarter of the eighteenth century (and for some time thereafter in North America) the physical form of the Anglican altar-table followed very closely the design fashionable for the ends of the secular banquet table. The top was rectangular or D-shaped, with an apron of six to ten inches in depth below its leading edge. Wood of especially fine figure was selected for the apron, which might be decorated with stringing or banding in a contrasting wood or with a little restrained carving. The table legs might be reeded or turned; in either case they were slender and rather taller than those fitted to their secular counterparts.

The pulpit, which stood behind the altar table in the Mohawk church, was partitioned vertically to accommodate the priest and

*I-12: St. Paul's Brantford, the King's Chapel of the Mohawks, 1906*

14

his clerk-interpreter. The division was, in all likelihood, expressed visually by finishing the front of the pulpit with panels having a moulded cornice at the top and a shallow plinth below. Above the pulpit was set the framed board bearing the Tables of the Law from the old Colonial chapel at Fort Hunter, New York. This board was the source of much controversy and soul-searching among the Six Nations. Brant's petition to the Crown on behalf of the unfurnished church at Brantford had eventually produced new furnishings, the gift of George III, which included the Royal Arms handsomely carved and gilded (I-11).

The proprietors of the Brantford church were delighted to have the Royal Arms but somewhat at a loss as to their proper placement in the building. It was customary to display such marks of Royal favour in the tympanum of the arch above the chancel screen. Alternatively, the arms might, with propriety, be set in the central panel of the gallery railing, a spot deemed to be especially fitting when it formed a part of the pew reserved for the King's representative. But they had neither a chancel nor yet a gallery. The obvious compositional solution was to maintain the formal balance of the end wall by placing the Royal Arms centrally in the apex of the gable. The spot of brilliant colour, high on the lime-washed surface, was grateful to the eye of the Georgian beholder, however much it was to exacerbate the Victorian.

The Mohawks loved their church and they strove always to adorn it fittingly. In so doing they unconsciously altered its appearance little by little—a metamorphosis gentle but so thorough that in time very little of the early structure was visible (I-12).

But one thing did not change. Services of worship have been held continuously in Her Majesty's Chapel of the Mohawks since the days of its building long ago, when Upper Canada was still a part of the colony of Quebec.

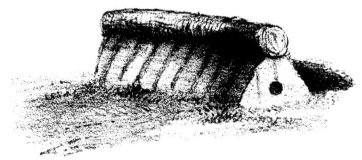

*I-13: Iroquoian grave marker. A small hole was left at one end near the ridge pole so that the shade of the departed might come and go freely. The soul went to the land of souls, happily reunited with its Creator. The shade stayed nearby, dependent on the benevolence of its kindred.*

# II
# *Loyalist*

*And they delivered the king's commissions
unto the king's lieutenants and to the
governors on this side the river: and they
furthered the people, and the house of God.*

*Ezra* VIII: *36*

Both the boundaries and the governance of the colony of Quebec tended to be somewhat confusing in the decade immediately following the American Revolution – or so it seemed to the loyal Americans settling in the western part of it (II-1). They spoke a number of different languages, but they had all lived under the British legal system in the Thirteen Colonies, and they had every intention of continuing to do so; they had just fought a war about it. So it came as a shock to them to realize that they would be subject to the provisions of the Quebec Act which, while introducing English criminal law, had retained the French civil code. Accordingly, in 1785 they addressed a petition to Governor Haldimand, then on leave of absence in England, asking that a new district be formed where "the mild tenures to which they had ever been accustomed" would operate.

Petition pattered after petition until the worn-down Colonial Secretary came to grips with the problem. Much struck with the impossibility of trying to direct the distant destinies of a stubborn people under a legal system which neither understood, the British Government began to work cautiously toward a compromise. Sir Guy Carleton, former military commander at Quebec, was sent out as Governor-General of British North America.

Carleton, now Lord Dorchester, divided the newly settled areas on the upper St. Lawrence and the lower Great Lakes into four large, open-ended districts. The districts, named in honour of the reigning House of Hanover, were generally defined by river boundaries – Luneburg from the Ottawa to the Gananoque; Mecklenburg from the Gananoque to the Trent; Nassau from the Trent to Long Point on Lake Erie; and Hesse from Long Point to the Detroit. Each district was to have a Court of Common Pleas and a Land Board.

After further delay the Constitutional, or Canada, Act was passed, on 18 May 1791. Under its terms Quebec was divided into two provinces – Upper Canada at the head waters of the St. Lawrence, Lower Canada downstream from the Ottawa to the Atlantic. The Act further authorized the Lieutenant-Governor to divide Upper Canada into "Districts, or Counties, or Circles, and towns or townships."

Ignoring the tacit permission to cover the map of Upper Canada with polka dots, the new Lieutenant-Governor, Colonel Simcoe, subdivided Dorchester's districts into nineteen regular counties from Essex to Glengarry. And the new legislature, in its first session, renamed the districts in logical geographic sequence – Eastern, Midland, Home and Western. Now everyone knew where they were on the map (if they had a map and if they could read), although the designations of "town" and "township" tended to overlap for some time.

Even the international boundaries were still a trifle fluid, espe-

*II-2: Notre Dame de L'Assomption (above). Bracing poles, visible in the water-colour of 1804, were set up after a hurricane which the outsize cock atop the belfry weathered without assistance. Frérot's floral panels from old L'Assomption (II-3 far right) still gracefully bedeck his Baroque pulpit (II-4 right), now set on a pillar in the later Gothic Revival church.*

cially on the upper lakes. And although Fort Detroit had been under intermittent attack since 1776, it was not ceded until 1796. During this time of uncertainty a considerable portion of the civilian population crossed the river to join French settlers already clustered about the old Huron mission at La Pointe du Montréal on the south bank, which had been the parish of L'Assomption du Détroit since 1761.

By 1781, L'Assomption du Détroit was deemed too small to accommodate the needs of a parish swollen by the arrival of townsmen from Detroit. Consequently, the parish priest, Father François-Xavier Hubert, former Vicar-General of Quebec, in a whirlwind of activity set up parish schools, built a new presbytery, and initiated the building of a new church. When, in 1785, he became co-adjutor to the Bishop of Quebec, supervision of church building passed to the new parish priest, Father Dufaux, but the distant hand of Bishop Hubert was still apparent in the furnishing of it.

The new church, Notre Dame de L'Assomption, which was completed in 1785, was built in the traditional timber style of French Canada. In this form of wall the infilling baulks of planked log were mortised into the framing timbers. It was a strong structure but not proof against acts of God. The bracing poles visible in an early water-colour (II-2) were set as a precautionary measure following a hurricane.

There had been earlier storms as well, during the furbishing of the church, but they had been of a parochial rather than a meteorological nature. There was the matter of the pulpit, for example. Bespoken from one Frérot, a woodcarver, for the handsome sum of "280 livres," it actually cost an additional 35 livres. But it was worth it. The parishioners, who soon became accustomed to concentrating on its opulent floral baskets (II-3) throughout the sermon, were very attached to it.

Frérot's pulpit was impressively Baroque. The strongly-sculptured corona of the sounding-board supported, visually and physically, a curvaceous angel joyously heralding salvation with a trumpet. In 1816, however, Bishop Plessis, on a pastoral visit, roundly condemned the statue as indecent, and it was forthwith removed. Nevertheless, the pulpit continued to please the congregation. They could not visualize L'Assomption without it, and when they built a larger church in 1846 they ensconced the pulpit in it, setting it high up on one of the piers and providing access by means of a short spiral stair railed in the Gothic style of the new building (II-4).

While Monsieur Frérot and his confrères were at work beautifying the sanctuary of Notre Dame de L'Assomption (II-5), the chief civic official in the parish was attempting to ensure that Caesar should also receive due recognition.

François Bâby held the obsolescent post of Deputy-Lieutenant for the County of Essex. As holder of that office it was his right to build an official pew at the front of the church on the Epistle side. Large box pews of this type were sometimes adorned with a canopy and blazonry, in addition to the mere creature comforts of soft cushions, upholstered kneelers and a table. Monsieur Bâby, proud of his ancient lineage as well as pleased with his official position, gave instructions to the carpenter. The pew was built and its owner occupied it in smiling complacency, blandly ignoring the indignant stares of the furious parishioners seated behind him. Three of them were so incensed that, waiting only for the celebrant to reach the outer door, they set upon Bâby's fine pew, wrenched it out of its position, and tumbled it ignominiously out of doors. Bâby restored it to its place in time for mass the following Sunday, but it was again thrown out. At this point the dismayed Deputy-Lieutenant appealed to Governor Simcoe, who ordered the instant restoration of Bâby's dignities. Whereupon, having won the round on points, Bâby graciously informed his priest that he would withdraw his claim "in order to prevent scandal in the parish."

Meanwhile, far removed from such unseemly squabbling, in a quiet workshop under the eaves of the convent of Les Soeurs Grises in Montreal, the sculptor Philippe Liébert was carving the last acanthus leaf on an altar tabernacle. Many years before Liébert had come from Nemours to New France, where he carved for the glory of God and a fair wage. This altarpiece was to be sent beyond that comfortable pale, however. As Monsieur Liébert had noted in his careful records, the commission was for "St. André, Rivière aux Raisins." "St. André" was actually a church then being built of rubblestone work on a loop of the Rivière aux Raisins, in the new District of Luneburg, to be dedicated to St. Andrew, Patron of Scotland.

Plans for building St. Andrew's had been set in train in 1790 when the altar tabernacle was ordered. The actual fabric would stand completed in 1803, after which time its furnishing could be allowed to proceed more slowly as necessary funds accumulated.

The preceding church, a simple log structure twenty feet square, sat rather closer to the river bank. It had served the needs of the parish since 1784, when it had been built by and for those Scots Loyalists on the upper St. Lawrence who were of the Roman Catholic faith.

At the close of the American Revolution the disbanded officers and men of the 1st Battalion, King's Royal Regiment of New York, together with some members of the 1st Battalion, Royal Highland Emigrants, Delancy's Corps, and Butler's Rangers, had been allotted land along the St. Lawrence from Pointe au Beaudette westward. These were citizen-soldiers, loyal militiamen of provincial corps from the old American colonies. Their families had made their way, as best they could, to refugee camps at Sorel, St. Regis, and Oswego, hoping some time, somehow, to be reunited with their menfolk.

The earliest party of these refugees to reach Upper Canada was a group of Highland Scots—women, old men, and children—who had fled from their homes in the Schoharie Valley in 1777 to escape capture by revolutionary troops under General Herkimer. The rudderless party would have perished in the mountains had not a few friendly Mohawks taken them in hand and led them to safety on the north shore of the St. Lawrence. As soon as their fighting men were free to join them, these Loyalists moved up the Rivière aux Raisins and established themselves on either side of the strip of land which had been granted to the loyal Six Nations. Most of the Protestant Highlanders settled to the east of the reserve, as far as Pointe au Beaudette. The Roman Catholics settled from the Indian Lands westward to a point on the river some ten miles due north of the Indian mission of St. Regis, Quebec. They at first called the place Rivière aux Raisins and later St. Andrews.

In 1784 Governor Haldimand, in response to earnest entreaty, appointed a missionary to the Indians at St. Regis, with responsibility to the parish of St. Andrew's as well. This priest, whose salary was fifty pounds per annum, was the Reverend Roderick Macdonell of Leek, who had received his education in France and at the Scots college of Valladolid in Spain.

The chief parishioner of St. Andrew's, Captain John Macdonell of Scothouse, wrote in 1801 to his son John, then a wintering-partner with the North West Fur Trading Company, demanding a donation for the church. He noted: "We are building a pretty snug and decent stone church at Rivière aux Raisins. It is Mr. Roderick's hobbyhorse. It is expected to be finished this year."

Mr. Roderick's hobbyhorse was a tall building, liturgically sited parallel with the river (II-6). It was constructed largely by French-Canadian craftsmen for a congregation of Highland Scots, to the order of a priest whose taste had been nurtured in Spain. What might one anticipate of such a combination? Certainly not a "preaching box." St. Andrew's, Rivière aux Raisins was Counter-Reformation Baroque in concept, a philosophy which demanded a church in which the emotive pageant of man's redemption might be forever re-enacted. But it was a modest essay in the Quebec Baroque tradition and it still retained something of the austere.

The finished appearance of the snug and decent stone church, to which the "Nor'westers" did subscribe two hundred and twenty-two pounds, was recorded by an early water-colourist (II-7).

*II-5: An elegant late eighteenth-century statue in wood, possibly by Frérot.*

There is a "peaceable kingdom" quality and naive charm in the composition. The unknown artist had some difficulty in reconciling the scale of the buildings with his vision of their relative importance, but they are delineated with radiant conviction. One can trust his eye for style. What an excellent witness! Certainly the priest pacing his verandah, breviary in hand, was not, in life, quite as tall as his drive-shed, nor is it likely that the primeval forest was composed of feather dusters, but the glowering gloom of that forest, inched painfully back from the little fields, had never been more vividly stated.

The greater number of the parishioners of St. Andrew's had never assisted at mass in a building as spacious and beautiful as this one. At the other extreme, the Scots gentlefolk among them were often more widely travelled and of greater sophistication than the majority of Upper Canadians of their time. Captain John Macdonell—once a student in Rome, a soldier of fortune in Spain, and aide-de-camp in the Stuart shadow court in St. Germain—regarded it simply as the decent church it still looks to have been. Furthermore, any Quebec bourgeois from that day to this would

*II-6: St. Andrew's, snug and decent by 1801, drawn in elevation (above) and in plan (on opposite page).*

have endorsed his verdict.

Indeed, the Quebec craftsmen employed by Father Roderick must have been surprised by the modesty of the specifications. Only one open pavilioned section to the clocher, no gilded cock above the bell-cast roof? Windows such as the Anglais set in their houses, but with a decent fan transom above each one, a small gallery, no fine pulpit, just a single altar on a low platform behind a straight rail!

But if the artisans were disappointed, the congregation was happy; the Liébert tabernacle had arrived (II-8). Intricately wrought, skilfully gilded, it was an instant success, and was set up with devout rejoicing. The parishioners called it the Spanish altar, happily ignoring its patently French origin but correctly attributing its inception to the Spanish background of their priest.

The Liébert tabernacle has suffered much at the hands of devotion since that day. It seems to have been converted for use on a side altar by unknown hands at an unrecorded date. St. Andrew and his canopy were amputated at that time and the roofs taken off the flanking pavilions. The supporting columns were

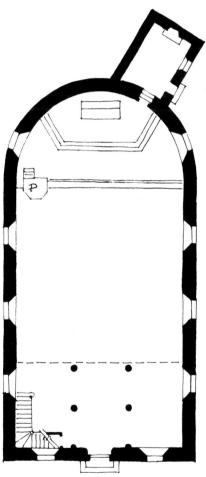

*II-7: St. Andrews West, c. 1820 (left). The wilderness Georgian hamlet stands against a lowering backdrop of primeval forest in the unsigned, undated water-colour hanging in the presbytery.*

II-8 above: Reconstruction (based on existing mutilated tabernacle and on other work by Liébert) of St. Andrew's altar as it appeared in 1800.

II-9 right: Detail of St. Andrew's altar. Liébert's angels, otherwise admirably Baroque, invariably display a touch of gout in hands and feet.

II-10 left: St. Andrew's, made Gothic with a tower and spire (below) in the 1850's, was cut down to the status of a parish hall (above) when a truly Gothic successor was built for it in 1861.

removed from the upper custode and four angels indifferently carved to a larger scale placed in their room. It is still possible, however, from the evidence of the mutilated tabernacle itself, and from other remaining examples of Liébert's oeuvre, to reconstruct conjecturally this historically important sculpture (II-9). Actual restoration, albeit more expensive, ought not to be too long delayed.

It would be equally possible to restore the church for which it was commissioned, a work of even greater historical merit. For here, in the guise of a parish hall (II-10), stands St. Andrew's, the oldest Roman Catholic church in Ontario but—more than that—the first church that looked like a church to be built by Roman Catholic Highland Scots since 1560. (The Relief Bill for Scots Catholics in Great Britain was not passed until 1793. And such Roman Catholic chapels as still existed in forgotten glens in the Highlands were at great pains to be as non-religious in appearance as was decently possible.) That in itself is much, but that it was built by a priest appointed and pensioned by the Government of Great Britain, for a people who just forty-five years before had been actively engaged in armed insurrection against it is even more remarkable.

A very long history of oppression also lay behind the Dutch and Palatine German Loyalists from New York whose ancestors had spent nearly the whole of the seventeenth century in migration—attempting to escape religious persecution.

Some of these Palatine Germans were of French descent. As Huguenots in Provence, they were hounded until, after the revocation of the Edict of Nantes, they took refuge in the Rhenish Palatinate under the protection of the Elector. There the tide of anti-Protestantism caught up with them again, and a generation later, as German-speaking Lutherans with teutonized names, they streamed out of the Palatinate to seek sanctuary in England. Queen Anne graciously settled them in Ireland. But the climate there was anything but ideal for dedicated Protestants, and after a brief stay they took ship for North America, convinced they would find true religious freedom in the New World. They had not been established long in the colony of New York, however, before the freedom to remain loyal to the House of Hanover (lineal descendants of their benefactors, the Counts Palatine) was denied them. So once again they set off, this time to Canada which they devoutly hoped would prove to be a land of enduring liberty.

The advance party, consisting mainly of women and children, came up through the woods in 1777. They were joined by the heads of the families as soon as the loyal regiments were disbanded, and all moved eagerly to their new lands along the St. Lawrence (in the townships of Osnabruck, Williamsburg and

*II-11 opposite: The much-travelled swan of Williamsburg, symbol of Lothair (Luther) the Swan-knight.*

Matilda). Soon they were settled in small communities and, as became people who had suffered much for their religion, one of their first priorities was to build churches.

In 1784 the Lutherans of Williamsburg Township petitioned the Governor for permission to build a church on the centre commons. They already had a lay reader who held regular services in their log houses; they had Bibles; and they had despatched a man on foot to Philadelphia to purchase, with a little hoard of money, a book of sermons and a copy of the Marburger Gesangbuch. But they wanted a proper church, and as soon as the licence of occupation arrived from the Surveyor-General's office in Quebec they began to fell and square white-oak timbers.

By 1789 the timber was sufficiently well seasoned, and building began. Colonel Henry Merkley, a member of the congregation, acted as master-builder, consulting now and then with Jacob Coons, the carpenter, on which details were feasible and which must regretfully be abandoned. The church frame was sixty feet by forty feet and some twenty feet from ground to eave. (Unfortunately, such inadequate pictorial records as there are show the church after it had been rebuilt, utilizing the early timbers and window frames, for a different denomination in 1836.) By June of 1790, the building, from its sturdy foundation to its fine weather-vane in the form of a swan (II-11), was complete. It was dedicated as Zion's Lutheran Church by the new pastor, the Reverend Samuel Schwerdfeger, late of Albany, New York.

Schwerdfeger had come from Martin Luther's own land of Saxony. As a Lutheran pastor he had ministered in Maryland and then in the Albany area of New York where he had provoked the revolutionary party exceedingly by his obstinate loyalty to the House of Hanover. Released from prison at the end of the Revolution, he was still living in a state of uneasy ostracism in Albany when the loyal Lutherans of Dundas County asked him to be their pastor.

While Schwerdfeger lived Zion flourished, its swan sailing serenely overhead. But when he died clouds began to gather. To state it baldly, the Lutherans of Zion Church were very poor. After building a handsome place of worship, they had gone on almost immediately to construct a parsonage—not as fine as the church but better than they could well afford. As a result, they had very little left with which to support a pastor. The Reverend August Frederik Myers, Mr. Schwerdfeger's immediate successor, departed to more lucrative southern fields after a brief ministry of four years. And the Reverend Johann Weigandt, who came to Zion in 1807, discovered the same problems which had beset Pastor Myers.

In this situation the pastor remembered that distant, imper-

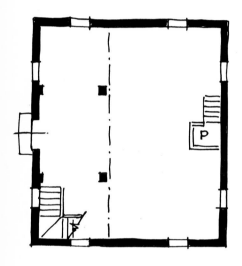

*II-12: Hay Bay Methodist meetinghouse in 1791.*

sonal source of funds, the Governor at Quebec, who had pensioned Father Macdonell in 1783. He recalled, moreover, that it had been the firmly stated opinion of Martin Luther that the civic authorities were the proper custodians of the physical welfare of a church—always assuming, that is, that the said authorities were not members of an actively hostile sect.

So supported, Mr. Weigandt sought assistance at Quebec. But 1811 was not, alas, 1783. Another Governor sat in Haldimand's room, one who viewed with an intolerant eye religious practices that differed from those favoured by the establishment of the Mother Country. Furthermore, there was now an Anglican Bishop at Quebec. Poor Mr. Weigandt was out-manoeuvered; he was advised that for the good of his people he should concentrate on the parallels in the Lutheran and Anglican confessions. It was a cruel dilemma. If he chose to remain faithful to his Church he must abandon his congregation; if he could, in conscience, conform to what was not actually, but seemed to be, a state Church, then the people of Williamsburg Township would have financial assistance and a clergyman who could further their interests with the authorities. The upshot was that the Reverend Johann Weigandt allowed himself to be persuaded, and was reordained by Bishop Mountain in Quebec.

The congregation of Zion was rent. Some members accepted their religion in translation; others refuted the arguments with scorn. The Anglican faction secured the church and the parsonage. The Lutherans withdrew, and in response to their urgent petition, Pastor Myers returned. But then, to their horror, he too joined the Church of England. The captive swan looked down on a troubled people.

At last, in 1826, the Lutherans were led out of despair by the Reverend Herman Hayunga, a pastor of valiant spirit though feeble frame. Within seven years of his arrival the repossessed swan sailed the sky again over the new Lutheran church of St. John in Williamsburg. When that church was rebuilt in 1863, the swan weathervane was placed on the top of the spire. And when, in its turn, St. John's was demolished by the imminence of the St. Lawrence Seaway flood, the Lutherans of Williamsburg took their swan with them to higher ground.

While singing the songs of Zion in the new land was still a novelty in Williamsburg, preparations were going forward with speed to raise a joyful noise unto the Lord in Adolphustown (II-12). A Methodist meetinghouse for Hay Bay in Hastings County was in the talking stage. It was 1791. By that date Methodism had been in Canada for some time.

Methodist exhorters were to be found among both officers and men in the British regulars as well as in the Loyalist list, including as it did the name of Barbara Heck who, with Philip Embury, had founded, in New York, the first Methodist class in North America. Born Barbara von Ruckle, in Balingrave, Ireland, she had emigrated with her husband, Paul Heck, and a number of other second-generation refugee Palatine Germans to New York. Loyal allegiance to the British who had given their parents religious asylum brought them to Quebec in 1778 and up the St. Lawrence in 1784. There they formed the first Methodist class in Canada, on the riverfront of Augusta Township.

There was a much greater concentration of Methodists among the disbanded 2nd Battalion, King's Royal Regiment of New York, which had settled in the Bay of Quinte area and along both shores of the Adolphus Reach. It was these followers of John Wesley's teaching who were planning to build a meetinghouse in 1791, the year in which their great founder died.

One does not usually think of Methodism as an expression of student unrest in the second quarter of the eighteenth century, but that is exactly how it came about. The discipline was initiated at Oxford by a group of thoughtful students under Wesley's leadership, as a method of ordering their lives so that they might encompass both scholarship and good work. A sceptical contemporary dubbed the group "the Methodists."

Wesley called his first houses of worship "preaching halls," for at that time all Methodists still repaired to the Church of England for Holy Communion, for marriage, and for baptism. And for some time thereafter all clergy within the Wesleyan Connexion had been ordained by the Established Church of England before embarking on a path of revival. By 1791 this was no longer true. The Methodist Church was now an autonomous body which ordained its own clergy. William Lossee, the first minister appointed to Adolphustown, had been so ordained. In addition to forming the first Methodist class in that community, he held preaching appointments in Kingston, Ernestown, Fredericksburg, and Hallowell townships, as well as covering a vast outlying territory. In this he was typical of most North American Methodist preachers—the storied circuit riders. (A Canadian member of the fraternity rejected the term "circuit rider" as inexact, saying, "I *travelled* the circuit; I rode my horse.")

No religious figure was more closely bound up with the traditions of North American folk history than the Methodist circuit rider. He operated within a system whose flexibility was ideally suited to the uncertainties of pioneer life. Responsible to the Presiding Elder of the Conference which appointed him to the circuit, he made appointments to preach at fixed times and in specific locations so that scattered settlers might congregate to listen. It was said by a preacher in Hallowell, a typical circuit where thirty-five preaching appointments had to be kept within four weeks, "The round was more like a horse race than anything I

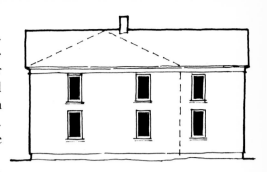

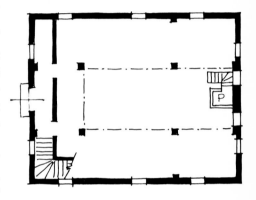

*II-13: Hay Bay meetinghouse as enlarged.*

could think of." Nor could the preacher expect to find ideal ministerial conditions. Almost invariably he had to conduct services in a settler's home or barn. Only in areas where there was some density of population would there be a meetinghouse.

Rather curiously, the deed of land "for a Methodist Episcopal house of worship at Hay Bay" (in Adolphustown) was dated 17 June 1811. The building had then been standing for at least eighteen years and looked very much as it did when described by the Reverend Anson Green, who preached in it in 1824. Green wrote, "The house is 30 by 36 with a gallery; it is painted blue on the inside and is rather a blue looking affair altogether."

A decade later it was decided to enlarge the Hay Bay meetinghouse, in celebration of the foundation of the independent Methodist Church in Canada. The rebuilding was carried out with such a will that the Reverend John Ryerson, in his report of 1834, described it as a new building (II-13). The refurbished meetinghouse sheltered the Methodists faithfully for another quarter of a century. Then it was abandoned, and all of its furnishings were transported to a new church several miles distant. From 1860 until 1912 symbolism became fact: the old meetinghouse was used as a sheep-fold and a storehouse for garnered sheaves. In 1912 it was somewhat drastically restored, and in 1963 all original material then visible was replaced.

A more reliable source for the study of an early Methodist meetinghouse survives in the neighbouring county of Prince Edward. It is the old Conger Meetinghouse, near Picton, (II-14), built between 1809 and 1811 on land donated for the purpose by Stephen Conger. The Congers were New Jersey Loyalists from Piscataqua where they had been brass-founders before the Revolution.

The Conger Meetinghouse has been altered very little over the years. It retains the basically square form of the New England meetinghouse, and the gallery, reached by a corner stair, contributes to the impression of squareness by shortening the apparent length of the north and south walls.

The Reverend Anson Green's opinion of the old Conger Meetinghouse was not a high one: "A more awkwardly arranged house for worship I do not wish to see. It has three galleries but the floors in them are level and only seated with rough plank or loose boards. They are much too high and, being level, the pulpit has to be stuck up toward the moon in order to see the people in them. The doorway is on one side and the pulpit opposite to it on the other side with a good sounding-board over it." This statement, made in 1825, does not coincide with existing conditions (II-15). The pulpit has been altered, but the gallery, about which Green was being deliberately provocative, has not. The beams which support the gallery were mortised into exposed timber framing which would clearly show evidence of change had any occurred. No such marks exist. On the other hand, the central wall space against which the pulpit stands was flush-boarded between plain beaded pilasters. On the outer surface of the pilasters cuts appear which indicate that the sounding-board was once suspended on a level with the lintels of the flanking windows, its wrought-iron suspension rod firmly anchored in the framing plate of the wall. The pulpit, then, stood at nearly double its present height, its cornice moulding level with the upper window sills.

There was historic precedent for cutting a top-lofty Methodist pulpit down to size. The pulpit in John Wesley's City Road Chapel, London, once soared to a dizzying fifteen feet—until the day when his reverend brother Charles, accompanying an oration with a flowing gesture, swept the heavy pulpit Bible from the ledge. It plunged floorward, stunning the unfortunate clerk in the reading desk beneath. So one stage of heavy mahogany was prudently removed from the massive height of the pulpit to lessen the force of future eloquence. The Methodists of Hallowell likewise shortened the pulpit, although no clerkly brother was imperilled by it. Upper Canadian Methodists seem to have dispensed with the office of clerk. Certainly no provision was ever made for the special seating of one in the early meetinghouses. Neither was there a kneeling step for communicants about the

*II-14: Four-square and forthright, the Conger Meetinghouse was built near Picton in 1809.*

*II-15: Simplicity reigns within the Conger Meetinghouse in the austere elegance of panelled pine galleries, chaste white walls and a reduced pale blue pulpit under a sounding board of threatening aspect. The earliest wooden marker left in the province guards the Conger family plot.*

unrailed altar table. These square meetinghouses retained the liturgical form of the preaching hall which had been designed to serve as an adjunct to an Established Church.

But was there an Established Church in Upper Canada? The Constitutional Act, in its inexact wisdom, had set aside certain lands for the benefit of "a Protestant clergy." It was a gift of no cost to the donor and of very little real worth to the recipients, but it excited a vast deal of vociferous envy among the Churches that were slighted. It is possible, even likely, that the parliamentarians of Great Britain realized how ambiguous the term "a Protestant clergy" was, and that they intended it should be so. All must have been aware that the Church of Scotland had been established in North Britain for a very long time, and that the Lutheran Church, also present in Upper Canada, was the State Church in His Britannic Majesty's Kingdom of Hanover.

In any event, the Constitutional Act had, by nebulous prose, endowed the people of Upper Canada with a bone of contention second to none. The very mention of the Clergy Reserves question was guaranteed to raise hackles in any company, and was more a political issue than a religious one. The sad part of it all was that when the need for financial support was most urgent none could be derived from the mere possession of uncleared tractless forest, reserved or otherwise.

*II-16: Interior view of enlarged and Gothicized St. Mark's, Niagara-on-the-Lake. (It has been recast at least twice since.) Drawing from J.R. Robertson's* History of Freemasonry in Canada.

Thus Upper Canada began the nineteenth century with the understanding that while the Church of England was indubitably the Church of the establishment it was not an established Church in the province. The cost of its churches would not be borne by the ratepayers generally, but by the congregations immediately concerned. It was not, in the circumstances, surprising that the churches built by that body immediately after 1791 should have been described as "meetinghouses for Episcopalians."

The Episcopalian meetinghouses of Upper Canada were superficially similar to the meetinghouses of other denominations in that they were unsophisticated in design and somewhat plain in detail. They differed from those of other denominations in their liturgical orientation, however. Indeed, they contrived to differ from one another in this respect, since they were built, on the basis of divergent memories, by North American Anglicans to whom the English mediaeval parish church was a distant symbol, not a well-loved reality.

The early Anglican churches, built by their congregations, were, in order of appearance: St. George's, Kingston; St. John's, Ernestown (Bath); St. John's, Sandwich; Holy Trinity, Cornwall; St. James', York; and St. Mark's, Newark (Niagara-on-the-Lake). Of these, St. John's, Bath and St. Mark's, Niagara-on-the-Lake survive, but in such a built-over condition that no profitable discussion of their early form can be embarked upon here. A sad state of affairs, as these were the two churches out of the whole group which were built under the liturgical eyes of those memorable English clergymen the Reverend John Langhorne and the Reverend Robert Addison.

The first Anglican church built in Kingston was dedicated to St. George in 1792. The simple frame structure, thirty-two feet by forty feet, which had been in the process of building since 25 October 1791, was the triumph of the devoted incumbent of Cataraqui parish, the Reverend John Stuart.

Stuart was a Loyalist who, having been chaplain to the Mohawks at Fort Hunter, New York, had been reappointed as chaplain to the Six Nations on the Bay of Quinte and the Grand River. Early documents offer a choice of birthplaces for him—"in Virginia" or "Harrisburg, Pennsylvania"—but they agree on his background and his subsequent existence. His father, who had emigrated to North America from Ulster was a devout member of the Presbyterian Church. While attending college in Philadelphia, John Stuart determined to take orders in the Church of England, or—as he invariably called it—the Protestant Episcopal Church. Philadelphia remained an inspiring memory to him, and when at long last he was able to build a church in Upper Canada he modelled it on the liturgical plan of St. Peter's Protestant Episcopal Church in that city. It was not a plan which commended itself to his Canadian ecclesiastical superiors, however, for the pulpit stood at one end of the long axis, the altar at the other. They disliked it even more after 1795 when the joiners, Francis Wyckott and Emmanuel Ellerbeck, at the behest of the churchwardens, built the gallery "over the altar" as specified.

Jacob Mountain, Bishop of Quebec, described St. George's as "a little blue wooden building with square windows; and with a steeple or cupola on the wrong end like the thing on a brewery." This was most unfair. Archibald Thompson, the builder, and the Reverend John Stuart had made the best spatial use possible of the forty by thirty-two foot room, fitting into it no fewer than thirty-seven rentable pews. The steeple had been erected over the pulpit end of the building for the excellent reason that this placed the bell rope within the clerk's reach and did not leave it dangling by the altar. Anglican Church usage of the time did not require frequent communion. The normal liturgical orientation was thus toward the pulpit, and during the infrequent communion services the communicants simply turned about to stand facing the altar while waiting their turn to approach it (II-17).

While the church had been a-building, the originator, the Reverend John Stuart, had been busy with his other duties. In addition to serving as rector of St. George's and chaplain to the Mohawks, he had, in 1789, been appointed Bishop's Commissary for Upper Canada by Charles Inglis, Bishop of Nova Scotia, the highest Anglican authority in British North America. The new office, which conferred on its luckless recipient the right to be called the Reverend Mister Official Stuart, considerably increased his problems. As a Loyalist officer he had been granted land in Cataraqui, which he had to clear and farm when not otherwise employed. His quadruple duties, as chaplain to the Mohawks and to the garrison at Kingston, as rector of St. George's, and as Commissary, brought him a modest salary, but the expense of travelling about his huge territory was great. The Mohawks, settled in two widely separated areas, had to be visited as often as he could manage. There was also the task of visiting the other outlying parishes to confer with their clergy on the Bishop's behalf.

The most remote of the parishes was that of Sandwich, in Essex County, on the Detroit River, where a number of devout practising Anglicans had congregated. Another group had located a few miles down-river, around Fort Malden. Sometimes there was a military chaplain at the fort; more frequently there was not. Where were the Anglicans of Essex to find a clergyman? Out of their need the clergyman came—Richard Pollard, Sheriff of the Western District, a Loyalist who had, as he himself recorded, "taken ship from the revolting colonies in 1776," and had been exceedingly busy in the Detroit area ever since. He believed

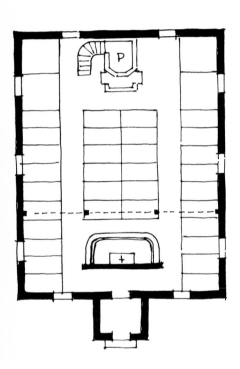

*II-17: St. George's Anglican Church, Kingston, 1792. Altar (+), pulpit (P). Dotted line indicates position of gallery.*

that if faith were sufficient grace would be vouchsafed. Accordingly, at the age of fifty he determined to re-educate himself so that he might seek ordination.

There was no seminary in which to study, had Pollard had the leisure to attend one – and he had not that leisure, having just been appointed Judge of the Surrogate Court, over and above his other activities. So he was forced to study on his own. After several years' work, feeling some confidence in his progress, he set out for Quebec. At the end of the long journey disappointment awaited him, however. Bishop Mountain did not feel that he could, in conscience, endorse him as ecclesiastically fit for ordination. Pollard went sadly back to Sandwich to attend to his farms, the fur trade, and the post office, to administer frontier justice, and to study with a new zeal.

The next year he went again to Quebec, armed with his own patient faith and "very satisfactory testimonials from the most respected people there, to which were added many testimonies of esteem and regard from persons of the first consideration." Bishop Mountain who made the statement in a letter to the S.P.G., identified two of those persons as Lieutenant-Governor Hunter and Chief Justice Elmsley. The desired ordination was at last achieved in 1802, and with it the appointment as missionary to Sandwich, Amherstburg and Colchester, in Essex, and to "the Thames"; as well as that of chaplain to the militia at Fort Malden.

The Reverend John Stuart, Bishop's Commissary, wrote to his superior describing Pollard's visit to Kingston on his way home from Quebec. The saga ended in amusement as Stuart remarked that he trusted that the new clergyman would be able to overcome the Sheriff's habit of swearing. Meanwhile, the reverend Sheriff, hurrying on to Sandwich, was determining to make his new charges the finest damn parishes in all Upper Canada.

He began with St. John's, Sandwich, which was built in 1803 – square in plan (thirty-six by thirty-six feet), the meeting-house form (II-18). It was constructed of stone, and seems to have had an internal porch, which suggests that there was perhaps a belfry or cupola requiring extra support. The altar rail extended across the far end, from wall to wall. It is highly unlikely that there was much in the way of church furnishing beyond a simple altar-table.

No working drawings of Pollard's pre-1812 buildings remain. But a seating diagram for St. John's, Sandwich somehow survived the burning of the building by Kentucky Mounted Riflemen in 1813. Regrettably, Mr. Pollard's personal library was destroyed as well. His papers were carried off and lost, while he himself was haled to Detroit as a prisoner – presumably in either his role of Sheriff or that of militia officer.

While Richard Pollard was building square little churches in

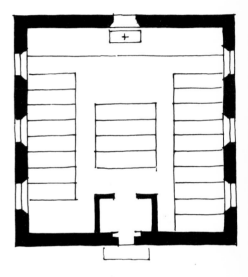

II-18: Plan of the first Church of St. John in Sandwich, burned in 1813.

Essex, another man, equally remarkable but half his age, was embarking on his ecclesiastical career in Upper Canada. On 26 May 1803 Bishop Mountain was writing of John Strachan, whom he had ordained just four days before, "He appears to be a young man of competent attainments, of fair understanding and great modesty and worth." The modest young man, who had just been appointed rector to the parish of Cornwall, was a twenty-five-year-old Aberdonian possessed of several characteristics not yet apparent to his Bishop. He was energetic, ambitious, and a born organizer. Moreover, he had some acquaintance with the building trades.

The little community of Cornwall was galvanized to spiritual activity. Mr. Strachan intended to set up a school for the sons of gentlemen; if there were not enough available locally, he was prepared to import them. And he was determined to build a worthy church. In a surprisingly short space of time both of these works were under way.

In his contract for the building of the Church of England in Cornwall, Abner Young, master-builder, convenanted to build a church "52 feet in length and 36 feet in breadth within the walls . . . the frame 18 feet high raised on a stone foundation 3 feet below and 2 feet above the ground." The foundations were to be laid in good lime mortar, "the sidewalls filled with wood and clay up to the arch, the whole to be lathed and plastered inside. The sides to be boarded up as high as the tops of the pews . . . the whole of the building to be painted except the pews and the floor, the roof to be covered with good sound eighteen inch shingles." It was further specified: " . . . there is to be a semicircular figure for the vesture or altar on the East end of the church the radius of which is to be ten feet . . . and the frame for a gallery to be erected in the west end of the said church." He agreed "to raise eight posts on the top of the frame of the said building at the west end that will form an octagon and will admit of a Belfry from which a Steeple may be raised." On 7 April 1806 an amendment was attached to the contract which stipulated "that the pews be painted a chocolate colour."

An original seating plan is still in existence but it is diagrammatic rather than architectural. It may be that the apse was not externally expressed. It does not appear in a water-colour of the church painted in the 1860's, but that, in itself, is not conclusive. By that date the church had been drastically Gothicized. The diagram seems to show a pulpit, semicircular in plan, encircled by segmental seats for the clerk and the churchwardens (II-19). The Holy Trinity of 1806 was a classical church designed for a late-Georgian Anglican liturgy. It had been built by Loyalist American craftsmen steeped in the severely elegant tradition of

New England building practice, to the exacting specifications of its young rector.

John Strachan had never been in England. And the only Church of England building of any consequence known to him was the Anglican cathedral at Quebec, a stripped-down late-Georgian design which had been produced by British engineers. Strachan seems to have copied its plan at Cornwall. In his *Memoir of Bishop Strachan* A. N. Bethune wrote: "He said of Holy Trinity that Cornwall had the finest church in Upper Canada—and that in the poorest parish."

York, the richest parish, on the other hand, had fared far worse. Yet here were congregated in greatest density those persons of the first consideration who had so kindly recommended Richard Pollard to his bishop. While the poor Cornwallians sat in their chocolate boxes, harkening to John Strachan, the rector of York had to report sadly that there was no money for a pulpit or a gallery in the church he proposed to build. How had this come about? In the first instance, although there were many people in York with a reliable source of income there were many demands on the public purse. And so long as religious services could be held in the government buildings, otherwise vacant on Sundays, the Governor and the Council had been reluctant to lay out money for a church building. Moreover, the first clergy in York had been regimental chaplains. Their military background did not incline them to be over-nice in their requirements, nor was church building an activity which fell within their province.

York's experience with its first resident clergyman had not been encouraging. The Reverend Thomas Raddish, appointed in November 1796, departed as soon as the St. Lawrence was free of ice in the spring. By that time he had made too personal an application of the provisions for the benefit of the Protestant clergy; he had disposed of over four thousand acres of Church land and had sold the parsonage park-lot to Chief Justice Elmsley. In his salaried absence, prayers and sermons were read in the government buildings and in the jail by William Cooper, the wharfinger. Finally, in 1799, Mr. Raddish found the grace to resign, whereupon a wiser government sought as a replacement someone nearer at hand and with a higher code of business ethics. They nominated the recently ordained George Okill Stuart, Harvard-trained eldest son of the Rector of Kingston. Stuart, who arrived in York on the first of July 1800, at once set up a fund for the building of a church.

In January of 1803 the church subscribers met to decide on a course of action. The substantial townsmen of York had turned out in ecumenical force; the minutes were kept by Sheriff Alexander Macdonell, a devout Roman Catholic. He recorded that it

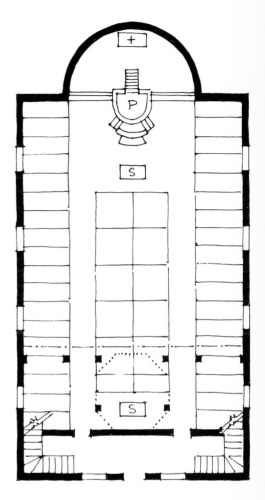

*II-19: Plan of Holy Trinity, Cornwall, 1806. Altar (+), pulpit (P), stoves (S). Dotted lines indicate the gallery position and the shape of the roof lantern.*

was decided to consult Mr. Berczy about materials and costs. This expert was William von Moll Berczy, an entrepreneur who had just come to York. Berczy was an artist of considerable skill with a taste for architecture. He seems to have advocated stone as the material, and must have drawn up a design on which his estimates were based. If he did indeed make such a drawing, it vanished with other early records in the disastrous fires which have consumed two successive churches of St. James' in York.

In 1805 the Reverend George Okill Stuart, in submitting his report to the Society for the Propagation of the Gospel in Foreign Parts, wrote: "The materials have been purchased and are on the ground intended for the site of the church. The dimensions will be 60 feet in length 40 in breadth and 22 in height . . . . They wished to have had the church in stone but found it impracticable."

Several years later Stuart wrote to the Society: "The church is nearly complete—the pews were to be finished in a few days; but their fund is not equal to the expense of a pulpit and gallery to the west end. There are 32 pews, 18 of which are called single pews —the rest double. The larger 6 feet 6 inches by 6 feet 6 inches and the smaller 3 feet by 6 feet 6 inches. There are three aisles. The middle is 6 feet in breadth, the side 4 feet 4 inches along which the range of wall pews is extended."

Within the next two years, however, Stuart was able to report the installation of a handsome pulpit and the building of a gallery at the west end of the church for the soldiers of the garrison. Placing the military in the gallery had been a bright bit of planning, as the cost of some thirty-two pounds, seventeen shillings, six pence, Halifax currency, must then be defrayed by the government. The handsome pulpit, constructed by Joshua Leach at a cost of twenty-five pounds, had been a gift of the new Lieutenant-Governor, Francis Gore, whose wife had promised to present a bell.

The eighth chapter of Dr. Scadding's history, *Toronto of Old*, which was published in 1873, begins: "The first church of St. James, at York was a plain structure of wood, placed some yards back from the road. Its gables faced east and west, and its solitary door was at its western end, and was approached from Church Street. Its dimensions were 50 feet by 40 feet. The sides of the building were pierced by two rows of ordinary windows, four above and four below." He then quotes from a description of York written before the War of 1812 by an American visitor: " 'It contains some fine buildings, though they stand scattering, among which are a Court House, a Council-house, a large brick building in which the King's stores are kept and a meetinghouse for Episcopalians.' " Dr. Scadding read the description "a meetinghouse" as a disparaging comment. He ought to have noticed that the operative word in the description of the buildings was "fine."

*II-20. Romantic inaccuracy. St. James', York as illustrated in Robertson's* Landmarks.

40

Something else was overlooked. In proof-reading his text he would have conferred lasting benefit on all people who consult his authoritative work had he checked the dimensions of the building; the church was, as the Reverend George Okill Stuart recorded, sixty feet by forty feet. But one must not complain; Stuart was directing the building of the church when Henry Scadding was just five years old, and St. James' had been extensively rebuilt by the time Scadding was sixteen.

The oft-quoted Dr. Scadding continued his narrative by saying, "The reservation of land in which the primitive St. James Church stood, long remained plentifully covered with the original forest. In a wood-cut from a sketch (II-20) taken early in the present century, prefixed to the *Annals of the Diocese of Toronto*, the building is represented as being in the midst of a great grove, and stumps of various sizes are visible in the foreground." They are indeed, but unfortunately the sketch was *not* taken early in the century. The engraving was the work of a professional illustrator who drew it in 1867, using as his sole reference a rough pen sketch made in that same year by George William Allen who had attempted to reconstruct the appearance of St. James' as it had been in 1816. Unfortunately for the visual accuracy of the drawing, the church had been remodelled before Allen was born, and completely demolished by the time he was ten. George Allen was relying on his recollections of descriptions of St. James' made by his parents and their contemporaries, none of whom seemed to have remembered the location or even the existence of chimneys. They would also appear to have forgotten to tell wee Geordie that the stumps had been cleared away in 1810.

It is unlikely that the first St. James' (II-21) ever merited the term "primitive." Scadding was writing of it at the high tide of the Gothic Revival, when a plethora of ornament, internally and externally applied, was considered essential to a tasteful building. Georgian architectural standards had been high and, where humanly possible, they had been met. The first St. James' was designed to the golden mean of antiquity and built by skilled wood craftsmen for an informed clientele who would not have considered the snake fence shown in the Scadding illustration suitable for church premises. Decent post-and-rail fences had been built in the remote Eastern District at a much earlier date. One cannot seriously believe the mechanics of the Home District were not equally proficient.

In point of fact, mechanical proficiency in church building was at the time an embarrassing topic in Glengarry, the most easterly county of the Eastern District. One fine morning in the winter of 1806 the Sabbath calm of Williamstown was shattered by horrid sounds—the shriek of splintering timbers and the crash of falling masonry. The anxious populace scrambled through the en-

*II-21: Reconstruction of first St. James', York, based on documentary evidence and known building practice.*

gulfing snow to gaze appalled at the wreckage of their new church. It was a staggering blow. They crowded into the old square log church nearby, to pray for strength to start again and for guidance to build well.

The log church had been the summit of possible ambition in 1787. They had built it on the practical plan of a block-house, using great squared timbers, and it had faithfully served in its dual role of church and schoolhouse ever since. But it was not a beautiful building, nor could the homesick Highland Loyalists ever consider a kirk truly a kirk which had not been constructed decently of stone.

Resolutely the congregation faced the task which they knew would not be easy. The stone churches they remembered had been built by an Established Church, the Church of Scotland, supported, as all Established Churches were, by the government of the country. In the colonies of New York and North Carolina they had already faced the fact that their Church was *not* established in North America and that if they wished a Scots Presbyterian church they must build it themselves. There was one favourable factor, however; their minister, the Reverend John Bethune, the first regular clergyman of the Presbyterian Church in Upper Canada, was not dependent on his congregation for his living. As former chaplain of the 84th Regiment of Foot (the Royal Highland Emigrants), he was on half-pay. He had, in addition, a modest subsidy from the Crown equal to that allowed Father Roderick Macdonell, the sole clergyman in Stormont County.

The Reverend John Bethune, born in Skye and a graduate of Kings College, Aberdeen had, after ordination by the Church of Scotland, emigrated to North Carolina. As a loyal subject of his King he had been imprisoned, then marched from New Berne to

New York. Eventually exchanged, he had proceeded to Halifax where he assisted in raising the 84th Regiment from among the refugee Scots Loyalists assembling there. (He had fallen temporarily from favour with those in authority at the close of the Revolution for reading the committal service over the ashes of the regimental colours when the Royal Highland Emigrants were disbanded.)

Many of the 84th had followed Mr. Bethune to Montreal and had helped to swell the ranks of his congregation there. For a time the Presbyterian services were held on Sunday afternoons in the old Recollet church—a courtesy for which the Recollets would accept no payment. When the Presbyterians finally achieved a church of their own they had the happy thought of presenting the good fathers with two hogsheads of fine Spanish wine, which were gratefully received.

By that time Bethune and his followers had departed to settle in Glengarry County. The lands granted to John Bethune as a Loyalist officer were on the Rivière aux Raisins in Upper Canada, beside Sir John Johnson's holdings at Williamstown. The county had been settled by Highland Loyalists. Of those who had settled in the Williamstown area and along the St. Lawrence to the Indian lands the majority were Presbyterians. The few Scots Episcopalians among them were prepared to waive the difference in ritual if they might worship in Gaelic. The Reverend John Bethune, as became a Skyeman, was bilingual—in Gaelic and English—and, ideally for their proximity to Quebec, his Swiss-American wife added French to the family store of linguistic accomplishments.

A veil of complete oblivion has been drawn across the history of the fallen church of St. Andrew's, Williamstown save for a terse item recorded in the church books, the payment of six pounds, eleven shillings, eight pence, in 1809, to Arthur Gilmore of Montreal for inspecting the ruin. The Gilmores of Montreal were master-masons much in demand and expensive, but the Presbyterians of Williamstown had already collected one hundred and fifteen pounds toward another stone church, and they wanted good workmanship.

The Reverend John Bethune knew that the congregation would not be able to meet Montreal prices, so discussed the matter with his good friend the Reverend Alexander Macdonell, parish priest of St. Raphael's. That worthy suggested another mason, François-Xavier Rochileaux, who was even then engaged in building a chapel in Kingston, an outpost of Father Macdonell's parish. Father Macdonell did even more; he undertook to convince the Presbyterian congregation that they ought to concur in their minister's decision without further argument. He is said to have concluded his address to them with these words, "Your minister is

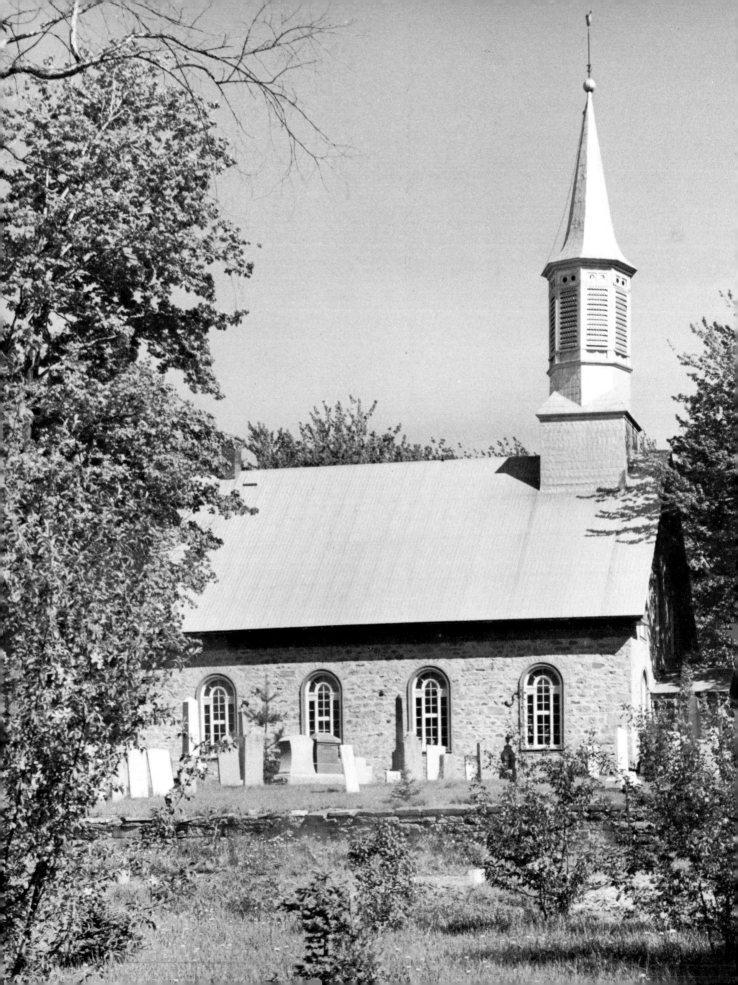

II-22: St. Andrew's United Church,
Williamstown, built by Church of
Scotland Presbyterians in 1813
to replace the log church of 1786.
In the register of first St. Andrew's,
Bethune recorded the marriage,
in 1812, of John Strachan,
rector of Holy Trinity, Cornwall,
and Ann Wood McGill, widow.

45

a good man who works very hard for you. You must not be ungrateful. Don't let me ever have to speak to you again." "Maister Alistair's" pronouncements seldom required repetition. The startled congregation sent for the Kingston master-mason immediately (II-22).

Most of Rochileaux's work in Kingston has disappeared. The church he built there in 1809 was recorded variously in the Alexander Macdonell papers and in Kingston histories as "the Old French Church," "St. Isadore du Kingston," or sometimes as "St. Columba's Church," and in extreme old age as "St. Joseph's." It was originally dedicated to St. Isadore who had been declared a Doctor of the Church in 1722. The side altars were dedicated respectively to St. Anne and to St. Columba whose claims on the loyalty of the French and of the Scots were long established. Early drawings show that in form St. Isadore's was similar to Rochileaux's masonry shell for St. Andrew's, Williamstown. The walls of both buildings were of thick coursed rubble. The Kingston church had three round-headed window openings to a side; St. Andrew's, Williamstown has four. And as the Kingston chapel was one bay shorter it was also more squat in proportion (II-23).

The contract for finishing the interior of St. Isadore, which was dated at Kingston, 24 July 1809, read in part: "I do hereby agree to make and put on the roof shingles and steeple of the Catholic chapel of Kingston also the flooring, ceiling, doors, windows, galleries, pews, altar and altar bannisters, pulpit, confessional, stair to galleries, partitions on each side of the altar to form the sacristy and another apartment opposite on the same level with the altar, also two small apartments of the same dimensions with the aforesaid above the altar with rails to look into the body of the chapel with any other timberwork that may be necessary ... for the sum of £350." The document was signed by the master-builder, Alexander MacLean, whose tribulations were to be many. He was alternately encouraged and hindered by advice from Father Macdonell, who had finally to be told that the contract could not be carried out as agreed because Rochileaux had not made the building as large as specified.

Rochileaux worked to approximate size—the familiar "more or less" of land titles. Certainly the dimensions of his other church, St. Andrew's, Williamstown—thirty-six feet, two-and-one-quarter inches by sixty-seven feet, eight-and-one-quarter inches—were somewhat strange, but for this Rochileaux may not have been wholly responsible. He died on the job, and the walls were completed under the direction of his works foreman, John Kirby.

Work on St. Andrew's ceased during the War of 1812-14, for although Williamstown was not on the exposed battlefront, the building force was from home defending Upper Canada. On its return the steeple of St. Andrew's was put up in a spirit of post-

*II-23: St. Isadore's or St. Columba's or St. Joseph's, Kingston, 1812.*

46

war celebration. Built by Pierre Poitras of Montreal for two hundred and twelve pounds, ten shillings, it was embellished with a copper weathercock, "gold-leafed" for a further ten pounds, seventeen shillings. In the belfry hangs a bell made by Mears of London in 1806 and given to Williamstown by Sir Alexander Mackenzie who, like his fellow fur-traders of the North West Company, had a special pew reserved for his use.

The most interesting detailing of St. Andrew's remains, mercifully left untouched by Victorian improvers. Each of its round-headed windows encloses a Palladian framework of glazing-bars – a central section whose rounded arch rises above short architraves supported by the capped pilasters of the sidelights. These, the original sashes, were the work of two carpenters, John Anderson and John Kay. The glass was supplied by Messrs. John and James Dunlop of Williamstown in standard eight-and-one-half by nine-and-one-half-inch panes.

The Reverend John Bethune had not lived to see his second stone church to completion. After his death in 1816, his widow sold the Williamstown property to the fur-trader-geographer David Thompson who discovered that he had inadvertently become ground landlord of the church which had been built on Bethune's property. Thompson hastened to transfer the church and churchyard to the congregation in whom it has been vested ever since.

St. Andrew's, Williamstown and "St. Isadore du Kingston" were the last churches to be built in Upper Canada in pioneer isolation. The War of 1812, which hampered the building of St. Andrew's, destroyed or ruinously damaged nearly all of the churches in the province. Their successors were more sophisticated structures, more architecturally competent and comparable.

# III
# *Neo-Classic*

*How amiable are thy tabernacles ....*
*Psalm* LXXXIV: *1*

Upper Canada emerged from the War of 1812 battered but cohesive. It had lost all its major buildings. Most of its fences had disappeared in a blaze of glory under regiments of camp kettles. There was little food about, and even less money. But there was a sense of community unknown before. As a massive lesson in practical geography the war had been a great success. In the line of duty the Fencible units from the Eastern District had actually seen Niagara Falls. They even knew where to find Beaver Dams. Militiamen returning to the Home District could compare Kingston with Chippawa, and Amherstburg with Cornwall, and all to the advantage of York. Canadiens from the Detroit had fought side by side with other Upper Canadians from the St. Lawrence who, to their infinite surprise, spoke only Gaelic or German. All had acquired a fuller comprehension of their land as they fought to keep it, and drawn out by necessity from the tight cocoon of pioneer isolation, they had found each other, for better or worse.

The churches of Upper Canada were in a sorry state when the war ended. All the better buildings had been on the shores of the Great Lakes or the banks of the international boundary rivers. Those which had not been burned outright had been used as hospitals, storehouses, forts, or as all three in turn. The furnishings had been removed from danger's reach by thoughtful hands—usually beyond hope of recovery.

But if the church physical had fallen on parlous times the church spiritual was in fighting trim. Two strong, determined religious leaders had moved to centre stage in Upper Canadian affairs during the war, mending the ravelled garment of civil order with firmness and dispatch. Alexander Macdonell, priest of St. Raphael's parish, Glengarry County, and John Strachan of Cornwall, newly appointed rector of St. James', York, had every confidence in their ability to cope with any contingency that was likely or unlikely to arise. They had, as well, a measure of confidence in each other, and would be prepared, each in his turn, to assist the other on the diagonal path towards the mitre.

If a line were to be drawn across Scotland from west to east, some ten minutes north of the fifty-seventh parallel, it would pass through Inchlaggan and Aberdeen, the birthplaces, respectively, of Alexander Macdonell and John Strachan. There were as many similarities of pattern in the religious background of the two men as there were deep and abiding differences in their religious profession. Both had been reared in homes in which harmonious solidarity had not been impaired by the fact that divergent religious beliefs were held by husband and wife. The fathers of both had adhered with stubborn zeal to denominations suppressed for political considerations in late-eighteenth-century Scotland. Macdonell *père* was a Roman Catholic; John Strachan senior was a member

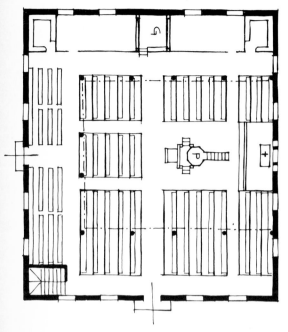

*III-1: St. James', York, as enlarged in 1818. The altar, ( + ), and the pulpit, (P), remained in their original locations but the processional axis of the interior changed direction. It now ran from the King Street entrance to the Lieutenant-Governor's pew, (G), flanked by pews for the legislators.*

of the Scottish Episcopal Church. Their sons had thus some early experience of the discomforts of non-conformity. The mothers of both churchmen, on the other hand, had enjoyed the assurance derived from membership in the Established Church of the land —in this instance the Presbyterian Church of Scotland. Both good ladies were to be equally proud of sons in orders in their fathers' faiths, but neither wavered in her devotion to her own Church; each was firm in her belief that it was predestined to be so. Strachan wrote of his mother, "She made religion amiable to me and a source of moral strength." Macdonell was given to saying that he "knew a lot of good Protestant prayers." He used them often, presenting them in his native Gaelic for the comfort of the afflicted who were not of his communion.

John Strachan, the younger of the two Scots, reached Upper Canada first, emigrating in 1799 on the vague promise of an appointment in a college as yet unfounded. As belief in the college mirage diminished, he became restive in his post of tutor to the Cartwright and McAulay children in Kingston, and when a vacancy occurred in the St. Gabriel Street Presbyterian Church in Montreal he toyed with the idea of seeking ordination in his mother's Church. Perhaps it was remembrance of her moral strength which deterred him, perhaps more worldly considerations prevailed. At any rate, when he did become a clergyman, it was in the Church of England. Thus Strachan, who as a boy had accompanied his father to furtive services in a humble little Episcopal chapel above a shop in the Gallowgate of Aberdeen, set his feet in the path of apostolic succession. The Scottish Episcopal Church, and more especially the diocese of Aberdeen, had done very well by North America.

John Strachan moved to York on the eve of the War of 1812. Six months later, when civil authority dissolved in the face of defeat, he bearded the victorious American invaders in their field headquarters and demanded that the looting and burning cease at once. Public panic had placed Strachan's hand on the helm; he would not easily let it go. But before he could get to work on the province he had first to set his church in order.

St. James' had been looted, dismantled, used as a hospital, and generally knocked about. Even had it remained intact, it was too small for a growing parish. Strachan marshalled his forces and pressed for immediate payment of the war-loss indemnity, determined to enlarge the building. The intention, as advertised in *The Gazette*, with the call for tenders, was to "lengthen the church forty feet toward the east with a circular end; thirty of which to form part of the body of the church and the remaining ten an altar, with a small vestry room on one side and a government pew on the other. To remove the Pulpit to the north side and to erect two galleries, one opposite to it and another on the west end . . . ."

The advertised intention was not fated to be realized, nor can the scraps of church papers which survived two major fires, be accepted uncritically out of context. A water-colour perspective and plan of a tall, narrow church with colossal windows (presumably submitted with an unsuccessful tender) remain to cloud the issue. They have been believed for years to show St. James' as it was in 1818, but the dimensions of the enlarged building, as described by Strachan himself in a report to the S.P.G., refute the attribution. He wrote in part: "The repairs and addition cost £1700, a sum which was subscribed for with great alacrity by the parishioners on condition of their being repaid from the sale of pews ... the church is sixty-six feet by sixty, with a neat altar and a steeple. The Hon. George Cruikshank, the Receiver General, presented rich silk damask coverings for the pulpit, the reading and clerks desks and the altar table ...."

Further descriptions of the completed St. James' exist from the personal observations of the Reverend Alexander Neil Bethune and the Reverend Henry Scadding. Bethune, who first saw St. James' in 1819, described the interior: "As you entered you found yourself in a building almost square. The aisle leading from the front door was bounded northwards by the Governor's large square pew: and midway it was intersected by one running east and west. Bounding this on the east was the chancel, in front of it was the pulpit, reading desk and clerk's pew."

On the basis of the descriptions a conjectural restoration of the floor plan can be made (III-1). The existing building was extended equally to the north and to the south —the old lateral framing replaced by superimposed turned posts to support the new gallery. It was a structurally practical solution within the means available. The seating capacity was doubled; the traffic pattern was admirable; but the visual orientation had had to be sacrificed. The altar remained in the east, but was no longer the processional focus of the building; that had shifted to the Governor's pew.

The only real difference between the plan of St. James', as recast in 1818, and that of St. Andrew's Church of Scotland, Williamstown (III-2), which was being completed internally in the same year, was that the altar table of St. James' was placed behind the pulpit, while that of St. Andrew's was before it. In both churches the pulpit was located to the right of the central long axis as it was in Gibbs' St. Nicholas West Kirk, Aberdeen, the handsomest Georgian church known to Bethune and Strachan, who were both King's College men. In seeking for a plan they had unconsciously followed a precedent already well established in North American church-building practice: when in doubt revert to Gibbs.

Dr. Scadding described St. James' as he recalled it: "An entrance was opened at the southern end, toward King Street, and over the gable in this was built a square tower bearing a circular bell turret, surmounted by a small tin covered spire. The whole

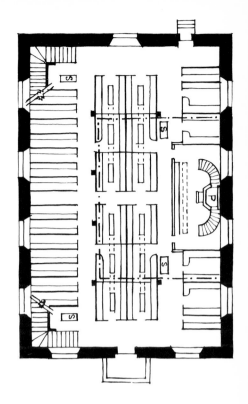

*III-2: St. Andrew's, Williamstown, as completed in 1818, retained the liturgical pattern of the eighteenth-century Church of Scotland. The pulpit, (P), centred on one side wall, was set in a railed communion place. Convertible communion pews ran the whole length of the building between two side aisles. Four stoves, (S), were set discreetly, their labyrinthine pipes warming the U-shaped gallery.*

51

edifice as thus enlarged and improved was painted of a light blue colour, with the exception of the frames around the windows and doors and the casings at the angles, imitating blocks of stone alternately long and short, which were all painted white." This Wedgwood elegance was further enhanced by placing round-headed windows at the gallery level on three sides of the building. On the eastern side the old altar window was raised and given a round-arched head and flanking lights in the Palladian style.

Scadding recalled some interior colour: "The pews everywhere were painted of a buff or yellowish hue, with the exception of the rims at the top which were black. The pulpit and its appurtenances were white." The worthy gentleman seems not to have found the colour of the walls and ceiling memorable; for lack of evidence to the contrary they may be presumed to have been white also.

It was not the church that Strachan had envisioned in York, but it would do for the time at least. He was gaining ground in other areas. He had just completed for his own use the largest and handsomest house in the town. Furthermore, in recognition of his services to the colony in the recent war, he had been appointed to a seat on the Legislative Council.

Strachan's large friend, the Reverend Alexander Macdonell, had been deedily employed in the war too. In 1812 he and the Reverend John Bethune had together sent around the fiery cross to call out their Highlanders for service in a re-formed Glengarry Fencible Regiment and an additional corps of the Canadian Fencibles. Both units had served throughout the war as British regulars and were entered as such in the army lists.

In the first days of peace the Lieutenant-Governor of Upper Canada recommended to Macdonell's ecclesiastical superiors that it would gratify him if the priest of St. Raphael's were given a position of authority. The Church concurred in this, and Alexander Macdonell was consecrated Bishop of Rhesina and named Vicar-Apostolic for Upper Canada. It was inappropriate for the Bishop of Rhesina – even *in partibus infidelis* – to set his cathedra in a log building. The Blue Chapel would have to go. Macdonell requested permission to visit Scotland that he might personally select stonemasons to build his church.

The "Blue Chapel" had been a misleading name for the first church of St. Raphael's, which was in fact a sturdy little building of weathered log. It had been built in 1789 by another Father Alexander Macdonell (of Scothouse) who had emigrated from Scotland in 1786 with some five hundred Roman Catholic Highlanders who had elected to settle near their Loyalist kindred in Glengarry and Stormont, forming in 1802 the second Roman Catholic parish in that area. The blueness of their log chapel was internal, and confined to the ceiling.

There was, however, a chapel in Upper Canada whose blueness was beyond question. This was the Blue Chapel at New Oswegatchie (now Maitland). Built by the Anglicans and used as a community church, it was destroyed by fire, but rose, phoenix-like, bluer than ever. The present structure, built on a reduced scale in 1845, eventually became a mortuary chapel.

Fire posed an ever-present hazard to the existence of isolated country churches in Upper Canada. In 1970 a disastrous blaze gutted St. Raphael's Church. Only the shell of Bishop Macdonell's pride stands, its austere date stone still making proclamation in beautiful uncial Gaelic that it was built to the praise of God in 1821 (III-3).

It had been an ambitious project for a rural community, but for the first five years of its spiritual life St. Raphael's was the premier Roman Catholic edifice of all Upper Canada. The Bishop had determined to build a large, substantial structure and had fetched stonemasons from Scotland to carry out his wishes. There was to be no repetition here of the Kingston nonsense about inability to fit the liturgical plan into the intra-mural space. The standing walls testify that the building contractor, Archibald Fraser, was a good master-mason; the archival records suggest that he was cantankerous, and also that the Bishop could be a high-handed Highland autocrat on occasion. The building costs exceeded the estimates—they always do. The Bishop had personally contributed some three thousand pounds to the undertaking, and he testily reminded the contractor that personal speculation had brought about his difficulties. Fraser, an autocrat in his own right, threatened the law and demanded payment in full. Where Greek meets Greek autocracy must go by the board, so the Bishop switched tactics and employed his considerable charm to advantage. The work proceeded, but it required the churchman's constant supervision to reconcile the exacting standards of the professional craftsman with the cheerful ineptitude of his labour force of parish volunteers.

In July of 1820, declining the invitation of Sir Peregrine Maitland to visit at Stamford Cottage, the Bishop wrote: "Have recommenced the work on the new church here. I find nothing will get on without my own presence. So difficult it is to get out of a mortar bucket once fairly deep in it."

Bishop Macdonell and Archibald Fraser had set their architectural objectives for St. Raphael's at an attainable level. The Bishop wished to build, within reasonable means, a large, well-lighted place of worship, but one which would allow for community growth. Fraser undertook to build a substantial structure of good masonry.

But then what happened? From there on the voice might be Jacob's but the hands were certainly the hands of Esau. The

54

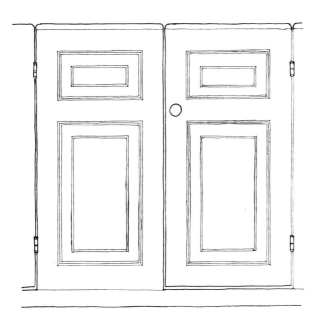

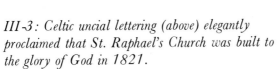

*III-3: Celtic uncial lettering (above) elegantly proclaimed that St. Raphael's Church was built to the glory of God in 1821.*

*III-4: Bishop Macdonell's pride, St. Raphael's (left), built in 1821, was for five years the most important Roman Catholic church in Upper Canada. Gutted by a disastrous fire in 1970, the ruin has been declared a national monument.*

*III-5: Elegant mouldings defined the panels of Neo-Classic slip pews and matching doors (top right).*

55

clumsy frontispiece of St. Raphael's, as built, was unworthy of a master-builder of Fraser's quality (III-4). Flanked by half-columns of a gigantic Tuscan order—which later hands reduced to flat pilasters—it had a stark, incomplete look. The stilted awkwardness of the fan-transomed overdoors and the square window openings set in an uncompromising row above them cried aloud for the vertical emphasis of the two additional attached half-columns with which Fraser had intended to pull the composition together. He had used the device to good effect in St. Andrew's Church, Kingston, the year before. The Bishop may have hoped to solve the problem more economically with a coat of harling and some stucco or fresco work. He undoubtedly meant St. Raphael to stand in winged splendour on the flattened apex of the gable wall.

As soon as all the principal masonry work was finished, Archibald Fraser departed, to range freely about Upper Canada in pursuance of his profession. In July 1833 *The Cobourg Star* reported: "Mr. Archibald Fraser who built the Hamilton [Township] Court House has taken contract for building the Scotch church [in Colborne]."

With Fraser out of the picture at St. Raphael's, work went on peacefully in the interior of the church. It was a large, light, uncluttered open space. Its flat ceiling had been painted a clear cerulean with a scattering of pale gold stars. The walls and the slip pews were white (III-5). Warmth and colour were concentrated in the sanctuary beyond the graceful double-bowed balustrade, with its polished cherrywood rail and simple slender white balusters.

St. Raphael's parish, happy in the completion of its church in 1826, was suddenly both jubilant and appalled. Bishop Macdonell had been recommended for further advancement. His new designation of Regiopolis (as nearly titular as the Lieutenant-Governor dared make it) was synonymous with Kingston where his cathedral must needs be. He would have to leave St. Raphael's.

Thereafter, over the years, St. Raphael's Church was changed, following ecclesiastical fashion. In the mid-1840's the pews in the nave were transformed with painted-graining in imitation of a dark hardwood of indeterminate species, to match new blocks of pews in the transepts vacated by the seminarians who had removed to Kingston. In 1900 the interior was extensively altered in the Beaux Arts style, and in 1970 it was destroyed by fire.

The completion of St. Andrew's, Williamstown, the alterations of St. James', York, and the building of St. Raphael's had all been part of the wave of energetic church building which followed on the heels of the War of 1812, yet all had been, for differing reasons, apart from it. St. Andrew's, removed from the direct path of the war, had been delayed for a time by the lack of both funds and builders, and was then completed in the old style. The second phase of St. James', York was frankly makeshift, and St.

Raphael's was architecturally eccentric according to the best North American standards.

Neither Macdonell nor Strachan was heir to the long English-Georgian tradition in either its native or its derivative North American form, although Strachan had come sufficiently under its influence to build in the style of Gibbs at Cornwall in 1806.

James Gibbs had, in 1728, very obligingly published *A Book of Architecture* in which he generously set forth plans, elevations, and sections, together with explicit directions for constructing several adaptations of his most famous buildings. The Gibbs book could have been found, with other architectural works, on the library shelves of a number of the principal pew-holders of Upper Canada's major churches before the War of 1812. Although many of those valued libraries had been lost in the course of the war, their bereft owners were not the sort of persons to sit bookless and moaning their loss while government officials and well-to-do merchants were crossing and recrossing the Atlantic. Neither did the colonial businessmen go architecturally blinkered when abroad. They considered with interest the new buildings in all the commercial centres visited, as well as the major monuments in London itself, and they brought back ideas, books, plans and craftsmen to assist them in their enterprises.

Many of the standard eighteenth-century architectural works of Campbell, Ware, Chambers, Gibbs, Adam and Soane were still available for study—to sharpen the perceptions of excellence and arouse longing and frustration in the ambitious. And there were other books, more suited to practical colonial needs, as well. Just when they were most urgently required, a seemingly inexhaustible flow of technical and pattern books was emanating from Thomas Kelly's publishing house in Paternoster Row. The list eventually ran to some thirty titles, which would be reprinted as late as 1853. The prolific author of the series was Peter Nicholson who had reached London and the Department of Public Works during the last years of Sir William Chamber's surveyorship (III-6). Nicholson wrote his builders' guides from a varied background of practical experience. Nor was his store of information simply derivative; he was himself a mathematician—the first to observe that Greek mouldings were based on conic sections. And he was as willing to pass on his own discoveries as those of other men.

Nicholson had a North American contemporary counterpart in Asher Benjamin who practised, wrote and taught his architectural skills to others in and around Boston. Benjamin's books and those of Minard Lafever, from the Finger Lakes region of New York, provided the working text for hundreds of master-builders scattered over the eastern United States, for almost half a century (III-7). It would be easy to assume that they were followed with equal assiduity in Upper Canada, but that would be too facile a judgment.

The pattern of reference to architectural texts would be simpler to plot had all the texts used remained in local collections. The task would be still easier had all of the churches remained more or less as built, or failing that, were at least standing for inspection. Alas, they have not. So it must suffice for the moment that reference works were used and that among the surviving texts those of Peter Nicholson and Asher Banjamin hold first and second places.

Given the problem of building for worship in Upper Canada in 1818, with architectural pattern books available, what might one expect the ideal solution to be? The fabric would be of masonry construction—stone, if available, for homesick British immigrants, brick for more seasoned North Americans. Or the building might be of fine timberwork and good honest weatherboard for those of limited means, whatever their origin. The nature of the material was truly immaterial if the quality of the workmanship was high enough. It was the nice adjustment in the proportion of enclosed space, the relation of void to solid, the number and profile of the mouldings, the fitness of its parts, which truly mattered in the production of a good Georgian church. Grace, dignity and repose—these were the components with which the Upper Canadians, following in the eighteenth-century tradition, sought to build houses of worship for their God. It was the most thoroughly domestic style of ecclesiastical building ever so offered, with the possible exception of the adapted Argive megaron.

The prototype of the ideal late-late-Georgian church of Upper Canada was proportioned to the classic golden mean of ancient Greece. The composition of its façade was centred about a doorway, or doorways, of some elegance, and one or more architecturally important windows. The side—or, as Nicholson would put it, the flank elevation—was made up of four bays externally expres-

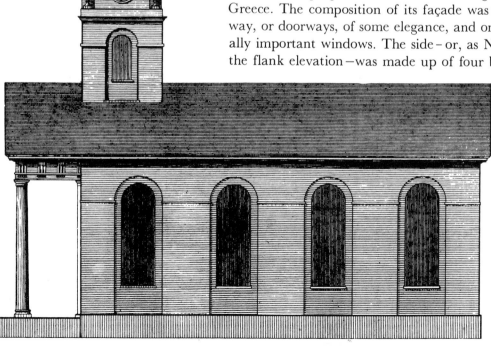

sed by four tall round-headed windows of two or more double-hung sashes, with small rectangular panes of clear glass inset in thin muntin bars. The principal doorways were finished with fan transoms either semicircular or, more usually, semi-elliptical in form. A finely detailed wooden cornice graced the eaves, frequently containing, among its complex member mouldings, one hollowed to form a rainwater trough.

The interior of this "ideal" Neo-Classic church was light, serene and graceful. At that time the focal point in most churches was still the tall pulpit with its ornamented sounding board. In close association with it there was usually an altar-table. The pews (box or slip), enclosed to the floor to exclude draughts, were entered by panelled doors. The box pews might be provided with kneelers or foot stools, and with foot warmers in cold weather. The Georgian church was a preaching church, and the congregations, trapped sitting throughout lengthy discourses, had to be encouraged with cushions and stoves.

Theoretically this was the Upper Canadian early-nineteenth-century house of worship in ideal form. It hardly needs to be said, however, that every church surviving from that date contrives in some way to depart from the rule. Most of the buildings have been altered many times. If one of them chanced to survive a hundred years in more or less pristine condition, loving hands proceeded to mutilate it in celebration of its longevity, carefully marking each fresh disaster with a small brass plaque.

Working alphabetically on the "A is for Anglican" principle which dominated government thought in Upper Canada in the relevant years, the major allowance for war-loss damage was paid first on the Churches of England destroyed between 1812 and 1814, and it was promptly paid — as government payments go. Thus it was that Richard Pollard, a major clerical sufferer on the Detroit frontier, could, by 1820, announce with satisfaction construction of two handsome brick churches — Christ Church, Amherstburg (III-8) and St. John's, Sandwich. And he could add that

*III-6 and 7: Most popular among Peter Nicholson's staggering output of thirty-two builders' pattern books was his* Principles of Architecture, *first published in 1795. The plate of a church in "The Grecian style" (III-6 right), drawn and engraved by Nicholson, shows the designer-author at his best. Nicholson's American counterpart, Asher Benjamin, satisfied his following with more reprints of fewer titles. Plate L (III-7 left) in the 1827 edition of* The American Builder's Companion, *ably blended Greek with Georgian elements.*

St. Paul's, Chatham (in wood) and Christ Church, Colchester (in stone) were already under construction.

The handsomeness of the brick churches was, in Pollard's view, largely due to the material, of which he was justly proud. They were the first churches to be built of brick in all Upper Canada. Archdeacon Bethune was to describe Christ Church, the elder by a year, as "a neat brick building, though at variance with all architectural rule." Architectural rule is more variable than the good Archdeacon realized. Christ Church, Amherstburg was a very free adaptation of the early Georgian style.

The west end of Christ Church, Amherstburg, save for a cumbering porch, stands more or less as Pollard knew it. A pair of pleasant round-headed Georgian windows were set under relieving arches on either side of a graceful fan-transomed doorway. The gable parapet, finished with a moulded coping stone and a pair of diminutive obelisks, rose on a pleasant Classical incline, to be suddenly cropped at the apex. This horizontal plane was the logical base for the lower register of the belfry. However, in 1819 when Christ Church stood ready for use, the belfry, although planned, had not yet been built. The roof must then have had a snub gable uncannily like that of St. James', Goose Creek, South Carolina, erected one hundred years earlier. The little Episcopal churches of the Carolina Santée were the work of French Huguenot masons and joiners. French masonry tradition, the needs of the Episcopal Church, and the Georgian architectural vocabulary may, in similar combination, have been responsible for the appearance of a group of snub-gabled churches which once graced the Upper Canadian side of the Detroit and the St. Clair rivers.

Christ Church, Amherstburg, the best of the lot, has retained the greatest proportion of its early fabric. Its initial superiority was due, in part, to the more abundant funds granted to garrison churches, but principally to the guiding hand of Robert Reynolds of Belle Vue house who donated the brick for the structure. Reynolds had served in the Commissary during the war and was thus in a good position to call on the engineers at Fort Malden for advice and assistance. There can be little doubt that the master-builders who constructed Christ Church had already been at work at Belle Vue. The pavilions there were even more thoroughly in the Georgian vein than was the façade of Christ Church, but the idiom was the same – a species of Whitehall Horse-Guards Georgian entirely familiar to British officers.

If further proof of Reynolds' influence were required, one has but to consider the second church of St. John, Sandwich, built by the same rector but with different pew-holders, and with no well-trained Royal Engineers conveniently at hand. Contemporary evidence for the original appearance of St. John's exists in a series of drawings made in 1821 by Colonel Claudius Shaw (III-9),

*III-8: Southern Georgian on the Detroit River. Christ Church, Amherstburg, 1819.*

signed and dated at Moy, an up-river fur-trading post.

Shaw lagged far behind the Royal Engineers in graphic skill; consequently some of the information conveyed in the drawings was ambiguous. The scale of the masonry would indicate stonework, but the church was built of brick, and oral tradition has it that the said brick was brought on scows from Buffalo. Why did the builders of St. John's boycott the brickyard at Amherstburg, where very good brick had been turned out for Belle Vue and Christ Church? And if they were set on buying material to build the new church from the people who burned the first one, why did they by-pass Detroit? But that was not Shaw's problem; he was drawing up a perspective visualization for masons who knew the quantity of brick required and how to lay it up in proper coursing without a brick-by-brick diagram from him.

There has been a degree of confusion about the dimensions of St. John's Church as actually built. Some evidence indicates it was thirty-six by thirty-six, like the first building; other authorities bear out Shaw's drawing which suggests that it was a church of four bays—that is, of a thirty-six by forty-eight proportion. A bay some twelve feet in depth, which was added at a later date, caused the confusion. It contained the chancel and vestry portion commended by Bethune in 1847.

One might doubt the probability of the elementary crow-stepped gable of the St. John's façade, which begs the addition of baroque scrolls or a segmental pediment or a bit of sculpture to complete it, were it not that the identical gable form appeared in Christ Church, Colchester, built of Pelee Island limestone. The latter building survived, although in a ruinous state, until 1959, when a replica of the church was built. There is no need to search for the prototypes of St. John's crow-stepped gable, which was neither Scots nor Dutch but inevitable, and which is reconstructed daily with building blocks in the kindergartens of the world.

Shaw's drawing for the sanctuary of St. John's was historically a much more important document (III-10). In it one can see the liturgical setting proposed for Anglican worship in 1821, which thirty years later still satisfied that zealous ecclesiologist, Archdeacon Bethune. The pulpit was certainly high and elaborate, but its canopied, swagged opulence was set decently on the Gospel side of the space. A less felicitous arrangement of the reading desk, the clerk's desk and a commodious pew occupied the Epistle side. In the centre, set beneath the Palladian window on a little raised platform, was an altar remarkable for its mediaeval form.

Having arranged the interior of St. John's with great decorum, Claudius Shaw became a trifle giddy on the roof. His "proposed elevation of a steeple for the Protestant church at Sandwich"—actually a perspective drawing—depicted a whimsical little pavilion of open arches supported on slender Tuscan columns. The re-

*III-10 below: His drawing for the interior of the second St. John's, Sandwich, while clean and explicit in the attenuated elegance of the Neo-Classic pulpit and the sturdy solidity of a surprisingly Gothic altar, faltered into incoherence in the reading pew.*

*III-9 left: The whimsical inefficiency of Colonel Shaw's design left a great deal to the builder's imagination.*

*III-11 right: A little mediaeval romance in salt-glazed stoneware. The S.P.G. gift font, Christ Church, Amherstburg.*

A. Pulpit
B. Communion Table
C. Reading Desk
D. Seat
E. Clerk

markable superstructure was given a semblance of credibility by an attached list of specifications. The square seems to have been set on its diagonals and the whole confection must have been weirdly akin to masque-scenery by Inigo Jones. The belfry was "strengthened" in 1833. No wonder.

The first breath of the changing winds of the ecclesiastical fashion reached the little Anglican churches of Essex County in the form of Gothic fonts—gifts from the Society for the Propagation of the Gospel (III-11). The fonts were little salt-glazed stoneware bowls with domed lids (ogival in section), ornamented with Gothic tracery derived from mediaeval sources, with a large disregard for the use of the original design. Sandwich and Amherstburg still cherish their stoneware fonts, but Colchester was either inadvertently overlooked in the original gift, or was deprived by careless packing. The parishioners were forced to improvise, and with the self-reliant spirit of Essex met the challenge. A matron of the congregation presented her best white stoneware soup-tureen; a pedestal was contrived for it, and the original lid was replaced by a more seemly covering of wood with a finial cross.

The post-1812 Georgian form favoured by the establishment in the Niagara Peninsula can best be studied in St. Andrew's, Grimsby (III-12). The parishioners of St. Andrew's were stimulated to architectural activity by the arrival, in 1817, of a resident clergyman, the Reverend William Samson. The masonry walls, of local stone, were laid up in record time, and the structure was roofed by the end of 1819, the year which saw the completion of the church in Amherstburg.

The design chosen for St. Andrew's was virtually identical to that being used in the rebuilding of war-damaged St. Mark's, Newark (Niagara-on-the-Lake). In both buildings a highly simplified colonial version of a Wren country parish church was

*III-12 St. Andrew's, Grimsby,*
*as it appeared in the*
*Neo-Classic serenity of 1824.*

followed. (Possibly designed by Captain Pilkington, R.E., who had married Margaret Nelles of Grimsby.) A stone tower, square in plan, occupied the centre of the façade, and was finished with a Doric pediment which carried forward the main roof ridge. And there the Grimsby builders rested from their labours, the sabbatical interlude brought about by the exhaustion of the available funds and the untimely death of the Reverend Mr. Samson.

In 1823 Grimsby acquired a new clergyman in the Reverend Alexander Neil Bethune, fifth son of the Reverend John Bethune of Williamstown and student in theology of John Strachan. Under Bethune's guidance sufficient money had been collected—or promised—by July of 1824, to make completion of the church possible. N.B. Goodell, master-joiner, who had already made the handsome Doric cornices for the main body of the building, set to work to complete the tower and fit the interior for use. The second stage of the bell tower was finished at the corners with paired Roman Doric pilasters (III-13). The belfry, a louvered, arcaded pavilion of octagonal form, was surmounted by a tall spire that slanted steeply up to the ubiquitous weathervane. Presumably the "four pine timbers" purchased for six shillings in 1824 were not proof against the hurricane which wrought such havoc among the churches of Niagara in the 1840's. Certainly the candle-snuffer spire which replaced the original one in the 1860's was a less daring structure. Nor are the windows at present seen in St. Andrew's those for which one hundred and sixty-four panes of glass were ordered from "Smith Griffin for two pounds fourteen shillings and eight pence." (By the 1860's the pointed phase of the Gothic Revival had passed, and the refenestration of St. Andrew's could be accomplished in the Venetian-Gothic taste within the existing openings.)

The parish records state that Charles Mullen, joiner, made music desks for St. Andrew's, Grimsby in 1831. Had he already worked on that walnut log purchased on 4 November 1824 for a pulpit? And was it Jacob Callarday, the steeple-painter, who mixed the quarter pound of lamp-black in a quart of whisky to take the glare from the limewash for the interior walls? Present evidence does not say, nor have any of the original interior installations survived for study.

The brick and stone late-Georgian churches of Upper Canada, like St. Andrew's Grimsby, were all subjected to alteration, but they stood a better chance of weathering the architectural rigours of the nineteenth century than did their timber contemporaries. Survival did not depend, as might be supposed, on ability to withstand the climate, but rather on a latent mediaevalism lurking at the back of Upper Canadian thought, which encouraged the belief that brick and stone as materials were more seemly than wood for the construction of sacred edifices.

*III-13: St. Andrew's, Grimsby, reglazed and re-spired.*

Of all nineteenth-century Upper Canadians, the New England Loyalists and their descendants were the most likely to build in wood. The white weather-boarded church was a part of their heritage, and they proposed to continue in the tradition. An agreeable example of the Georgian timber style survives in Port Burwell where a church was built by one of the many Lake Erie Baptist communities (III-14).

The first Baptist settlers along Lake Erie were largely Loyalists from New England, an area that had been founded by Puritans seeking freedom of worship in the New World. As with all people, they really meant by this freedom to worship after their own manner and no other. The southern colonies had received a large mixed group of Royalists and dissenters escaping, in their turn, from Puritan persecution. (Every religious belief ever held by mankind has been opposed, if not persecuted, somewhere, at some time, by someone.) In the southern colonies the Baptists had been one religious group among many. None was predominant, although one Church – the Church of England – was officially established. In New England, on the other hand, the Congregational Church, founded by the Puritans, was entrenched in strength. Many New England Baptists had learned to prefer the indifferent tolerance of the official Church to the active hostility of the dominant Puritans. They had to consider which party was likelier to accord them total religious freedom, and during the Revolution quite a number of them decided to ensure the degree of freedom already in hand. They emigrated to Nova Scotia, to Quebec, to the Niagara Peninsula, to the Bay of Quinte, and to the sandy northern shores of Lake Erie.

*III-14: Two Georgian churches in the New England tradition. Port Burwell Baptist (left) in Norfolk County and White's Methodist (III-15 right) in Hastings.*

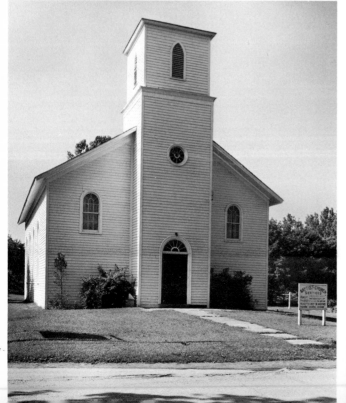

The central core of Baptist belief—the practice which gave the sect its name—was in the saving ordinance of baptism. And by baptism the Baptists meant the total immersion of adults on profession of faith. The architectural implications of this practice differed greatly from those deriving from the baptism of infants, even when this was solemnized by immersion, as in the Eastern Orthodox rite.

The pioneer simplicities of Upper Canadian living precluded the building of special baptistries, and inhibited the development of special functional areas within the church building. All early Upper Canadian Baptist churches were located on or near a considerable body of water, however, so the lack of special provision was not immediately acute—though the clergyman who cut a hole in the thick ice of a frozen river for the purpose was felt by some to have demanded rather too Spartan a degree of endurance on the part of the faithful.

As the years went by, the little Baptist church in Port Burwell and others built in the days of early settlement were altered to suit changing practice. Inward change was expressed externally at Port Burwell by the insertion of fashionable Gothic tracery in the windows of the flank walls, and by adding a belfry stage of mildly Gothic mien to the tower. In its pre-belfry day the tower was capped by a pyramidal roof like that which was to be seen on White's Church, Bayside (III-15) from 1841 until its demolition in 1970.

White's Church was a small but charming building, harmonious in its proportions, bold in the attenuated height of its windows and in the drama of shadow cast by the entablature of the entrance doorway. The Neo-Classicism of that doorway and the fine scale of the cornice moulding were old-fashioned by 1841, but the builder either did not know this or, more probably, did not care. He was continuing to build in the best timber tradition of the Bay of Quinte region. The doorway of White's Church had a slim Tuscan pilaster on either side, supporting the handsome entablature. The uppermost member of the cornice was cut after the fashion more generally associated with interior door casings and mantelpieces of the Neo-Classic style. Its central section was curved in a shallow semi-elipse; the terminal portions were rectangular and of slightly deeper projection.

Of the timber churches which were designed in the continuing Georgian tradition, one of the handsomest yet standing is Christ Church, Vittoria (III-16). Built in the late 1840's, this structure displays a number of Regency characteristics. In it the fine-drawn, almost fragile scale of the Neo-Classic had been replaced by a more robust approach to surface treatment. Mouldings had become broader and thicker; and new proportional relationships in the glazing of windows had replaced the old regular rectangular grid.

*III-16: Plank masquerading as ashlar masonry in the Regency manner. Christ Church, Vittoria.*

Christ Church, Vittoria, was clad with flush-boarding, bevelled on either matching edge, and grooved to imitate the vertical joints of ashlar masonry. All arrises were finished with heavier pieces of plank similarly moulded and arranged to form quoins. The textural illusion of stone was strengthened when the church was first built, by dashing fine sand against the freshly painted walls. Casings for the round-arched windows and door openings were given keystones and fillet mouldings at the springing of the arches. The lower portion of the bell tower, serving as usual as an entrance porch, now gives access to two small vestries set on either side of it. These little single-storey projections, finished with quoins similar to those of the main body of the building, were later additions.

The same Regency-Gothic taste gouged descriptive channels about lancet forms in the supporting piers of the altar-table (III-17) which was presumably set on a small platform raised by a single step above the floor of the altar place. The finely scaled altar-rail appears to be original but there is clear evidence that it was once a little taller. A matching rail guards the pulpit steps. All the mouldings of this fine piece of cabinetwork are flat fillets arranged to enhance the beautiful figure of the wood (III-18). The pews, now minus their doors, are panelled with equal simplicity, imparting a great sense of unity to the whole interior of this interesting church. One suspects that the graining which now covers the pews was added after the Gothic Revivalists had pronounced oak to be the authentically Early English wood.

Fortunately the parishioners of Christ Church confined their mediaevalism to the painting of the pews and left undisturbed the pleasant glazing of the windows. The distinctive Regency glazing pattern followed here was designed for French doors and casement sash. Larger panes of glass had recently become available, and these were used as full panes in the central area of the window,

*III-17 below left: The altar-table became bolder and faintly Gothic under Regency influence.*

*III-18 below right: The moulding of the Regency pulpit tended to be crisply-cut flat fillets.*

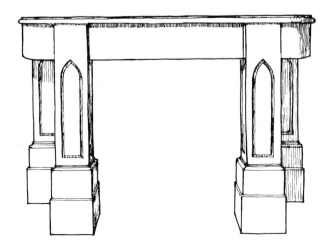

with a border of half panes at either side. This type of Regency glazing made its first appearance in Upper Canada in the late 1820's and was at the height of its popularity when the Roman Catholic parish of L'Orignal was founded in 1836.

Father Roderick Macdonell, the first parish priest of St. Andrew's and missionary at St. Regis, had in his will left money to assist in the building of a church at L'Orignal, once the site of the only French seigniory in all Upper Canada. His executors, Alexander Grant of Duldregan, *de facto* seigneur, and George Hamilton of Hamilton Hall, Hawkesbury – both Protestants – as in duty bound, took the matter in hand. They induced a third Protestant to donate land for the church site, and they themselves subscribed jointly one hundred and twenty pounds toward the project. The money was well spent. The church of St. John the Baptist was built in a suitable blend of the Lower Canadian and Upper Canadian Georgian styles, with Regency windows and a French double-pavilioned clocher (III-19).

Because it had made an economic use of space and was at the same time commodious, dignified and beautiful, the Georgian style continued to inspire builders to the eve of Confederation. At its simplest, the Upper Canadian Georgian church was a towerless preaching hall – a rectangular structure of classic proportion, with a pitched roof. The compositional balance was always pleasing, however meagre the claims of the little building to architectural pretension. If it were true, as one is constantly being told, that all Upper Canadian architecture was vernacular, then the common tongue in the early nineteenth century was still under the influence, however remote, of persons well versed in the classics.

How much poorer has rural Ontario become by the loss of buildings such as the old Methodist Meetinghouse at Switzerville (III-20)! It was both handsome and historic, for it was there that the first Methodist Conference in Canada was convened. And it was there that the first ordination of a Methodist clergyman in Upper Canada took place, as a corollary of that event.

The Switzerville Meetinghouse was simple in form, in the continuing tradition of wood construction, but the building date of 1826 placed it well within the best period of the Loyalist Neo-Classicism of the Bay of Quinte region. The builder of so engaging a principal façade may be forgiven his eccentric treatment of the upper windows, which hung like bath towels suspended from the frieze.

Switzerville Meetinghouse is gone, but there are still, at the time of writing, three small late-late-Georgian stone churches of great worth and charm in southern Ontario. They are the Old Stone Presbyterian Church in Thorah Township, near Beaverton; St. Anthony of Padua Roman Catholic, in South Easthope Township near Stratford; and Zion Lutheran, a short distance east of

St. Agatha in Waterloo. All are sturdy structures of local stone standing by country roadsides, each surrounded by the silent witness of its neat little churchyard. Much patient effort went into their building.

It was a full ten years from the early summer morning, in 1840, when the Presbyterians of Thorah vied with one another as to who would first arrive at the building site with a load of Lake Simcoe stone, to the winter day when the pews were all in place. John Morrison, the building contractor, awarded the prize for the stone-race to George Ross of the Fourth Concession of Thorah, who presumably had either the greatest driving skill or the best horses.

The initial incentive toward building the church had reached the new Lake Simcoe community in 1832 with a gift of fifty pounds from the King, William IV. A piece of ground in a suitable spot was purchased immediately, and over the next eight years the settlers subscribed enough money to begin building. Once the stone walls were up (III-21), the congregation set up benches and cheerfully endured day-long services in the roofless building, eating their frugal lunches in the churchyard in the brief respite between "the English" and "the Gaelic." By 1851 they had carefully amassed a sum sufficient to complete the building, and after yet another decade of zealous thrift, enough to install a U-shaped gallery.

John Morrison, within the narrow limits of a very tight budget, made skilful use of his materials. The best flat stones from the lake bed were set aside for the construction of the slightly cambered door arch and the round-headed window openings. They were beautifully laid, slightly projecting from the wall surface, and keyed by a stone but little larger than the rest. Wooden nailing blocks were let into the east façade, at eave height, for an anticipated returning eave of graceful form. But this either never materialized or unfortunately succumbed to expedient reroofing in the more robust 1860's. It is difficult to believe that the joiner who made cob-web fine muntins for the windows would have been

*III-19 opposite page: English Regency glazing (above) and a double clocher in the Quebec style (below) express the dual origins of St. John the Baptist Church, L'Orignal.*

*III-20: Outward, as well as inward grace clothed the Switzerville Methodist Meetinghouse.*

71

*III-21: Areas of secondary settlement were still building Georgian churches in 1840. The rubble stonework of the old Presbyterian church in Thorah (III-21 below) was set with discriminating care. Mitred velvet cushioned the pulpit's rim (III-22 right above) and twin stairs curved down to the railed communion place in the old style. But its pair of stoves (III-23 and 24 right below) celebrated the industrial present in every cast-iron frond of their Regency crests and every braided puff of smoke.*

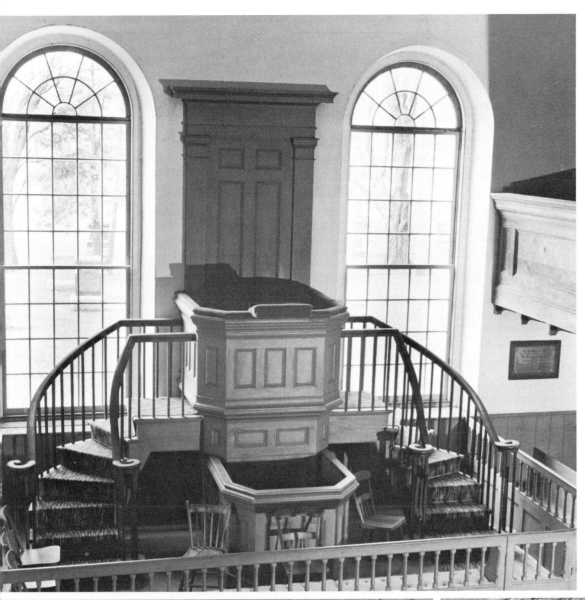

satisfied with the abrupt edge of the present roof. For the mould-ing of the muntins was fine-drawn—so fine-drawn, in fact, that the semicircular member at the centre of the window fans had actu-ally to be made of metal. A similar metal hoop muntin was used in the circular window in the gable.

On the other hand, if the same joiner was responsible for the finishing of the communion place there were narrow limits to his sensitivity (III-22). Stair building was not one of the areas in which he excelled, nor had he had direct access to the excellent treatises of Nicholson or Benjamin on that difficult subject. He built his ambitious double-scrolled staircases from fading recollec-tion, one would say, of a higher pulpit in a more spacious com-munion place.

The communion place in the Thorah church was designed to accommodate the liturgical needs of the Presbyterian Church of Scotland service. This railed space was not a choir, in any sense of the word, nor was the long built-in bench which faced the pulpit designed to hold a row of songsters, although some of its occupants may have been musically gifted. The side-chairs which now clutter such spaces in the Presbyterian churches of rural Ontario were later accretions. For the regular observance of the Sabbath the communion place had but two occupants—the minister, the in-habitant of the pulpit, and the precenter, who took his seat at the small desk immediately beneath it. The precenter, equipped with a tuning fork and, one would trust, a degree of musical training, led the congregation in the singing of the Psalms and, if the church were a Church of Scotland or United Presbyterian, in the singing of the Scottish Paraphrases and a few approved hymns as well.

The design of the communion place becomes comprehensible in the light of the Presbyterian communion ritual of the early nineteenth century. It was celebrated quarterly, and pre-com-munion preparatory services were held daily for as much as a sennight, if convenient. At the last of the preparatory services those members of the congregation who were professing Christians and who had, as far as the minister and the kirk session were aware, led exemplary lives, were each presented with a communion token. The tokens were small lozenges or discs of silver or pewter engraved or stamped with the name of the church and/or that of the minister. On the following day—the Sabbath itself—at the close of the prayer following a sermon of great length and strong feeling, the minister would descend from his high pulpit by the second stair (if the carpenter had made a provision for such a proceeding) and would take his seat at a narrow table of some length which had been set up in the communion place. Facing him across the fair linen cloth were the members of the kirk session seated on their special bench. They were the elders of the congregation, elected by their fellows and dedicated to their office. (After the Reformation some churches set the communion table thus in the devout belief that they were following the practice of the Early Christian Church in re-enacting the first communion at the supper table in the Upper Room in Jerusalem.)

When the Scots practice of setting a long table in a railed communion place originated, all the communicants proceeded to the gates in the communion rail, presented their tokens to an elder standing to receive them, and passed within to communicate. Long before the settlement of Upper Canada this form of procedure had been abandoned by the Church of Scotland as impractical, however. A table was still set up at each communion season within the railed communion place, but it was now reserved for the use of the minister and the elders of the kirk session. The congregation received the elements of communion seated at tables provided by modifying the structure of several of the pews in the front portion of the central section of the church seating.

In Thorah the pews were of single slip form—all democratically equal in comfort or discomfort. By hinging the bookrests attached to the backs of the first four rows of pews in the centre section, the transformation was achieved. When the pews were to be used at the communion season, the hinged flanges were raised to a horizontal position and supported on butterfly brackets. Narrow linen table-cloths were then spread over them and the communicants sat effectively on one side of a very narrow, very high table, and were served by the minister and the elders.

The joiners of Thorah did their best to provide a balanced liturgical arrangement within the limited space at their disposal. The pulpit was set centrally between a fine pair of windows. It was panelled, chamfered at the corners, and provided with a pair of curving staircases. The minister stood in an architectural setting backed by a panelled false-door set between pilasters supporting a solid entablature in the Roman Doric style. When he chose to sit, a shallow bracketed shelf with a cushion was ready to receive him but did not encourage long repose.

The minister was expected to derive all necessary inspiration from non-tangible sources, so that no special consideration seems ever to have been given to the rear wall at which he had often to look. In the small churches of rural Upper Canada the most exciting feature of that end was generally a box stove or two. The church in Thorah has a pair of stoves (III-23) of lively and imaginative design, manufactured by William Rudden of Montreal. And, in order that the unseemly clatter of poking and stoking should not disturb a congregation concentrating on higher matters, the stoves were set in a low heat-hole in the partition wall, with the body of the stove (III-24) in the principal room and the lesser portion, with the stoking doors, projecting slightly into the narthex.

*III-25 and 26: Plain Georgian excellence informs St. Anthony of Padua, South Easthope (III-25 below left), endearingly tempered by the rule-of-thumb common sense expressed in the simple confessional screen (below right) and the durable rows of thick pine benches (III-26 opposite page).*

The twin stairs, which rise in the narthex and give access to the gallery, were more expertly constructed than the pulpit steps, and suggest that they owe their form to the builder of the later gallery. If the same joiner worked on both, then he had in the interim had a look at one of Asher Benjamin's excellent books. The curve of the step and the rail are Benjaminian in form, and the turned newel follows his exact specifications. The stairs do not rise directly into the gallery in Thorah, as they do in other churches of similar size and date, but into two small lobbies on either side of a little room whose glazed doors allow for borrowed light. In this little room, which may have served for meetings of the session, is a long narrow table whose size suggests that it was once set up in the communion place, before the precenter's box was enlarged to its present dimensions. It also contains a relocated corner cupboard which undoubtedly stood in the body of the church before the gallery was constructed and must always have held the communion plate and linen.

The other two members of the trilogy of late Georgian stone churches, St. Anthony of Padua, South Easthope (III-25) and Zion Lutheran, St. Agatha, which were being planned when the final touches were being installed at Thorah, were designed around different liturgical practices. Their structural containers, the buildings themselves, although having a stylistic likeness to the

*III-27: Zion's purity has been dimmed a little by the insertion of tinted and leaded Art Nouveau glass in its round-headed Georgian windows.*

Thorah church, have a much closer relationship to each other. They may even have been the work of a single team of builders. Both were erected by and for Upper Canadians of German extraction. And they were built, of variegated local fieldstone, in the adjoining counties of Perth and Waterloo. The two buildings were roughly the same size and proportion, with pitched roofs, returned eaves, three round-headed windows on either side, and a central doorway in one end, with a blind fan-transom of sunburst pattern above it. There was also a small enclosed belfry on the roof ridge. The roofs and belfries of both little buildings have been resurfaced, and in the process the belfry of St. Anthony's has lost its louvered voids which may have been similar to the charming fan-transomed openings still in place under the elf's cap spirelet of Zion.

St. Anthony's, on the other hand (as behoves the patron of those who seek that which is lost) has retained its original window sash and all its original furnishings (III-26). The harmonious beauty of this small church was still intact at the time of writing, although disquieting rumours were current that it was to be "saved" by having murals depicting the growth of the lumbering industry smeared on its clean white walls—a desecration abominable to believer and pagan alike. How could anyone standing—or better still kneeling—in this quiet abode of peace not wish to keep it exactly as it is? Its lovely proportions and restrained colour are a delight to the eye—white walls slightly shadowed by the sanctuary arch, the fitful gleam of pale gold on the high altar, the cheerful square of scarlet carpet spread before it, the dark linear pattern of the austere altar rail, the air-burned russet of pine plank pews, and the wide ebony frames of the tiny engravings high up on the wall marking the Stations of the Cross.

Life has passed by St. Anthony of Padua and St. Andrew's, Thorah. Both have largely become mortuary chapels. Zion, St. Agatha (III-27) has suffered greater structural change over the years, but still serves a congregation. All three bear witness to the importance of their role in the formative years of Upper Canada when the late Georgian churches of every denomination proclaimed in every line of their sturdy structure the social worth of those things which were lovely and of good report.

# IV
# Regency

*. . . What are the names of the men that make this building?*

*Ezra* v: 4

Upper Canada was somewhat underprivileged in the first decades of the nineteenth century as far as monumental professionally-designed architecture was concerned. Its churches suffer by comparison with those built in Australia at the time, and even more invidiously with those built in Lower Canada when that area was in a similar stage of colonial development. Unfortunately George IV, although quite as fascinated by building as Louis XIV had been, was even more self-centred. It would not have occurred to him to dispatch designers and artisans to an unimportant North American colony to improve the quality of its church building, as had been done for New France. And while one cannot seriously regret that Upper Canada was never a penal colony, there is no denying that when English architects found guilty of the more obvious forms of malpractice were transported to Australia on permanent government service it resulted in a colonial gain of marked visual importance.

The architects who eventually reached Upper Canada were self-propelled, and occasionally their professional status had been self-bestowed. Almost the only professional training in architecture to be had at that time was as an articled student in the office of a designer of recognized ability. The architect and the student had then to decide when professional proficiency had been attained (IV-1). Medicine and law were still being studied under parallel circumstances, and the standards in all three professions were somewhat fluid. On the other hand, it remains to be proven that a tight regimen produces good design or that a rigid standard of professional acceptance separates all of the sheep from the goats.

There was nothing outside the limiting contents of his own skull to prevent a draftsman in the Office of Works from thinking about the plans he had been given to execute and devising more exciting schemes for his own edification. There was nothing to prevent his counterpart in the building trades from observing the spatial solutions and uses of material made by a number of architects, and drawing his own conclusions therefrom. Neither was there anything to prevent a craftsman with a good visual memory from reproducing the working drawings for future reference. From such situations well-trained draftsman and astute builders could, and did, export their knowledge to less sophisticated communities. Some of them were content to coast on borrowed ideas for the rest of their working lives, but if they were intuitive designers in even the slightest degree, they would be compelled to adapt and invent within the idiom—or beyond it—and if, in so doing, they contrived to compose imaginatively in the interests of specific function and of aesthetic satisfaction, then the title of architect had been well and truly earned.

When Upper Canada was ready for them, the builder-engineer-architects arrived. By their works they are known, and all too often by their works alone. The clients who were so eager to pick their brains were reluctant to give credit where it was due. A search through church archives will usually uncover much information about the chairman of the building committee, the whole building committee, who subscribed to the building fund, how much (and if not why not), but it may never divulge the name of the designer whose idea it all was. The agreement will naturally have been between the contractor and the building committee. It may reveal the name of the clerk of works, who may or may not have been the architect of the building, although usually a member of the profession.

It is significant in this context that of the architects who practised in early-nineteenth-century Toronto, the best known should have been John George Howard. Howard was a competent designer, but he was memorable for having the forethought to publish an autobiography which was as remarkable for the vital information deliberately withheld as for that set forth. Frederick Cumberland, coming on the architectural scene some twenty years later, had to build a railway and raise a regiment to win second place in popular memory—although of the two he was the better architect. However, when the chips were down posterity has not played favourites; it has obliterated the works of both with cheerful impartiality.

Who then were the builder-architects who came to Upper Canada in the opening years of the nineteenth century and what did they build? One would expect to find evidence in the capital of the colony. J.S. Buckingham, in his work *Canada, Nova Scotia, New Brunswick* published in 1843, had this to say of the churches of Toronto (built while it was still a town called York): "The largest

*IV-2: St. Paul's, Lot Street (Queen East), 1823, the first Roman Catholic church in York.*

and handsomest is that for the Established Church of England. This was partially destroyed by fire a few years since and has been recently rebuilt from the subscriptions of the inhabitants nearly all of the more wealthy families here belong to the Establishment. It is built of stone, has a spacious and comfortable interior, a lofty tower of good architecture but crowned by an abridgement of a spire above this, which is mean in its proportions and the meanness is not at all redeemed by the glittering coat of white tin plate with which the spire is covered. The Kirk of Scotland, also an Established church in the colonies stands near it, and though smaller is a fine building. The Roman Catholic Church in size and rank of architecture comes next to the two named." The three churches (which had been built in reverse order) were all the work of John Ewart, the first architectural designer of demonstrable merit to appear in York.

Born in Tranent, East Lothian in 1788, John Ewart stemmed from the Scots background which had sent Watt, Nicholson, Telford and the Rennies to London to join that milling reserve of building practice, His Majesty's Department of Works. As a group they were inquisitive, inventive and prepared to experiment, generally basing their imaginative flights on a good sound training in practical building. John Ewart was a typical example of the export model of the species. While modestly styling himself a builder, he emerges from the mists of sparse documentation in 1823 as the architect of St. Paul's Church, York (IV-2), and recedes from view in 1846 in the guise of a director of the Toronto and Lake Huron Railroad.

In the interim he had not been idle. It has been established by Dr. Eric Arthur that John Ewart, aided and abetted by Dr. W.W. Baldwin, designed the earlier wing of Osgoode Hall for the Law Society of Upper Canada. Osgoode Hall was a pilastered Classical building in brick, stone and wood, in harmony with two earlier works by Ewart and Baldwin, the courthouse and the jail on King Street in York. At the same time Ewart designed the sham-Gothic courthouse still standing in London, Ontario.

John Ewart's churches stood in close relation to Osgoode Hall in their bold Classicism, but all had about them a touch of the London romantic. He designed two of the major churches of York in the second quarter of the nineteenth century: St. Paul's on Lot Street, built for the Roman Catholic community in 1823, and St. Andrew's Church of Scotland, fronting on Church Street, built in 1830. He also rebuilt a third, the 1839 version of St. James' Church of England on King Street.

The Honourable James Bâby, one of the leading parishioners of St. Paul's, writing to Bishop Macdonell on the first of February 1825, said in part, "I have however to observe that if the cost is great the Building is well worth it, for on Inspection it is, and will be found, I can truly say, the neatest Building of the kind in U. Canada—To this may be added the cheapest—the roof, steeple, a neat Gallery, a beautiful arched ceiling with cornices all in Plaster of Paris complete and painted—the whole ready for Public Worship . . . ."

Dr. Scadding recalled that St. Paul's had been a substantial brick building, the north and south walls of which had been worked into "a kind of tessellated pattern, which was considered very extraordinary." John Ewart had built well and handsomely for the congregation of St. Paul's. He had employed brick, the logical building material in muddy York, thus reducing expenditure. He had then instructed his masons, including the aptly named Thomas Bond, to lay up the brick in the Flemish manner— the tessellated pattern which had so intrigued the citizens of the wooden town.

Sufficient archival evidence remains on which to base a reconstruction drawing of the principal façade of St. Paul's, and in it one can sense the quality of Ewart's feeling for proportional relationships. He had a designer's eye for the degrees of drama, solemnity, economy and light relief required in a building of urban importance in a semi-pioneer community. All three of his churches would seem to have been based on a close personal knowledge of the design produced by William Stark, in 1808, for St. George's Parish Church in Glasgow, a fanciful Regency simplification of the Baroque idiom, borrowed freely from Nicholas Hawksmoor's London churches. Ewart very sensibly cut his designs to suit his cloth—the townscape of York—telescoping the stages of his bell towers to relate to the mass of his buildings. St. Paul's was dignified but never pompous, and did not mock its humble secular neighbours.

But if the façade of St. Paul's, Lot Street was all peaceful gentility, the early history of the parish was tempestuous in the extreme. St. Paul's had the distinction of being the only church in the city ever to have been placed under an interdict. This unhappy situation arose when the political opinions of the parish priest, the Reverend William John O'Grady, brought him into sharp personal conflict with his ecclesiastical superior, Bishop Macdonell. Father O'Grady had been appointed to York in 1828 in the wake of a major influx of Irish immigrants. He had been made Vicar-General in 1830, but working as he did among the very poor, his political sympathies were with Mackenzie and the Reform Party. Bishop Macdonell had a poor opinion of violent reform and a lively sense of the precarious position of the parish of York. The principal parishioners of St. Paul's—the Honourable James Bâby, an executive councillor; Alexander Macdonell, the Sheriff; Mrs. Henry John Boulton, wife of the Attorney-General, and her nieces, Mrs. Elmsley and Mrs. King—were all members of

*IV-3  Soane mannerisms*
*on Church Street. St. Andrew's*
*Church of Scotland, York,*
*John Ewart's church, built in*
*1831. The spire was added by*
*John Howard in 1841.*

the ruling oligarchy whom it was financial madness to alienate. The Bishop advised Father O'Grady that he was to remove to Brockville at once. O'Grady refused, and locking the door in the Bishop's face, he petitioned the Lieutenant-Governor, Sir John Colborne, asking him to declare himself head of the Roman Catholic Church in the Canadas. Colborne, a level-headed veteran of Waterloo, had no desire to play the role of Henry VIII, and truly sorry for the unhappy parish, exerted his powers of persuasion on both sides of the dispute. A priest of sympathetic moderation was found and St. Paul's resumed its proper role in the life of York.

The parish history of St. Andrew's Church of Scotland (IV-3), which stood at the corner of Church and Adelaide Streets from 1831 until the turn of the century, was less exciting. It was commissioned by a number of the citizens of York who met together in 1830 with the intention of forming a congregation in connection with the Established Church of Scotland. At the time York already had a Presbyterian church, but it was small, and moreover was under the ministry of the Reverend James Harris, a member of the Secession Church in Ireland, who preached in Canada under the aegis of the American Presbyterian Church.

Dislike of the Secession Movement cut across political alliance in York. Presbyterian legislators (like William Dunlop of Goderich and William Morris of Perth) wished to worship as a body in a Church of Scotland when attending the session in York. William Lyon Mackenzie became a founding member of St. Andrew's because he disliked the tunes selected by Mr. Harris for the Psalms. The whole thing came to a head when the 79th Regiment of Foot was stationed in York. The 79th, Scots to a man, could not all be seated in Mr. Harris' little church even had they approved both his music and his doctrine. At the meeting, which he and Morris had called, Tiger Dunlop proposed that a congregation be formed in connection with the Church of Scotland. The motion was duly noted by John Ewart, who chaired the meeting. (That St. Andrew's would be built well was never in question; in addition to its designer, there were numbered among the faithful that excellent builder Jacob Latham, John Jacques, the cabinetmaker, and Robert Hay, "upholsterer to the trade.")

St. Andrew's, as built in 1831, was a handsome, dignified structure in brick, stuccoed and lined in imitation of ashlar. It had all of the monumentality of St. Paul's in the treatment of its masonry, and had in addition—as became a more costly structure—a little discreet detailing in the manner of Soane. Ewart, while working in London in 1812, had become acquainted with the architectural designs of John Soane, either through simple observation—a designer's intense interest in all that was being built—or because he was employed as a mason on some of Soane's projects.

An early photograph of St. Andrew's exists, but as an example of Ewart's style, one should regard it with some reserve. The same caution should be even more narrowly observed when contemplating the likeness of St. James' Anglican Cathedral of 1839. Both buildings, as pictured, had had the upper registers of their towers redesigned by John George Howard, an architect with whom Ewart enjoyed an agreeable association.

Ewart's unenviable task at St. James' had been to rebuild that edifice following its destruction by fire in 1839. He had been instructed to reproduce the preceding building but to give it a higher ceiling, greater length in the nave, and a different pulpit – all this while James Grant Chewett, the clerk of works for the demolished structure, was not only living in York but was actually a member of the congregation. It was very much a church designed by the building committee, and the grateful sigh with which its builders turned over completion of the bell tower to John G. Howard carries down the years. Howard does not appear to have fared much better at the hands of the building committee; the abridgement of a spire which incurred James Buckingham's censure was his contribution.

The third St. James', in its turn, was to be destroyed by the fire of 1849 which swept away the heart of the old town of York. It would be rebuilt by a younger generation in a style more in step with contemporary church design in England and the United States.

While John Ewart was busily building his urbane places of worship in York, a remarkable essay in the Palladian-Baroque idiom was under construction at the Head of the Lake (IV-4). The town of Hamilton, forging ahead of its parent community of Dundas, was flushed with civic pride and was prepared to build for future expansion. Moreover, they had, in Robert Charles Wetherell, a resident architect who was young, enthusiastic, and professionally trained in England. The Anglicans of Hamilton had placed their future church in his hands without a qualm, confident of his ability to design just what they were wanting. Had he not just completed Dundurn, that charming villa on the York Road at Burlington Heights, for Allan MacNab?

The architect was ambitious. The building committee was swept along by MacNab's buoyant optimism. And John Gamble Geddes, the newly appointed clergyman, was just twenty-four years old. In the hands of such a team Christ's Church could not have been other than exciting for its place and time. Nor was it.

What did Hamilton want – this town won so recently from the bush? Robert Wetherell knew. They wanted the most monumental and urban building possible for the sum promised, and they wanted that sum stretched to its utmost limit. They wanted an instant sense of city. And, in so far as one building could ensure it, that was precisely what they received.

Christ's Church (the incumbent rejected with horror the local tendency to call it Geddes' Church) was a Baroque building of some distinction executed in stuccoed wood, lined and painted in imitation of Bath stone. For its composition Wetherell had drawn on his recollections of two of the impressive Baroque churches of London, St. Paul's, Deptford, and St. John's, Smith Square, designed by Thomas Archer a century earlier. Christ's Church, Hamilton was set on a platform-plinth in the Deptford manner – but a plinth of brick and rubblestone which housed a Sunday School in place of a crypt. The first bay of the wooden church, narrower than the rest, formed the base of the tower. The auditorium was one hundred feet in length and sixty feet in width in the aisled area.

The contract was undertaken by Messrs. Simpson and Tovell, builders, of Hamilton. Kenney Fitzpatrick was employed as mason, and William Hill, who had already demonstrated skill in his craft at Dundurn, was engaged to finish the exterior with three coats of "plaister called Bailie's cement." Presumably the excellent Hill, a frustrated sculptor at heart, was given a free hand with the ornamental plaster work within. All painting and glazing was under the charge of one Craig – "if recommended by David McNab" for whom he had worked. He seems to have been paid, so he must have given satisfaction.

On 24 May 1837 the diminishing building fund was given a boost to the tune of two hundred and twenty-five pounds raised by the zealous ladies of Christ's Church at a bazaar. The occasion, carefully recorded in the minutes, was the birthday of the Princess Victoria. Thus encouraged, the building committee proposed that "by November 15th the first length of tower be encased and finished with wood. Lower part to be sealed and nailed with rough boards. Agreed to give the tinning of the spire to Paul Filion on condition that the price of the said tinning be £1.10.0 per box. Beads and astricle [astragal] to be made of wood and tinned for one shilling per running foot extra, tinning key or keying 6d. per running foot; lower cornice 2/6 running foot; making and tinning. Mr. Filion will expect payment as work advances at the rate of $6.00 per week for each man employed." One hopes that the project was well under way before the end of November, for by December 1837 tin, or more properly speaking *fer blanc*, was no longer being shipped up from Quebec, and the men were being paid rather less than six dollars per week in the militia. The Reformers of Upper and Lower Canada had risen in revolt under Mackenzie and Papineau, and the architect and mechanics of Christ's Church were marching with the Men of Gore, under the leadership of the chairman of the building committee, to suppress the insurrection.

*IV-4 opposite: The unfinished Christ's Church, Hamilton so impressed Thomas Glegg, visiting Canada in 1842, that he gave it a full page in his engineering diary.*

88

Sketch of the English Church at Hamilton, U.C.

N.B. A Frame building. the Body & lower part of Tower unfinished.

N.W. View.

Architect Mr. Wetherell.

6/4/42

By 1842 the ladies had accumulated "one thousand dollars," and building operations were resumed under an agreement of 18 October which read in part: "A good one and one half inch floor planed and painted and neatly laid (boards not to exceed 8″ in width) upon the whole of the platform around the said church including the landing, covering the planks that are now spiked down on the landing with the same kind of floor. Six columns, three quarters round to be made, put up and to be properly cased with 2″ boards and to have a base and capitals as shown on the plan. Six square columns made with 1″ stuff to be put up and finished in every respect as marked on the plan. Four round columns made of 2″ lumber with capitals and base each to be finished as marked on the plan and according to the original design balustrades to be made and put up around each side of the outside stairs and around the whole of the platform. The balustrades not to be less than 9″ thick and to be properly secured in rail not less than 7″ by 12″ and to be finished as shown on the plan and a proper facing to be put all around the platform and to be brought out as far as the brick ... being the plan drawn up for the finishing and completing of the said church by Mr. Wetherell of Hamilton aforesaid architect."

On the roof ridge were set "two thick copper stovepipes, ten feet long and ten inches in diameter indented at the top thus ... and secured to the ceiling at foot of pipe with a copper plate fastened to the ceiling," as specified by Wetherell. The "stovepipes" which the iron founder, Alexander Carpenter, called "copper chimneys" had separate tin linings and "umbrellas." Carpenter also supplied four thirty-six-inch stoves with stove trays and baskets, and six wooden standards of black walnut. The walnut standards may have supported stovepipes or may have held aloft some of the "fifty lamps" which occupied the attentions of the clerk, when he was not stoking the stoves or leading the responses.

With all these shining accretions, Christ's Church was so beautiful by 1842 that it was described, with pardonable local pride, as one of the finest in North America. Its period of glory was short, however; in 1852 it was disfigured by an incongruous addition—a chancel and the first two bays of an aisled Gothic nave in stone. Twenty years later Wetherell's Classical church was demolished to make way for the completion of the stone nave, a portion of the ubiquitous cloak of decorous Gothicism which Henry Langley was to draw over the face of Ontario in the 1870's.

Earlier architectural errors and omissions were set right by John George Howard who had arrived in York after eleven seasick weeks, in 1832. Some time during that nightmare voyage from London the young architect, hitherto known as John Corby, tidied up the ravelled thread of his own beginning by assuming the aristocratic name of Howard, patronymic of the Earls of Carlisle from whom the Corby family claimed descent. His second momentous decision, taken on arrival in York, was to abandon at once and completely his intention to settle in Goderich. Resolutely setting aside all memory of the blandishment by which William Cattermole, the Canada Company's agent, had lured him to emigrate, he rented lodgings in the colonial capital and looked about him for patronage. It came, as it often does, obliquely. Howard went to call on an old acquaintance, William Dibbs, then located in Hamilton. Dibbs introduced his young friend to the local fount of architectural commissions who advised Howard to send some drawings to Peter Robinson, then much in need of building plans for his new community, Peterborough (IV-5). Robinson, preoccupied with many matters, set the roll down in a welter of papers and forgot about it. Howard then sought out another entrepreneur, Hiram Capron, at his farm on the Grand River. This time he had immediate success; Capron commissioned Howard to lay out the land for his projected village of Paris.

In the meantime, Howard's first approach was coming to the surface. Reminded that he had had a roll of drawings for some time, Peter Robinson looked them over and advised Howard to take them to Colonel Rowan, Secretary to the Lieutenant-Governor, Sir John Colborne. Rowan obligingly placed the plans

*IV-5: The Goths arrive. Upper Canada's first Perpendicular windows in St. John's, Peterborough.*

on a table in the Governor's drawing-room. The Governor was impressed, and offered Howard the position of drawing master in Upper Canada College. It was both a useful source of income and an ideal introduction to the notice of nearly everyone in the colony who might some day require architectural assistance.

Howard meant to be remembered. He left a quantity of drawings lying demurely in a cupboard in Colborne Lodge, the Regency cottage which he built near the Humber River and later gave, with its park, to the City of Toronto. A number of his office time-books for the years 1833-43 also survived, and became city property as well. Both journals and drawings are in the Toronto Public Library and are available for study. The drawings were not catalogued by Howard, and many of them are unsigned. Some are obviously practice copies from source books, while others, which seem not to have been by Howard at all, may have come to his drafting office as reference for alterations to existing buildings. The entries in the journals were often cryptic, and the earnest researcher is discouraged by the discovery that the architect, in his publication *Some Incidents in the Life of J. G. Howard*, occasionally contradicts the entries in his day-to-day journal.

The early pages of Howard's daybook show that his first church problem in Canada was not very exciting. He seems to have been asked to plan alterations for St. James'—that is if the "bishop" of the journal was, in truth, John Strachan and not Bishop Macdonell or the Bishop of Quebec; and a later reference to measuring the site with William Dibbs holding the tape would seem to rule out the Bishop of Quebec as a sponsor. In any case, the church alterations dragged on in the talking stage, and Howard went glumly back to drawing ornamental chimneys and "groining" for Henry John Boulton's alterations at Holland House on Front Street.

The first genuine church commission to come Howard's way was a belated request from Peter Robinson. On 2 September 1833 Howard entered in the daybook a note to the effect that "the plans" had been dispatched to Peterborough. If these were the plans and specifications of St. John's, Peterborough (intended to guide and encourage Joseph Scobell, the local contractor who completed the building in 1839), then in this, his first Canadian church, Howard embarked on the design of romantic Gothicism with great caution.

When John Howard left England to try his fortune in the colonies the Gothic Revival in architecture was still in the exploratory stage. This early phase produced works which have been described as "Ivanhoe Gothic"—an architecture derived from a mediaeval world which had never existed. As an idiom it had great appeal for a young architect who claimed descent from Belted Will Howard, and who entered in his daybook the hours he

*IV-6: Regency sham-Gothic crowned Holy Trinity, Chippawa, in 1840. Serious Goths corrected most of its glazing thirty years later.*

spent in drawing up a coat of arms for his new cutter. Unsophisticated Upper Canadians were as pleased with his Gothic style as they were impressed by his heraldry, and they were completely untroubled by the doubtful authenticity of both.

When examined carefully, John Howard's churches seldom completely merit the description "romantic Gothic" in the sense in which the term is generally applied to those essays in mediaevalism which preceded the serious academic mid-nineteenth-century Gothic Revival. The most important Howard churches were romantic only in so far as they were not constructed in the true Gothic manner but the majority of them were more Gothic than not. In order of appearance they were: Holy Trinity (IV-6), Chippawa, 1840; St. Paul's, Yorkville, 1841; Snake Island, 1842; St. John's, York Mills; Christ Church, Tyendenaga and Christ Church, Holland Landing, 1843; and Holy Cross, Wikwemikong, 1844. There exists some evidence for attributing to his authorship as well St. John's, Peterborough; All Saints, Tyendenaga; a Roman Catholic chapel in Barrie, since destroyed; and two small chapels now converted to other use, one in Aurora and the other in Queenston. Howard also, at various times, made plans for additions and alterations for St. James' and St. Andrew's in York and for St. Mark's, Niagara-on-the-Lake. He was consulted, if only to settle a dispute about sash-weights, on St. Paul's, Woodstock in 1834.

Of all John Howard's works the most romantic confection by far was Holy Trinity, Chippawa, designed to replace the church destroyed in the Mackenzie Rebellion of 1837. It has the advantage of being the least altered of his buildings, but it was also least typical of his work. The parish, through the building committee, appears to have requested a virtual replica of their earlier building. It stands on the outskirts of its river town, well back from the highway, in an extensive churchyard that is still well treed, although the sweeping drama of the avenue is no more.

The principal façade of Holy Trinity had drama enough on its own. Composed in brick, with freestone dressings and much of its superstructure in wood, the design was Gothic of the Regency picturesque kind, as its predecessor undoubtedly was also. Structurally the church was, like Ewart's churches, a late Georgian Classical hall, with projecting entrance tower and a high panelled parapet to conceal the low gable roof. The crenelated cornice of the parapet and the ogee-arch of the louvered windows in the bell tower had their counterparts along Lake Erie, and similar needle-sharp pyramids had been pointing heavenward all over Upper Canada for well over a decade. In these details the church at Chippawa was old-fashioned for 1841. However, the English architect had some subtle distinctions to bestow. The stone quoining of the entrance-door transom and the window above it was not

94

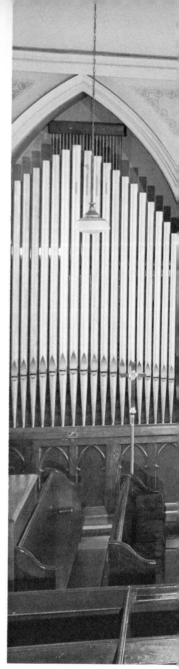

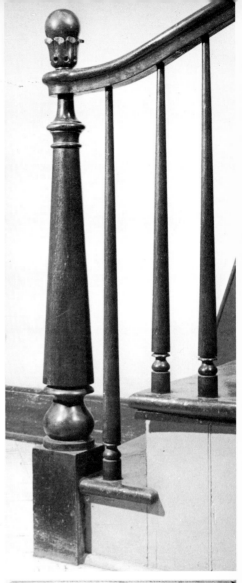

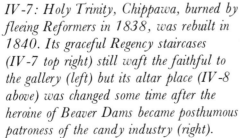

IV-7: Holy Trinity, Chippawa, burned by fleeing Reformers in 1838, was rebuilt in 1840. Its graceful Regency staircases (IV-7 top right) still waft the faithful to the gallery (left) but its altar place (IV-8 above) was changed some time after the heroine of Beaver Dams became posthumous patroness of the candy industry (right).

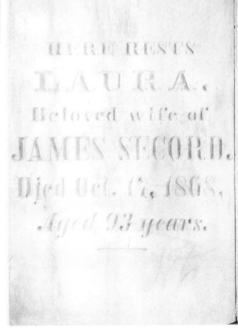

HERE RESTS
LAURA,
Beloved wife of
JAMES SECORD,
Died Oct. 17, 1868,
Aged 93 years.

*IV-9: Simple Regency-Gothic charm in altar (right) and bench end (below). All Saints Church, Tyendenaga.*

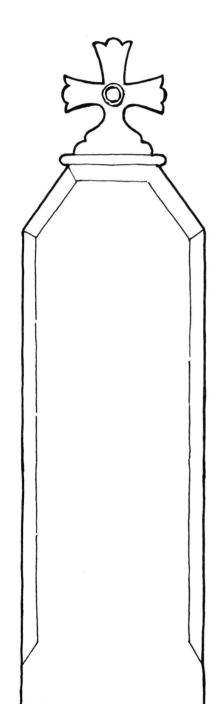

composed of blocks of alternating length but was cut, as a low relief pattern, on larger voussoirs. The tower window (IV-1) followed the form of a *vesica piscis*, the aureole indicative of sanctity which often surrounded the blessed in mediaeval manuscripts and Byzantine ikons. (One feels that had they really tried, the Ecclesiologists might have found a name more euphonious than "fish-bladder" for the odour of sanctity made visible.)

The interior of the church now fulfils the processional aspect once established by the avenued approach; the entrance doorway opens directly on the major vista—straight through the tower base and up a central aisle to the triple arcade of the chancel wall. However, there is no evidence that any of J.G. Howard's churches were thus designed and there *is* evidence in the narthex of Holy Trinity, Chippawa that originally there was a very different arrangement. As planned, the parishioners entering the church were directed to right or left, either up the curving sweep of open staircases to the gallery or, passing between the newels and the baffle wall which joined the internal columns supporting the tower, they moved up either of two aisles to their enclosed pews.

The view from the chancel was quite handsome, a rare occurrence in Upper Canada. The officiating clergyman looked out over a congregation seated in walnut pews whose end and door panels made up a blind Gothic arcading which matched that of the gallery rail. On either side of the baffle wall the very handsome stair rails rose in fine linear patterns of dark brown against the white plaster walls (IV-7). However, the ritualists won in the end; the baffle wall was removed and a central aisle of processional width was provided. It was a fine idea, beautiful on the drawing board, lovely in execution, but bitterly cold for too much of the year. The stairways had to be enclosed and the vista from the chancel sacrificed in the interest of comfort.

The chancel itself suffered over the years a number of the alterations which afflict chancels. An altar of greater elaboration than Howard intended appeared, one which has since been moved forward, leaving the retable section stranded against the reredos (IV-8).

Howard seems to have had a preference for semicircular altar rails with vase-turned balusters of the late-Stuart Baroque solidity he used at Holy Trinity. Those in St. John's, Peterborough and St. Paul's, Woodstock have been shifted about, but their former locations can still be determined. The best surviving example of the altar, as John Howard conceived it for many of his Upper Canadian Gothic churches, is in All Saints, Tyendenaga (IV-9). It was designed in 1851 with a breadth and simplicity suitable alike to the scale of the church and the quality of the wood; and it has the dignity inherent in the intention of a parish commemorating a beloved rector. The Greek cross of the central panel has been repeated in a finial form on the bench ends and painted a cheerful scarlet.

That the fanciful Gothic of Howard's Chippawa was more Chippawa than Howard is apparent on examination of the main body of his work. The commission which gave him the freest hand was private, and in it his Gothic was much closer to the mediaeval churches remembered from his English youth. In January of 1834, he was at work on an altar-piece for the Honourable John Elmsley, who had been converted to his wife's Roman Catholic faith in 1833. As his conversion coincided with the vendetta then being waged between Father O'Grady and Bishop Macdonell in the parish of St. Paul, an alternative place of worship was in order. Elmsley commissioned John Howard to design him a private chapel (IV-10), a drawing for which would seem to be in the Howard papers still.

Howard's next essay in the Pointed style (the beautifully general term employed by Carter, and subsequently by Pugin, to describe all English building from the Normans to the Stuarts) was a simple wooden structure for the Anglicans of Yorkville, a place simply identified in the architect's daybook as "up Yonge Street." He was proud of St. Paul's, Yorkville, but his pride stemmed from a successful feat of engineering rather than an artistic triumph. He had contrived—with the assistance of Robert Wetherell of Hamilton, to whom the mysteries of steeple structure were evidently revealed—to erect the tower and spire in a single day and in absolute silence. The church, described by Scadding in *Toronto of Old* and illustrated by Eric Arthur in *No Mean City*, has long since been demolished. It was the forerunner in wood of the rural Perpendicular churches which Howard was to design in brick for York Mills and Holland Landing and in stone for Deseronto and Manitoulin.

In this group of churches, built between January 1841 and December 1844, Howard came as close to the perpetration of academic Gothicism as he was ever to do. He was aware of the furore in England emanating from the spiritual revivalism of Oxford and the artistic mediaevalism of Cambridge. He was a regular subscriber to such trade publications as *The Builder*. And he had, in 1836, purchased a copy of David Laing's recent book on architecture—not, perhaps, a happy choice, for Laing had written his work in precipitant retirement following the collapse of his major building. But there were other oracles more reliable; Howard could, and did, appeal, in the matter of a major Classical

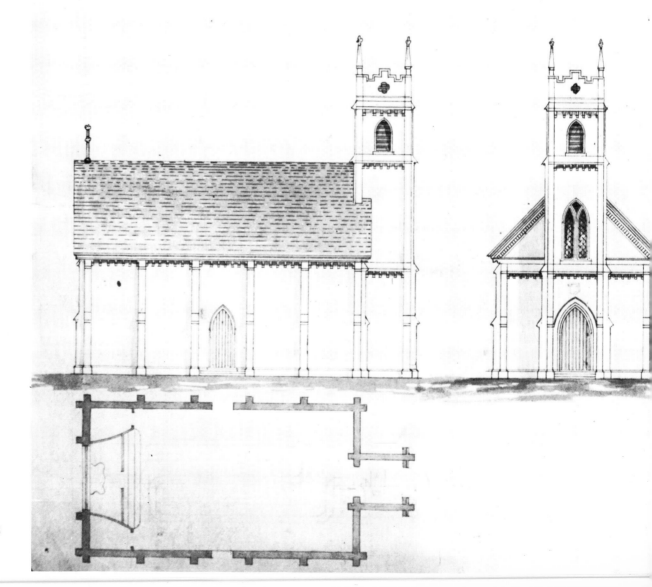

building, the Queen Street lunatic asylum, to Charles Barry, through that worthy's brother-in-law, Henry Rowsell, bookseller of Toronto. In the ecclesiastical arena of Upper Canada Howard and the hour were admirably matched. He was quite equal to the task of meeting the proto-Gothic yearnings of his clients—outlying Anglican congregations and the Superintendent of Indian Affairs—who were not yet ready for academic exactitude.

The churches of St. John, York Mills; Christ Church, Tyendenaga; and Christ Church, Holland Landing, varied not at all in form and but little in detail. All three were originally square-ended hall-churches with four windows to a side. All were buttressed suitably—the brick churches having angled corner buttresses, the stone, diagonal ones. The bell towers were in three stages, with bracketed set-offs, and all were crowned with stepped crenellations which have since been rebuilt. Externally the churches of York Mills and Holland Landing differed only in the colour of their brickwork and the termination of their angled buttresses

*IV-10: William Boulton wrote of Elmsley's private chapel, in 1833. "It's to cost £12,000. I think he must be a little cracked."*

*IV-11: Christ Church, Holland Landing (opposite), like all churches in Howard's Pointed Gothic style, had a large choir pew (IV-12) in its gallery.*

— open gables at St. John's, closed, with trefoils, on Christ Church. The battlemented crown of the York Mills tower was lightened by the insertion of arced triangles carrying the vertical movement of the lancet windows to a triumphant conclusion. Holland Landing's rebuilt battlements (IV-11) may have lost their recessed ornament but have kept their pinnacles.

Christ Church, Holland Landing still has some of its original interior installations. In the first seating plan the gallery at the west end was furnished with slip pews for parishioners and a large central box pew for the choir. The gallery pews remain, but the body of the church has been reseated. And when the white brick chancel was built the old altar-table was displaced.

John Howard's Gothic churches scarcely had time to be furnished (IV-12) before they were damned by the new liturgists. Archdeacon Bethune wrote of York Mills in 1847: "St. Johns is an exceedingly handsome and beautifully situated religious edifice. Constructed of white brick in the Pointed Gothic style. The interior too is respectably furnished but it would be improved, as I ventured to recommend by adapting the seats in the centre to the general construction of the pews. At the same time I cannot here, or in any other church, feel reconciled to the absence of a centre aisle."

But if Howard's liturgical plans did not meet with the high-churchman's notion of the seemly, his major church building—Christ Church near Deseronto—had been commended the year before (IV-13) by a fellow member of the Toronto Society of Artists. In *Canada and the Canadians* Sir Richard Bonnycastle wrote: "A church has recently been erected by them [the Six Nations] on the Bay of Quinte, in the Township of Tyendenaga, or the Indian woods. It is of stone, with a handsome tin covered spire and replaces the original wooden edifice they had erected on their first landing, the first altar of their pilgrimage which was in complete decay.

"They held a council, and the Chief made this remarkable speech after having heard all of the ways and means discussed: —'If we attempt to build this church by ourselves it will never be done, let us therefore ask our Father, the Governor, to build it for us, and it will be done at once.'

"It was not want of funds but want of experience he meant: for the funds were to be derived from the sale of Indian Lands. The Governor, the late Sir Charles Bagot was petitioned accordingly, and the church now stands, a most conspicuous ornament on the beautiful Bay of Quinte.

"They raised one thousand pounds for this purpose; and proper architects being employed, the contract was entered into for £1,037 and was duly accepted . . . . The first stone was laid by S.P. Jarvis, Esquire Chief Superintendent of Indians in Canada:

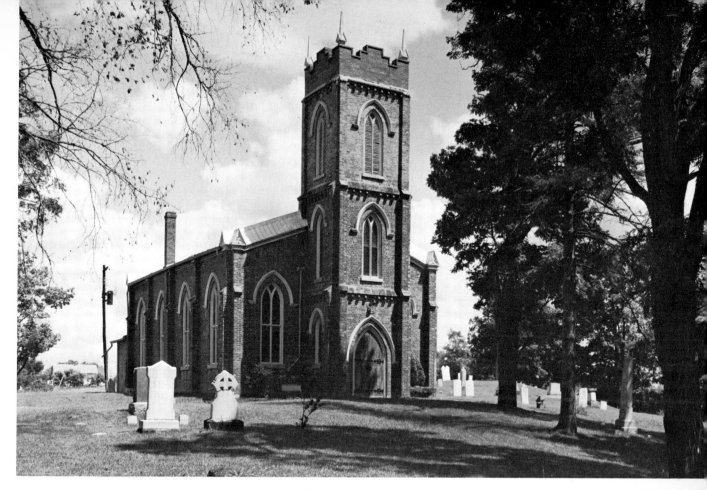

and the Archdeacon of Kingston, the truly venerable G.O. Stuart conducted the usual service which was preceded by a procession of Indians, who singing a hymn, led the way from the wharf where the clergy and visitors had landed from the steamer ... they reached the site of their new Temple ... I saw this edifice lately: it is Gothic with four lancet windows on each side, and buttressed regularly. Its space is 60 feet by 40 feet with a front tower projecting and the spire, very pointed and covered with glittering tin, rises out of the surrounding woods from a lofty height of 107 feet. It is certainly the most interesting public building in Canada West."

Alas for the most interesting building in Canada West. The triumphant spire was struck by lightning and the interior of the church badly damaged in the resultant fire. The handsome grey-stone font (IV-14) still shows horizontal cracks induced by exposure to extreme heat. The treasured carved coat of arms of George III over the west door, which had been in the direct path of destruction, was replaced by new Royal Arms, a gift to the Six Nations of Tyendenaga, the Keepers of the Eastern Door, from King George V. The fire and consequent rebuilding explain the incongruity of the building as it stands—the un-Howard aspect of the roof and ceiling.

One of Christ Church's most interesting features escaped the

blaze. This was the screen designed for the much shallower chancel originally beyond it. Supported on clustered colonettes, the three shallow arches once neatly framed the pulpit (entered through the Gospel arch), the altar (surmounted by the Creed, the Decalogue and the Paternoster in Mohawk), and the reading desk (entered by the Epistle arch). The choir originally occupied the central pews of a west gallery, or choir loft, for which borrowed light had been provided.

Christ Church, Tyendenaga, standing proudly on its height, was destined to be John Howard's finest ecclesiastical monument. Holy Cross, Wikwemikong, a Roman Catholic mission church, built the following year for the Ojibwa of Manitoulin, was not its equal stylistically nor did it survive a fire in its centennial year.

Although Howard recorded many discussions with both Bishop Strachan and Bishop Power on the subject of cathedrals he did not secure the commissions for those edifices. At one point, in response to a request from Bishop Strachan for a cathedral "like Tyendenaga only bigger," Howard actually made drawings and plans. Unfortunately it was all too much like Tyendenaga—a cautious Perpendicular cloak on Georgian bones. By the time the drawings were finished the Bishop had visited England and had been converted to the romantic richness of the Gothic Revival at its source. The Gothic cathedrals of Toronto were to be designed by younger men, who were at ease in the new ecclesiological Zion.

Bonnycastle, in his description of the building of Christ Church, Tyendenaga, recorded that the cornerstone carried a long inscription concluding with the information, "John Howard, Toronto Architect: George Browne of Kingston, architect having

*IV-13: Lightning consumed the spire of Christ Church, Tyendenaga (IV-13 right) and cracked its font (IV-14 far right) but failed to daunt a congregation which had taken its first communion in Canada around an upturned canoe.*

undertaken the supervision of the works and John B. Pringle being the builder." Well might George Browne be styled "of Kingston" on church cornerstones. Although his architectural training had been in Belfast and Dublin and his principal office in Quebec, his major work was the city face of Kingston. Imported from Lower Canada expressly to alter both the hospital and Alwington House for official use, Browne remained in Kingston for several years. He found it a provincial garrison town and left it a classical urban community.

Much of Browne's contribution to the elegance of Kingston lay in his ability to put architectural rivals on their mettle. Civic and religious authority needed no urging; Kingston, making a determined bid, in 1841, to be chosen permanent capital of the new United Province of Canada, was building with a joyous abandon. Churchmen, caught up in the excitement, re-examined their fabrics in the light of future ceremonial occasions. The Anglicans and the Presbyterians were moderately complacent. But the Kingston Roman Catholics, augmented by the Church's principal Upper Canadian patrons, in town for the session, were appalled. St. Joseph's (once St. Isadore's) was too small, and was dowdy beyond belief. What must the Quebec legislators think of them! Bishop Gaulin found, in their chagrin, the leaven needed to build his cathedral (IV-15), which must also be a worthy memorial to Bishop Macdonell with whom he had served as co-adjutor before the latter's death in Scotland in 1840.

St. Mary's Cathedral of the Immaculate Conception is indeed worthy of both its founder bishops, but unfortunately there does not seem to be any record of that other founder—the designer. As it now stands, it represents the cumulative work of many designers. (The two-hundred-foot tower and impressive front, added in the last quarter of the nineteenth century by Joseph Connolly lie well beyond the scope of this study.) But about the unaltered portions of the nave and the chancel, for which tenders were being called in 1843, one senses the distant guiding hand of Henry Bower Lane.

Lane, who was born in London, England in 1787, studied architecture at the Royal Academy Schools. He then entered the office of William Inwood where he may have been in some degree responsible for the spidery Gothic of the few Commissioners' churches which emanated from that most Greek of all Classic Revival firms.

Lane came out to North America in 1840 but did not reach Toronto immediately. On 15 April 1842 John George Howard entered in his daybook: "Mr. Henry Boulton came with Mr. Lane to introduce him to me." Lane was based in Toronto—but not without remission. Bishop Gaulin, was frequently there too. Moreover, Lane's friend and patron, Henry John Boulton, although himself a

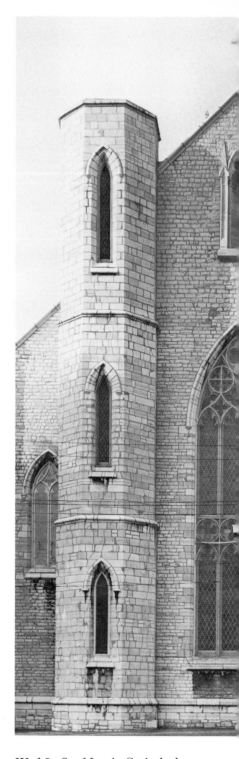

*IV-15: St. Mary's Cathedral of the Immaculate Conception, Kingston, the last resting place of Bishop Macdonell.*

staunch Anglican, was vitally interested in Bishop Gaulin's projected cathedral. And Mrs. H.J. Boulton and her sisters, Mrs. Stuart and Mrs. Sherwood, were among the most influential of the good Bishop's far-flung flock, representing as they did the Roman Catholic wing of the Family Compact.

St. Mary's Cathedral of the Immaculate Conception was already far advanced structurally in 1844. It was in that year that a mob of over-excited Kingstonians destroyed the dressed stone already cut for its entrance doorway. The indignation of the rioters, members of the Orange Order, was not directed against the Cathedral itself, but rather aimed at one of its builders – a stonemason who had had the temerity to criticize their entry into the arena of Upper Canadian politics. The stonemason, Alexander Mackenzie, a zealous Baptist and future Prime Minister of Canada, was not easily intimidated. He restated his opinion of them, cut new stone, and proceeded with the doorway.

The doorway of 1844 has gone. The interior of the building has been recast several times, but externally the east end, with its Perpendicular window and octagonal chancel towers, still looks hauntingly like the known Toronto works of Henry Bower Lane. The flank walls also retain the Commissioners'-Gothic window form adopted by Lane for Little Trinity, King Street East.

Little Trinity was Lane's first Toronto church and as such was of consuming interest to John Howard, who was slightly involved in its building. On 27 August 1842 he noted: "Morning, went to Mr. Lane's office to see the plans of the new church for the East end of Town." And again on 8 May 1843: "Morning at 1/4 to 7 with Mr. Ritchey [builder] to set out Mr. Lane's church. Back at 9." Howard recorded in his published work that Mr. Boulton wanted him to take Mr. Lane into partnership but that he had refused to do so.

By the middle of 1843 Lane had far too much work on his dish to lay out the footings for his first church. He was well into plans for Toronto's first City Hall, as well as proposed editions for Osgoode Hall. He was also designing a new church for the west end of town – St. George the Martyr, John Street, built on land donated for the purpose by D'Arcy and Sarah Robinson Boulton of Boulton Grange. In 1846 Lane designed a third Toronto church, Holy Trinity, Trinity Square.

Lane's Toronto churches all belonged in feeling to the late Regency, early Victorian, "somewhat Gothic" school. All were designed to be executed in brick and were very sensibly of the late Perpendicular-cum-Tudor parish church form – expressing externally the unpretentious aspirations of their building committees. Little Trinity, King Street East (IV-16) was a disarming confection of warm red brick with white brick octagonal buttresses on its square tower, principal façade and false-transept faces. The large

*IV-16 and 17: Little Trinity, King Street East (IV-16 above) and Holy Trinity (IV-17 below), sitting precariously in a commercial complex, are the least damaged of Henry Bower Lane's Toronto buildings.*

windows in the side walls were of that order of skeletal Perpendicular stigmatized by Sir Nickolaus Pevsner in *The Buildings of England* as "Commissioners' conventions ... of three lights, horizontally subdivided in this case by a transom with panel tracery below to house the galleries which the interior originally possessed." Sir Nickolaus was describing St. Peter's Church, Brighton, by Charles Barry—a building of great charm if imperfect scholarship. Little Trinity's charms belonged to the school which designed useful buildings in a flexible, romantic, late-mediaeval idiom, as an antidote to the exacting correctness of the Classical Orders. Henry Bower Lane was not delivering sermons in brick, and Toronto, happily worshipping in warmth and light in his three churches, was pleased with him.

The Church of the Holy Trinity, Trinity Square (IV-17) had a lesser proportion of glass to wall but was, in its heyday, provided with four large stoves, two burning wood and two coal. The church was erected as the result of a generous anonymous gift to the Bishop of Toronto, for the building of a church which should have free seating. Holy Trinity thus owed its origins to an early protest against the comfortable pew. Lane and the building committee complied with the unknown benefactress' dislike of box pews, and furnished Holy Trinity with the spindle-backed seats known to the antique trade, for some obscure reason, as "deacon's benches." In 1857, William Hay, another architect at work at Holy Trinity, introduced seating of a more Gothic character. He defined the free and inalienable right of each individual to eighteen inches of dark brown discomfort by nailing transverse strips of moulding at intervals along the benches.

The Church of St. George the Martyr, on John Street, was more reticent in form—a restrained Perpendicular structure whose three deeply recessed west doorways were echoed within by the three pointed arches of the chancel wall. The gallery was tripartite as well; the choir and organ were lodged in the centre, after the custom of the time, and over the north and south doors were private galleries, or parvises, with separate access staircases. The parvises were furnished by their lease-holders with armchairs and curtains. In 1888 the church purchased the lease of the south parvis from the Boulton family, but the north parvis remained in the possession of the heirs of John Cawthra for another quarter-century.

St. George's well-proportioned bell tower alone survived the fire which destroyed the building. Its tall spire—so long an ornament of the Grange Park scene—had been removed a few years earlier in the mistaken belief that it was unsound. Those who put their trust in reinforced concrete have little faith in the tensile strength of wood, but in the day when Lane designed and Richey built and Kivas Tully was a churchwarden of St. George's they understood it better.

Lane returned to England in 1847 – his reasons for going as mysterious as those which led him to emigrate. His mantle of romantic Gothicism (IV-18) had fallen to Kivas Tully, a young Irish architect who had emigrated to Canada in 1844, fresh from apprenticeship in a London office. Tully was the last formally trained practitioner, in Upper Canada, of the light-hearted Regency school. He was employed initially to refurbish an older building, St. John's, Peterborough. St. John's, designed in 1833 by an absentee architect, was by 1851 neither sufficiently large nor sufficiently Gothic to please the parishioners. Kivas Tully brought it up to date – or took it back in time, depending on one's point of view – by installing Gothic pillars inside it and by strengthening the exterior with quoined East-Anglian buttressing.

Kivas Tully was an eclectic. His largest and finest building, Victoria Hall, Cobourg was as formally Palladian as his Trinity College was Cambridge-Tudor. His additions to Osgoode Hall were unexceptional and uninspiring. But his churches, designed to enclose the essential simplicities of early-nineteenth-century piety, had style and charm.

The vestry of St. Peter's, Cobourg (IV-19) placed quite a problem before their architect in 1850. They wished Tully to build them a new church around the existing church, and they wished to continue to use that building until the new one should be ready for occupation. Out-numbered by Bethunes and Boultons, Tully obligingly did just that, and if the interior was never quite to their satisfaction and had to be reworked by Henry Langley twenty years later, it was not a matter for wonder.

*IV-18: The skeletal Perpendicular window (below left), much favoured by British Church Commissioners, was used in Canada West by both Lane and Tully.*

*IV-19: Built as an overcoat around an existing church, St. Peter's, Cobourg (below) was re-lined after its predecessor had been removed.*

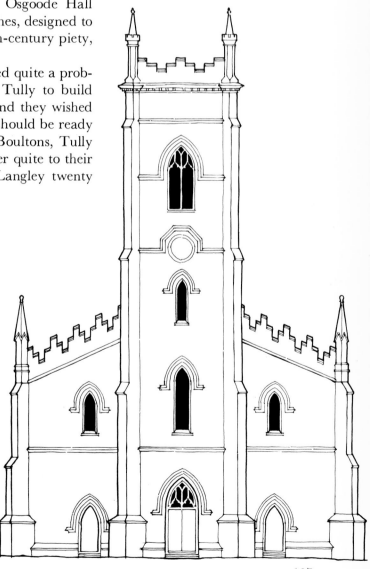

*IV-20: Bought for St. John's and resurrected for St. Mark's (above), the voice from the bell tower (opposite) sounds over Port Hope.*

In 1851 Tully was making over another church, St. John's, Port Hope. The task was rather simpler there, for the building material could be easily adapted without leaving visible scars. Once the chancel and transepts were added, the whole could be covered with weather-boarding. Tully altered the windows as directed, again employing the Commissioners'-Gothic form—with a transom at the centre division because of the galleries.

St. John's had been outgrown by the late 1860's. It was closed and its name conferred on a new church which had been built on the other side of the town. A stubborn churchwarden removed the bell, before it could be taken to the new building, and buried it in his orchard. When Tully's old church was reopened four years later and rededicated as St. Mark's, the bell was resurrected and returned to its proper place (IV-20).

By 1853 Kivas Tully was at work on a church commission further inland. Of all Tully's buildings, Christ Church, North Douro (IV-21), built in Lakefield in 1853, most truly merited the epithet "romantic." The minute stone church, Gothic in spirit and structure, exuded nostalgia. It was built for a parish of transplanted English gentlefolk, some of whom were active participants in the Romantic movement in literature. They selected their site with an eye for the contour of the ground, the protective stand of well-grown trees, and the possibility of reflections in placid water. The architect, entering into the spirit of this, gave them a solid little building crouched in the grass like a nesting bird. The interior (IV-22), which has been restored, was simple and direct, a place for worshippers who followed the faith of their fathers but in the clear strong light of the New World.

Kivas Tully was doing very well. He had designed to the satisfaction of the local establishment in both Cobourg and Port Hope. Better still for a rising young man in the United Canadas, in designing Trinity College he had won the approval of the ageing but still powerful Bishop Strachan. Moreover, he was working on the Town Hall which was to be both the glory and despair of Cobourg for years to come. It was fitting that Christ Church, North Douro, should have been his most romantic as well as his last church, for in it Kivas Tully contracted an alliance with the establishment; he married the daughter of Colonel Samuel Strickland of Lakefield, and after a suitable interval was appointed architect to the government of Upper Canada.

The early builder-architects of Upper Canada, although practising largely in the early nineteenth century, had been of the late eighteenth century in their philosophy of design. They were products of the Romantic movement, and their clients had been prepared to accept a romantized Classicism or Gothicism as the appropriate shell for prayer and praise. But the serious Gothic Revival was at hand. Soon the church building committee would be

*IV-21 and 22: Ivy-mantled Lakefield (top), restored to Kivas Tully's vision of well-bred reverence (below).*

asked to examine its conscience as minutely as its budget before choosing a building style. And when that choice had been made, it would seek out an architect of earnest sincerity who would, with prayer and fasting, design the edifice. Remarkable as it may now seem, such architects would be found in the United Province of Canada, and the rigorous course of archaeological probity would be followed, but not by Ewart, or Howard, or Tully, who made their escape into the freer fields of railway building, engineering and town planning.

Romantic buildings would not vanish overnight, however; the builder-architects might have introduced the style and skimmed the cream of the commissions, but the larger company of builders which had worked for them, or had worked on parallel projects, would continue in the tradition for an appreciable time.

# V
# *Picturesque*

*... not of the letter, but of the spirit ...*
*Second Corinthians* III: *6*

Coincident with the appearance in Upper Canada of the builder-architects, there arose a wave of picturesque churches and chapels whose authorship, always vague, has been increasingly blurred by time (V-1). Many of these humble, beautiful little structures have disappeared. Some were replaced, within a decade or two of construction, by expanding congregations who were prepared to accept in their stead commodious, comfortable buildings of lesser character. Others have been so modified in the interest of conformity, sobriety or economy that the original architectural intent has been obliterated. And once the tangible evidence of that intent was destroyed, it was impossible to refer to the master-builder's drawing. The builder's drawing board was, more often than not, a handy piece of pine plank, and the drawings incised therein with the point of a penknife seldom conveyed detailed information. They were simply directives to fellow initiates in the ancient craft of building, who were expected to solve minor problems for themselves. The system flourished because the standards of apprenticeship were exacting, but inspiration occasionally cropped out in surprising form. The handsome fantasies of builders' architecture stand or fall, as folk songs do, on the combined sensitivity and structural skill of the craftsmen concerned in their making, and their roots are as deeply embedded in the parent cultures.

The basic structure of the builders'-picturesque church continued to be that of the Georgian auditory hall, with a tower projecting from the façade or growing out of it above the roof ridge. But whether executed in weather-boarded or stuccoed frame, in stone or in brick, it was embroidered with battlements, needle-sharp pyramidal pinnacles, or fanciful cantilevered, over-sailing balconies. In some giddy compositions all three ornamental units were combined. Windows were "Gothick" in form—sashed with pointed mutations of the small-paned, round-headed Georgian muntin-grid.

As a rule these buildings were pleasantly sited—usually well back from the thoroughfare in a spacious treed churchyard, sometimes fronting on a lake or river. Vista buildings, designed to improve the townscape or the landscape, they were the direct heirs of European parish churches designed in the late eighteenth century to be the focal points in picturesque estate villages. In Upper Canada they had to forgo the romantic gloom of the "yew tree's shade," but, in the churchyards about them, forests of willows wept in stone for public and private loss in infant mortality and epidemic.

The second quarter of the nineteenth century—the building time of the picturesque churches of Upper Canada—was also the era of massive emigration from the British Isles. And while there was little romance about the potato famine, the Highland clearances, or the industrialization of England, many a building tradesman skilled in the picturesque style reached North America because of their apocalyptic pressures—accompanied on his journey by hope, ship's fever and cholera morbus. A few happy rows of wooden battlements (V-2) and a pinnacle or two may surely be forgiven him here.

Some of the early migration schemes were underwritten by philanthropic noblemen, which lent a mediaeval air to the enterprise at the outset. A more forthright feudalism awaited many luckless settlers at the speculative hands of Upper Canadian entrepreneurs and land companies.

One of the more colourful practitioners of philanthropic self-interest was Colonel Thomas Talbot of Malahide, County Dublin, Ireland and of Malahide, St. Thomas, Upper Canada. Talbot had hoped to raise hemp in marketable quantities on the north shore of Lake Erie. He convinced the British Government—in need of rope but reluctant to allow emigration—that he could people his lands with American settlers. He then sold his commission as a colonel for five thousand guineas and immediately invested part of the capital in building saw mills and grist mills in his wooded principality. The hempen dream proved to be just that, and his American settlers showed a lamentable tendency to join with the invaders during the War of 1812. However, after the Napoleonic War emigration from the British Isles was resumed, and Talbot secured settlers of the type he had vainly sought for so long. They came in from Sussex, Yorkshire, and Wiltshire—outnumbering the Irish and Highland Scots who had given him such trouble.

It would seem to be these settlers who constructed the little parish church in St. Thomas, for it still wears a polygonal Cotswold spire, with roll-moulded angles, above the battlements of the stumpy, weather-boarded tower added in 1824. The church had then been standing for two years, a sturdy little brick building redeemed from the commonplace by the charm of its site and the graceful elegance of its windows.

One feels that the incredulous Thomas, patron of architecture, must have been pleased with the exterior aspect of the pretty church which bears his name, but that he might regard the history of its interior with a degree of reserve. St. Thomas' Church has galleries in its transepts. Other churches have transeptual galleries too, but few have a gallery with no visible means of access. The south transept gallery in St. Thomas' Church was reached by a staircase still in place, and the seating of that gallery was designed to accommodate it. The north transept gallery has no such stair. There is no visible evidence of it ever having had one, nor does the seating plan make any provision for it. The enquiring are offered the remarkable explanation that the north gallery was designed to contain the captive devotions of prisoners from the local jail who

*V-2 opposite: Old St. Thomas',
the picturesque heart of the
Talbot settlement.*

114

trooped in on Sunday morning carrying a ladder. The jailer then placed the ladder against the front of the gallery, the prisoners climbed up to their roost, and the ladder was removed for the duration of the service. Perhaps they did. The gallery fronts have been worked over extensively. The south transept gallery has every appearance of having been relocated from some other position, and both galleries have at some time had much alteration in the returned box sections on either side of the chancel recess. It is possible that the transept galleries (V-3) were returned across the chancel space—the reused south gallery having occupied a similar position in the 1824 arrangement before the chancel and transepts were added. But it is unlikely. The transepts were added after 1848 when such aberration would be unthinkable. It is also possible that there was another stair whose location could only be determined now by structural dissection.

The west gallery of St. Thomas' was altered too (V-4). Originally stretching straight across the width of the building, it was later broken forward in the centre to accommodate the choir. The projecting bay, supported by three small turned columns, was given a panelled front, somewhat lower than that of the original section, which had been supported by capped reeded piers. And apparently when the gallery was reseated the stair (V-5) from the tower base which gave access to it was, for some reason, reversed in position.

Fastened to the centre front of the west gallery there now hangs a wooden panel on which are painted the Royal Arms of Great Britain (V-6). In 1830, the Reverend John Strachan, in a letter to the Lieutenant-Governor Francis Gore, wrote of a resolution which had been made in St. Thomas "to procure to be taken by some respectable artist at home the Portrait of the Honourable Colonel Talbot, at half length, to be placed, with the Talbot Arms, immediately below the King's Arms, in the St. Thomas church, to remain there forever as the property of the people of the Talbot settlement." So much time was consumed in collecting the money to fund this enterprise, however, that when the time arrived for the arms to be painted, they were no longer those of King William IV—with the escutcheon of Hanover superimposed on the shield—but those of the young Victoria, Queen of Great Britain.

Once completed, where did the Royal Arms hang in St. Thomas' Church? Not in the present location, obviously, for the panel is taller than the parapet against which it hangs. Nor could the "Talbot Arms and Portrait" have hung suspended in tandem beneath the gallery front. One cannot, however, believe it possible that Bishop Strachan would countenance, for as much as a moment, the obvious alternative position of honour. Upper Canadians might, in their pre-Tractarian darkness, locate a three-

*V-3 opposite: Mysteries abound in the old recast church interiors — galleries without access (V-3 top left), relocated seating (V-4 bottom left), reversed stairs (V-5 top right), and wandering heraldry (V-6 bottom right). Old St. Thomas' Church, St. Thomas.*

116

117

*V-7 and 8: Trees crowd protectively about St. James', Maitland (V-7 above), hiding its pinnacles, but those of Christ Church (V-8 opposite) point clearly skyward above Burritt's Rapids.*

decker pulpit in the centre of the east end of a church, in front of the chancel recess. They had even been known to set the Royal Arms high up in the gable above it. But no congregation, however feudally besotted, seriously intended to hang Tom Talbot—even at half length—in such a place.

The galleries of old St. Thomas' Church in the Talbot settlement throng with teasing questions but other picturesque church galleries were memorable for builders' reasons. The west galleries of three interesting churches built within a decade of each other in the united counties of Leeds and Grenville remain largely unaltered. In them one can trace the hand of a builder-designer of quality working out church interiors (with the aid of the locally available joiners) for differing clerical and congregational criteria, and within varying financial boundaries. The churches—all begun about the same time—were, in order of completion, St. James', Maitland (V-7), St. Peter's, Brockville and Christ Church, Burritts' Rapids (V-8). Arthur McClean, an Irish-trained master-builder, has long been recognized as the designer of St. Peter's, Brockville; stylistically the other two churches appear to have been his brain children also.

One must not, however, fall into the error of believing that the townships of Augusta, Elizabethtown and Oxford had been completely church-less and forgotten before 1812. Loyalist settlers had built the Blue Chapel near New Oswegatchie, to which travelling missionaries were eagerly welcomed, and church services had been held on a regular basis in the courthouse in Elizabethtown (Brockville) as soon as resident clergy were available. It would seem that the first of these was the Reverend William Smart of the Church of Scotland, who arrived in Elizabethtown in 1811.

In 1814 the Reverend John Bethune was appointed by the Church of England to the cure of souls in the townships of Elizabethtown and Augusta. Bethune (third son of the Reverend John Bethune, first Presbyterian minister in Upper Canada) was born in Williamstown, Glengarry County, Upper Canada in 1791. At first a pupil, and then assistant master, in John Strachan's school in Cornwall, he had taken orders in the Episcopal Church, the communion to which his Swiss-American mother belonged. Bethune rushed about his extensive parish holding services and teaching in the schools for four hectic years. He then exchanged parishes with the Reverend John Leeds of Montreal.

By 1821, the concentration of settlement in Eastern Upper Canada was such that the parish had to be divided. The old area of Elizabethtown (now officially renamed Brockville) went to the Reverend John Wenham, and the newly formed parish of Augusta to the Reverend Robert Blakey. Both clergymen had recently arrived from England and both were interested in architecture for its own sake—not always a clerical attribute.

New Oswegatchie, in the meantime, had exchanged its difficult designation for that of Maitland, and to Maitland there came, in 1826, George Longley from Westmorland. Longley had no sooner acquired land in the town than he donated a portion of it for a church building. He then proceeded to build mills and, in partnership with Ziba Webster, an American settler who understood the terrain, to establish a lumber business. In his spare time he acted as churchwarden, member of the building committee, and general driving force in St. James' Church.

The Anglicans of Brockville had been catapulted into a building programme too. Their old standby, the courthouse, had inconsiderately burned down. As a result they had been forced to lay aside—temporarily at any rate—the differences which had earned for their fair community the byname of "Snarlingtown." William Buell, founder and still a leading citizen of Brockville, offered a site for the church on the Courthouse Square. The Family Compact, in the person of Charles Jones, countered with another location farther removed from the vulgar bustle of secular affairs. The Jones site was selected. The decision was never really in question; William Buell could not be allowed to give land to the church. The fellow was actually a Reformer. Buell had already presented a church site on the opposite side of the Courthouse Square to the Presbyterians who, although not necessarily Reformers, were somewhat less sure of their mandate to refuse gifts offered to the glory of God. William Buell, unrebuffed and unrepentant, went

*V-9: Prayer books and hassocks in the ancestral pew (below), still serve the descendants of Solomon Jones, U.E.L. of Maitland.*

*V-10 and 11 opposite: The stream of time washed out McClean's altar rails but spared his galleries in Maitland (V-10 top) and Burritt's Rapids (V-11 bottom).*

on giving land for church buildings—to the Methodists and to Bishop Macdonell's Roman Catholics.

Arthur McClean designed all three of his church interiors as harmonious compositions—relating the shape of the gallery to that of the altar-place. In St. James', Maitland the altar rail extended in a straight line across the east end between the principal box pews (V-9). Centred before the rail was an octagonal pulpit. (It has been removed but the floorboards still show the cuts of its original location.) The gallery front, carried on two turned posts, extended in a matching straight line from wall to wall (V-10). It was finished in plaster, with a finely moulded base and cornice in wood.

Christ Church, Marlborough Township, across the Rideau from Burritts' Rapids, was clearly designed by McClean also. In it the gallery, supported on four turned Tuscan columns, took a more interesting form. The gallery face was curved in plan in a semi-elliptical U-shape, and benches in the front row of the gallery—constructed with a complementary curve—provided seating accommodation for the choir (V-11). Portions of the original altar rail, relegated with other antiquated lumber to the bell-loft, indicate that in this building also the altar-place and the gallery were complementary in form. The rail curve would have been convex when viewed from the body of the church.

St. Peter's, Brockville was McClean's most elaborate structure, and was in consequence a much longer time in building. All its intricate joinery was executed in black walnut, a wood which was not available locally in sufficient quantity. Cost accounts exist for matching walnut, used in the alteration of the church in 1851, which give some indication of the problems involved: "The black walnut necessary for the construction of the pews was ordered from the shores of Lake Erie last winter and is daily expected; every effort possible was made to procure this Lumber last fall but it was found impossible to obtain it sufficiently seasoned for immediate use."

Bishop Strachan, in his *Journal of the Visitation of the Diocese of Toronto*, wrote of St. Peter's Brockville in the summer of 1840: "The church is elegantly fitted up—even sumptuously, being all carpeted and finished with black walnut." Strachan was not given to fulsome praise. St. Peter's *was* elegantly fitted up. The ladies of the parish had installed red carpeting in the church and provided matching hangings for the pulpit and reading desk. The box pews, panelled in the Neo-Classic style under the direction of Benjamin Chaffey, had been executed by Miller, one of those expert joiners who had already finished the handsome interiors of such fine houses as Poplar Hall, the Blakey rectory, Maplehurst, and the Sherwood and Jones houses.

But it was the beautiful gallery which gave St. Peter's its spe-

cial distinction. Arthur McClean's classical Irish training was evident in the Roman Doric dignity of its supporting columns, turned from the long-awaited walnut logs of Lake Erie and fluted with care. While McClean's plan for St. Peter's called for a gallery in the Doric Order, the parapet of the gallery above the Roman architrave was panelled in the Neo-Classic style of the pew ends. When St. Peter's was enlarged in 1859 quadrant projecting box pews were built at either end of the gallery front (V-12). The matching sobriety of their Doric parapets visually supported the rector's contention: "They would tend further to secure order and propriety in that gallery, which being so far removed from the eye of the minister is particularly exposed to infringement in that respect."

The enlarged St. Peter's continued to be sumptuous. The parish had, in 1849, been the fortunate recipient of a bequest under the will of Sir Charles Metcalfe, the late Lieutenant-Governor. (Fortunate, that is, once Bishop Strachan had managed to extract the bequest from the unwilling grasp of the residuary legatee then on active service in India.) It was decided at that time that all pews in St. Peter's should henceforth be slip pews but executed to match the earlier box pews in black walnut (V-13). The sombre taste of 1850 cushioned the church in black leather—which, despite its stygian tone, made St. Peter's the most comfortably pewed edifice in Canada West.

The gloom was relieved by the installation of gaslight in 1854. Opulent branched standards, with walnut barley-sugar-twist columns and ormolu mounts, replaced the branched candle-lights "supplied by George Mallock" in 1834. Indeed, wooden light standards affixed to the box pews at one time supported the illumination in all three McClean churches. The turned rudimentary Tuscan posts, (V-14), which once served in lighting Christ Church, Burritts' Rapids, now languish, with the early altar rail, in the lumber-room of that church.

The Gothicization of St. Peter's in 1850 may perhaps be attributed to John George Howard. All through the 1840's there were entries in his daybook of work and alterations for a "church for Mr. Jones." Jones was not an uncommon name, but the town with the greatest concentration of influential Joneses in Upper Canada was indubitably Brockville. Furthermore, the fact that the Classical pillars had to wait until a suitable carver could be found to execute them suggests that they were being made to the exacting requirements of a distant architect.

*V-12: Comfort embowered the Anglicans of Brockville (top left)*
*in panelled walnut pews (V-13 bottom left). Gas lamps blossomed*
*on twisted stems overhead, to be relit by the electricity which banished*
*the lamp standards of Burritt's Rapids (V-14) to the tower (opposite).*

*V-15: St. Paul's, Fort Erie, a Regency whimsy, redrawn from archival evidence.*

The same team of builders who had worked on Howard's Brockville courthouse—Benjamin Chaffey and John Sheppard—toned down the wilful exterior Gothic of the nave of St. Peter's, while they were about it, "altering the cornice and Battlements to correspond with the new addition," as instructed. The tower of St. Peter's, on the other hand, was continually undergoing repair, if not outright rebuilding, from 1837 to 1851. John George Howard and John Sheppard gave it stability. They also bestowed the sobriety of conical pinnacles and authentic Gothic dripmoulds.

The strong-minded parish of Chippawa alone succeeded in bending Howard to its will in the use of the picturesque Gothic style for a church design. It must have been one of the few instances in which an architect has been asked to follow the style set by a master-builder. But this was a builder well worth following—"the master of St. Paul's, Fort Erie," no less, (if one may use the art historian's method of identifying an unknown artist by his masterpiece). The people of Chippawa won their battle of the styles by the simple expedient of demonstration. St. Paul's, Fort Erie (V-15), the prototype of their lost church, which was still available for study, was the epitome of Upper Canadian picturesque Gothic in wood.

For some reason, the most exuberant picturesque churches built in Upper Canada were those in the charge of the two Leeming brothers—St. Paul's, Fort Erie; St. John's, Ancaster; St. John's, Stamford; and the first Holy Trinity, Chippawa. The Reverend Ralph Leeming had come to Canada as an S.P.G. missionary to Ancaster in 1816. Two years later the people of Chippawa had addressed a petition to the Honourable and Right Reverend Charles James Stewart, Bishop of Quebec, begging for a resident clergyman. He had sent their petition on to the Society for the Propagation of the Gospel, and in 1821 the Society had sent out the elder brother, the Reverend William Leeming. The Leemings had studied theology amid romantic ruins at St. Bee's in Cumberland—which probably predisposed them toward the picturesque in architecture. They were, moreover, clearly in a position to draw on, and to direct, the design resources of the Niagara Peninsula in the first quarter of the nineteenth century.

The Reverend William Leeming, in Fort Erie, had a special source of architectural inspiration under his nose in Stamford. There the Lieutenant-Governor, Sir Peregrine Maitland, had built a summer home, Stamford Cottage, for his young wife, Lady Sarah, who found the York summer oppressive. One can picture a group of Maitland's aides-de-camp—young officers trained in draftsmanship at Greenwich and Woolwich — whiling away the boredom of warm summer afternoons planning little whimsies for the reverend brothers Leeming to build. St. Paul's, Fort Erie certainly had an *al fresco* look about it, a brave insistence that grace and charm could be superimposed on the grim realities of the frontier. Its pilasters, terminating in pyramidal pinnacles, created the illusion of a marquee-church, its façade suspended from tent poles or supported by four up-ended lead-pencils. It may have been too ephemeral. At any rate, St. Paul's, Fort Erie was replaced in 1870 by a more substantial though less imaginative building.

The churches of St. John in Ancaster and Stamford were stouter from the beginning. The walls were of rubblestone work, stuccoed to a more pleasing surface. The windows and door openings of both were made in the approved Gothic form. But from that point they diverged. St. John's, Ancaster was built by the united efforts of the Churches of England and Scotland, and was not, therefore, liturgically identical with St. John the Evangelist, Stamford, an Anglican church under the direct patronage of the Lieutenant-Governor. An early water-colour depicting the Ancaster church from the rear, clearly delineated two large windows in the east wall, a spacing which implied the presence of a central two- or three-decker pulpit. The bell tower rose from the ground on the east façade—its superstructure a fantastic tiered composition of rectangular boxes of diminishing scale (V-16).

The lost tower of St. John's, Stamford was probably very like it. One can easily picture such a belfry going merrily up under the impetus of the five-and-a-half gallons of whisky solemnly entered in the Stamford church accounts against its raising—a proceeding in which the existing dumpy, buttressed bell chamber could never have had a part. Nor would anyone in possession of his senses now have a vista cut through noble woodland so that he might view it—as Sir Peregrine did. Vista-cutting had become a dying pursuit in Niagara by 1866, at which time the original tower was thoroughly repaired, weather-boarded, and chastened. A decade later the church was re-roofed. The "fine cornices" for which a builder, John McMicking, had been paid "seven pounds seventeen shillings six pence" were not renewed. Their scale was out of step with the more robust taste which buttressed the tower, reglazed the windows, and a little later, ran riot in the chancel.

In the church papers of St. John's, Stamford there is a half page from a letter dated March 1887. It reads in part: "I have asked Henry Sudan if he can shorten the communion table and he can do it if therefore you approve and it meets with the approbation of Mr. Buck I will do it but as for adding to the height or putting filigree skirt between the legs that is out of the question...." Nevertheless a filigree skirt *was* inserted, a somewhat incongruous addition to the elegant altar-table which had been constructed, together with the altar rail, by one Mariam for five pounds in 1825.

*V-16: St. John's, built in Ancaster by Job Loder at the behest of the Churches of England and Scotland.*

There was worse to come. The original subscription list recorded, among other items, that Steven Brown, the building contractor, had made "windows and galleries, etc. for forty-seven pounds ten shillings eleven pence ha'penny and the pews for fifty-five pounds thirteen shillings nine pence." The etceteras had included the pulpit and a panelled walnut reredos with moulded pilasters, Classic architrave, and a mildly Gothicized frieze. Above the central area of the architrave was a low-pitched walnut pediment, in the apex of which had been painted a sunburst radiance emanating from the sacred monogram executed in Roman lettering.

The spirit which added the filigree to the altar-table in 1887 had seen fit to remove the pediment from the reredos and to replace it with flamboyant foliations. The old pediment was shortened and, with its angles blunted, was then inserted between the front legs of the altar-table at floor level. Later taste, pardonably displeased with its appearance, encased the unhappy table in a decent plywood box for use as a chapel altar. There it remained until 1963 when it was placed, with the greater portion of St. John's early chancel furniture, in the hands of the Ontario St. Lawrence Development Commission, for installation (V-17) in the restoration of Christ Church, Moulinette which had been removed to safety in Upper Canada Village.

Originally Christ Church had faced the frothing waters of the Long Sault, which indirectly gave the community its name. The original Moulinette was not, as one would suppose, a small mill. It was, in fact, a windlass built on the riverbank by the *voyageurs*, to draw their craft through the rapids on the upriver passage. And as such it was marked on the beautiful terrestrial globe in the library of Louis XIV in Versailles. There had been no permanent French settlement at the Moulinette, however; the *coureurs de bois* simply winched their boats upriver and went on in search of furs—adventure—Cathay. It was the British North Americans who put down roots there in 1783, when they established the river communities of Mille Roches, Moulinette, Dickinson's Landing, Wales, Aultsville, Woodlands and Iroquois—communities which, together with the early portion of Morrisburg, were to vanish in the flood waters of the St. Lawrence Seaway Power Development in 1959. Christ Church, Moulinette alone survived the obliteration of its community.

Built on the north bank of the St. Lawrence in Stormont County in 1836, Christ Church was a munificent gift to his community from Adam Dixson, mill owner of Moulinette. Grandson by the left hand of the Loyalist leader Sir John Johnson, Dixson, an innovator and Reformer, had daringly harnessed the St. Lawrence for his use, and had built, before 1821, a very handsome house in the finest style of Upper Canadian Neo-Classicism. Then, a decade later, he had set about the realization of another

*V-17 opposite: Regency church furniture from St. John's, Stamford (V-17 bottom left) was installed in battlemented Christ Church (V-18 bottom right), Adam Dixson's gift to Moulinette, now relocated in Upper Canada Village (V-19 top).*

dream—the construction of a church in the picturesque Gothic style (V-18). He did not live to worship in it, however. Business reverses and interminable law-suits which sprang up over his interference with the shipping lanes of the St. Lawrence shortened his life. And when he died, in 1836, Christ Church (not as yet known by that name), though structurally complete and externally finished, was utterly devoid of interior fittings. Oral tradition has it that the Dixson ballroom chairs were carried into the church for his funeral service, and that a "D-end" of the family dining table served as a temporary altar.

Christ Church, Moulinette was chosen by the Commission to represent the houses of worship of the drowned riverfront in Upper Canada Village (V-19) for three reasons: it was an early church; it had retained to a large extent its original appearance; and it was of timber construction, which made it possible to uproot the structure and transport it bodily to the chosen site on the man-made shoreline of the new Lake St. Lawrence. There, ironically, the church built by a Reformer was fitted with the furniture from St. John's, Stamford, the Lieutenant-Governor's church. And so Christ Church ceased to be "of Moulinette" and became, in truth, "of Upper Canada."

Unfortunately the spatial and liturgical arrangements of the early ecclesiastic interiors of Upper Canada can now be found only in those churches relocated in museum village complexes. And somewhere during the lengthy process of restoration the church interior becomes "typical" — akin to many; truly like none. The ceremony of deconsecration has rinsed out its life. The spirit of worship has gone away. It must come back, if it comes at all, in the mind of the viewer who strives in imagination to repeople the pulpit and the pews.

The shades of Peregrine Maitland and of Adam Dixson would both be confounded by the interior of Christ Church, Upper Canada Village. The liturgical setting has been, perforce, a compromise. Few churches of the period had a central altar freed from association with a central pulpit. St. John's, Stamford had such an arrangement, but it also once had an octagonal reading desk which matched the octagonal pulpit and was set on the other side of the altar. Some time in the course of many alterations Stamford lost its reading desk altogether. The restorers of Upper Canada Village, receiving the altar-table, reredos and pulpit on permanent loan, did not feel free to convert the octagonal goblet-pulpit into a two-decker by enclosing it in a reading pew. The restoration budget would not permit the manufacture of a new matching reading desk, nor would it have been typical of the Eastern District in 1836 had it been financially possible. The same consideration applied to the replacement of the "red velvet furniture" with which Sir Peregrine Maitland had bedecked the pulpit. However,

*V-20: St. Alexander's, Lochiel, a late essay in the picturesque.*

the serene semi-elliptical cove of the white plaster ceiling, the cheerful buttercup yellow of its walls, and the dignified simplicity of the banks of white pews (as restored) were native to Christ Church, Moulinette.

The vestry minutes of Christ Church, Moulinette show that in 1893 a committee was appointed to prepare a scheme for church improvement. Among its enumerated duties were: "... to take out the old windows, and put in new lancet windows and repair the tower." The comprehensive instructions had not, fortunately, included any change in the glazing of the transom above the entrance doorway. It remained in position, a factual archive for the restoration of the early windows. The original pointed windows of Moulinette contained sixty small panes in two rectangular grid sashes below the springing of the arch. The arched sash, of true Gothic proportion, had been formed by the intersection of arcs whose radii were the full width of the window and contained ten interlacing curved muntins of the same constant radius. This was Upper Canadian Regency picturesque glazing in its most classic form.

The ten tall nave windows of St. Alexander's Roman Catholic Church, Lochiel—consecrated in the adjacent county of Glengarry in 1851—were constructed in the same style. But whereas the windows of Christ Church, Moulinette had sixty panes, those of St. Alexander, Lochiel had sixty-six. The greater height of these slender windows compensated for the section blocked from inside view by the gallery. St. Alexander (V-20) had been built to the plan of the first church in its mother parish, St. Finnan, Alexandria, and was provided, like it, with side galleries rarely seen in Roman Catholic churches. But when the church was enlarged by the addition of shallow transepts and a large apse, the side portions of the U-shaped gallery were removed. Under the remaining end gallery still stand the original handsome stone font (V-21), with its unusual reeded basin, and a stone holy-water stoup which bears the legend "Presented 1845 by John Macdonald [of] Sandpoint." St. Alexander, Lochiel was thus a beneficiary of the lumber trade of the Ottawa.

Builders'-picturesque was never, at any time, particularly popular as a building style with the Roman Catholic Church in Upper Canada. St. Alexander, Lochiel, and the earlier St. Finnan's, Alexandria, were isolated phenomena, the work of designers accustomed to build churches with U-shaped galleries for other denominations. If the Church of Rome in Upper Canada had a design preference in the second quarter of the nineteenth century, it was for the picturesque qualities of stark mass and silhouette—the working vocabulary of the master-mason—the memory of Erin.

Those were the decades of the great Irish migration to North

*V-21: Carved stone font, 1851, St. Alexander's, Lochiel.*

*V-22 overleaf: Our Lady of the Assumption, Windsor, designed in 1834, open for service in 1846, and altered in 1874.*

America, when the Canadas received well over one hundred thousand emigrants from that island in comparison to some forty thousand English and twenty thousand Scots. The initial migration from Great Britain and Ireland had been well organized, semi-military in character, and directed towards strategic location in the colony. Many immigrants had been settled along the projected route of the Rideau Canal system; others had been dispatched to dilute the concentration of radicalism—real or imagined—in the Talbot settlement, while a number had been encouraged to settle along the Detroit and the St. Clair rivers. Economic recession in the British Isles impelled the next migrations; it was a time of rapidly increasing population in a tightening economy, of gruelling poverty in the United Kingdom and desperate search for survival.

Luckily those were also the decades of Upper Canada's major public works projects, and the demand for both skilled and unskilled labour was great. The engineers, sappers and miners who had been especially recruited in Britain for work on the Rideau Canal were, on completion of the project, disbanded and settled in new communities along its length. Private building contractors and their employees swelled the ranks of the skilled artisans wherever there was a need for locks, mills, timber slides, forts, barracks, courthouses, roads or bridges. Many of the artisans were migratory, but some inevitably elected to remain near each building site, and a taste for the picturesque remained with them—the evocative silhouette of the masonry church on the horizon, the bell-voice of the day hours calling from its tower. It would be tempting to read into the architectural form of the churches which the immigrants built a commemorative grimness—a reluctance to let even the stones forget the hunger and the privations of their passage, but it will not do. The monumental simplicity of coarse rubblestone makes the woeful heart to sing if the texture speaks of home, whether the mason comes from Yorkshire, Perthshire or County Cork.

In point of fact, however, the major edifice in the picturesque style built by the Church of Rome in Upper Canada (V-22) was executed in brick, in 1843, from a design especially drawn for it by a professional architect in 1834. The parish of Our Lady of the Assumption in Sandwich (now a part of Windsor) had been interrogated in 1826 by Alexander Macdonell, Bishop of the new diocese of Kingston, to which the parish belonged. The Bishop had asked how long the existing church was likely to be usable. He was told some eight or ten years. He then demanded to know what was being done to build anew. He was informed that material was already being collected.

Thereafter parish affairs became confused. When L'Assomption had been an outpost of the diocese of Quebec the material

130

affairs of the church had been in the hands of the fabrique—that is, of a committee of churchwardens under the guidance of the curé. The parish priest, Father Crevier—accustomed, as were his parishioners, to the old system—was not a statistician. His haphazard bookkeeping exasperated the Bishop almost as much as did his tendency to campaign for the Reformers during general elections. The Bishop sent Vicar-General O'Grady from York to remonstrate. O'Grady, not yet the militant reformer he eventually became, arrived, quarrelled with everyone, and placed the church under an interdict. Not the climate to foster an ambitious building programme.

In 1831 Father Crevier returned to Quebec, to be replaced in Sandwich by the Bishop's nephew, the Reverend Angus Macdonell. It was not a happy choice. Father Macdonell was bilingual, but French was not one of his languages, and it was largely a French parish. However, by 1834 a degree of concord had been achieved, sufficient at least to warrant the commission of plans for a new church from "Mr. Elliott," an architect newly arrived in Detroit. This would seem to have been Robert Elliott (although some sources call him Richard) who emigrated from Tipperary to Quebec in 1819. Elliott had worked as a draftsman in Quebec until 1827, then moved on to Rochester, New York, to practise as an architect and builder. His next move, in 1834, took him to Detroit where he established an architectural school.

Although Robert Elliott came from Ireland, his formal architectural training had a strong English basis. The octagonal buttresses he designed for the Church of Our Lady of the Assumption, Sandwich, owed more to Cambridge than they did to Cashel, County Tipperary. It may be that Elliott considered the limitations of his budget and the possibilities of the media, and having decided for brick which could be manufactured on the site, chose to adapt the amenable Perpendicular Gothic style to the needs of the parish. One hopes that he was able to use the plans of Assumption for demonstration purposes in his architectural school, while awaiting a just reward for his pious labours, for his earthly rewards were not excessive. The accounts for 1834 in the parish of Assumption recorded in part: "To Mr. Elliott for church plans $10; 6,508 ft. of lumber for the church—$65; 5½ toises of stone taken from the foundation of the old mill $11; 200 cords of wood for the brickyard $250."

The accounts named Abraham Johnson as contracting brickmaker in 1835. But when the brick for the church was actually made, in 1849, it was with a "new brick-making machine invented by Collins of Sandwich" in 1836.

Upper Canada in general and the parish of Assumption in particular had suffered much in the intervening years. The Reformers had risen in rebellion and had been suppressed—under the constant threat of possible intervention from across the border, uncomfortably close at Sandwich. The parish enjoyed—or rather did not enjoy—the ministrations of an absentee priest. Father Macdonell spent much time in attendance on his ailing uncle the Bishop, who was not always as appreciative of his devotion as one might expect. Bishop Macdonell, who never made a move without considering its merits, had settled Father Angus at Sandwich—as far from Kingston as the bounds of the diocese would admit. He had intended him to stay there. But he was not insensible of the needs of the parish and he withdrew his nephew from time to time leaving other priests in his room.

The deteriorating political situation in the Canadas, culminating in rebellion, darkened the declining years of the good old Bishop who died while on a visit to his native land in 1840. He had accomplished much; now the task would be taken up by other hands.

In 1841 the Roman Catholic diocese of Kingston was divided, the western portion becoming the diocese of Toronto. In that eventful year the architect, Robert Elliott, died without having had the satisfaction of seeing Assumption, one of his major buildings, even begun. Better times were at hand for the parish however, for on 8 May 1842 Michael Power was consecrated Bishop of Toronto. The building committee of Sandwich took heart of grace and on 9 June Jacques Reaume was employed as master-mason at $1.75 for an eleven-hour day. The cornerstone was laid on 9 July 1842, and in a little more than a year the shell of the structure stood completed. In July of 1843 the Jesuit Order returned to Assumption, the old mission of the Hurons.

The church the Jesuits came to was a rectangular structure one hundred and twenty feet by sixty feet, for which a tower had been designed but not yet executed. The tower and the sanctuary which stand today were added in 1874—intensifying considerably the Gothic image of Assumption. However, the flank walls still stand very much as Elliott designed them; six bays defined by octagonal supporting buttresses, with a pierced balustrade (supported by little octagonal pinnacles) strung between the buttress-pinnacles above the cornice moulding of the wall. The fenestration was "Pointed" rather than Perpendicular, for Assumption was picturesque rather than scholarly in all of its details.

Our Lady of the Assumption was opened for service on 20 July 1846, and as the excellent history of the parish by Father Lajeunesse, C.S.B., records, "In August of that year a five by seven foot representation of Murillo's Assumption of the Blessed Virgin was hung over the main altar. This beautiful work of art was executed by the renowned Canadian painter A.S. Plamondon and was the gift of Judge Philippe Panet of Quebec."

The painting is not over the altar now for the excellent reason

V-23: Wood and plaster were substituted for stone in the piers and vaults of Assumption, Windsor and in those of St. John's, Perth (above).

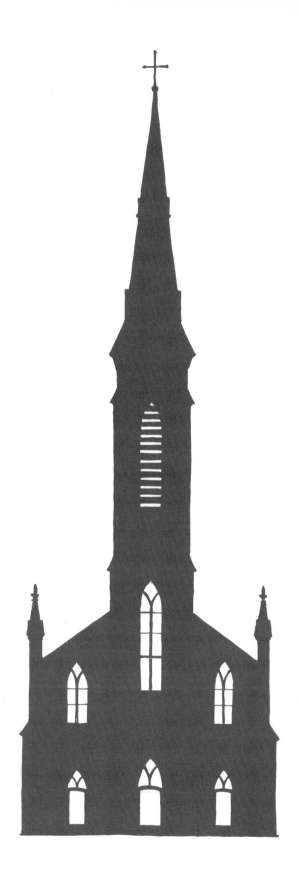

*V-24: Ottawa Valley silhouettes. St. John's, Perth,
left; St. Edward the Confessor, Westport, centre;
and Our Lady of the Visitation, South Gloucester.*

that the altar installed in 1848 is no longer in use. The very wall against which it stood was removed when the new sanctuary was built in 1874. The eighteenth-century pulpit, from the earlier church, is still in Assumption, however, although not, perhaps, supported by the pier to which it was attached in 1848. The piers of Assumption are more or less Early English (the style selected by the Ecclesiologists as worthy of patronage), which was very much admired in Upper Canada around the middle of the nineteenth century (V-23). Though not academically sound, the piers are structurally useful, as they carry the wooden underpinning of the sham-Gothic plaster ceiling vaults. The secondary function of the piers was to define the tripartite spatial division desirable for a liturgy which demanded a principal focal centre between two side altars. In all churches of the 1840's in Upper Canada such piers and vaults were invariably executed in wood and plaster innocently disguised as stone and marble. Everyone was aware of the substitution and happy with the result. The exponents of the picturesque felt no compulsion to express the nature of the materials; their concern was to enhance the gladness of those who went into the House of the Lord.

It was with such gladness—mixed with much anxious discussion of the heavy mortgages involved—that four Roman Catholic parishes in the Rideau area planned their impressive churches. As a result St. John's, Perth was completed in 1848, Our Lady of the Visitation, South Gloucester in 1849, St. Francis Xavier, Brockville in 1855, and St. Edward's, Westport in 1869. As a group the churches were distinguished by a stark, impressive simplicity of silhouette. Three of them were dramatically sited, exploiting the distant impact to the full. The fourth—hampered by re-use of an earlier building site—cannot be fully appreciated visually. In all, colour and warmth were reserved to the interior, in dramatic progression toward the ritual heart of the enclosed space. Surface detailing was minimal, chaste and rather severe.

The ecclesiastical author of these churches was not far to seek, he was the Right Reverend Patrick Phalen, co-adjutor of the diocese of Kingston from 1843 to 1857. Credit for the design of the individual buildings would be harder to assign. For although in all four churches the character was determined by the massing of forms, and must therefore be indicative of the Bishop's taste, they differ from one another (V-24) as greatly in quality of design as they do in skill of execution.

St. John's, Perth, beautifully sited on a street vista and skilfully composed, was the work of a superior masonry designer—a designer who chose to express the triune liturgical space without, as well as within, the walls. There are three entrance doorways, three lancet windows above them, three towers, three widths of vertical plane diminishing from centre to side in the principal facade. Un-

*V-25: Economy dictated grid-glazing, but Regency charm prevailed, in St. Andrew's Church, L'Orignal*

fortunately, the tall lancets in the flanking towers have been closed up with imitation stone, leaving narrow square-headed slits. The composition of the flank walls has been less disturbed. The well-placed lancet windows have retained their mullions—the vertical glazing supports interlaced in the arched head—but have lost the thinner horizontals of the early muntin bars in the lower sections.

The picturesque silhouette of Our Lady of the Visitation, built in South Gloucester Township one year later, was very different. This must surely have been the only church ever to have been built with a clerestory in which there were no windows. The designer simply enclosed a high ceilinged nave and lower side aisles with stone and tin—puncturing the flank walls at regular intervals with narrow lancet windows. Two wider lancet openings, one above the other in the centre of the façade, served as the principal entrance and the major source of light. Two lesser doors, approximately half the area of the main doorway, stood on either side of it. High up on the gable wall above the apex of the window, this most austere designer unexpectedly set a grace note—a little crown-shaped niche housing a minute statue of Our Lady of the Visitation. The squat ogee arch of the little recess would, at a later date, inspire the design of similar ogival arches for the far more graceful belfry. It was a surprisingly successful building, albeit somewhat grimmer now at ground level than its builders intended. Twentieth-century vandalism has made it necessary to lock the faceless slabs of plywood which have replaced the old panelled doors.

The design motif of the ogival arch surmounted by a cross had been used before in the Rideau area. Smoothly cut from well-dressed stone with turned moulded corbels and one elementary poppyhead, it constituted the principal external adornment of St. Francis Xavier, Brockville, on which work was begun in 1855. The cramped building site—which discouraged unnecessary lateral adornment at the time—makes it difficult to appreciate the clean austere lines of the façade now. It is almost impossible to photograph. It was not that the parishioners of Brockville were less appreciative of the beauties of the vista than were their friends in Perth and Westport, nor that they were insensible to the visual impact of the important silhouette. But theirs was the oldest Roman Catholic parish in the area and they had had a smaller church on the site for many years. They were naturally anxious to make use of their land—which, incidentally had been given to them by the ecumenical Presbyterian William Buell at a time when the parish was small and comparatively poor and the site generous and open.

St. Edward's, Westport, on the other hand, which was essentially the design of St. John's, Perth, simplified, commanded an excellent prospect. It was by no means the first church in the parish, however. Settlers from Ireland had first reached the Westport area in 1825. In 1830 they were joined by many more, and by 1848 had built a log church. This was followed a year later by a larger frame church which was destroyed by fire almost immediately. Sorrowing but determined to build well, they slowly accumulated the money to begin again. Bishop Phalen, who visited the parish in 1852, encouraged them to plan for a building scaled to future growth, and in 1859, under the immediate inspiration of a zealous builder priest, Father Foley, the stone shell of St. Edward's slowly rose in its appointed place. Although the building was in use within two years, the interior was not completed until the 1870's. And the tall spire-tower, which was to bring the church to full flowering, did not rise until 1881.

The post-Napoleonic depression had respected neither denomination nor national boundary. Thus it came about that in the late 1820's the old Eastern District of Upper Canada received the first craftsmen from Ulster. They came up the Ottawa to work on the locks and barracks of Carillon and Grenville or on private commissions for the lumber merchants of Hawkesbury, Point Fortune and L'Orignal, and from thence went inland. In 1832 one James Dowal—variously spelled Dowall, Dole and McDowall—was, as its architect, advertising for workmen to assist in building a stone church in Martintown. The next year he was working on a church for the Presbyterians of L'Orignal (V-25). Both churches were somewhat picturesque in design, well executed in stone, and when completed as specified, attractive. Both were dedicated, in the confusing Presbyterian fashion, to St. Andrew. St. Andrew's, Martintown, which rose under the managerial eye of Alexander McMartin—mill-owner, postmaster, sheriff and member of the legislature—prospered, and has been altered twice. St. Andrew's, L'Orignal, despite generous gifts by three Episcopalians and two Roman Catholics, was under-financed, and in its incompleteness remained picturesque. Most of the Ulster craftsmen, unable to wait for the necessary funds to be accumulated, moved on to Bytown and the Rideau or went back to Montreal. Only a few master-carpenters and cabinetmakers remained, happily unaware that as Orangemen—a form of life hitherto unknown to the Eastern District—they were the subject of much uneasy speculation.

The long days of peaceful religious coexistence were unfortunately drawing to a close, and Upper Canada—recovering from its political upheaval—was about to be shaken by the revivals, both spiritual and architectural, which were even then exercising Western Europe. The mid-Victorian conscience—honest, devout, relentlessly analytical—ceaselessly belaboured the mid-Victorian delight in materialistic success and sentimental romanticism. Under this pious bludgeoning, romanticism was transmuted to mysticism.

*V-26: The stones of strife — Knox Free Kirk, Perth, 1854.*

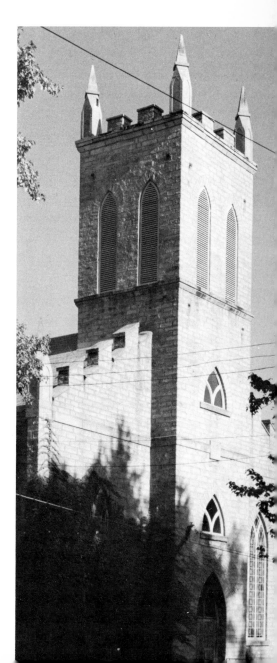

The joyous inconsequence of the Regency picturesque style was rejected with loathing, on the ground that it was not only frivolous but "untrue," and a revived academic-Gothic style, which was about as mediaeval in spirit as the crinoline, was adopted.

Architecture, the mother of the arts, less volatile than her daughters, requires a breathing space to gather stylistic momentum, and church building generally responds more slowly to change than does the domestic architectural field. It was perfectly logical—or so it must have appeared at the time — for some congregations, constrained by conscience to follow the newest liturgical trend, to house the new wine of the spirit in the old bottles of traditional architectural style.

Many of the Free Presbyterian churches of Canada West—the churches of the Disruption—continued to be built in the picturesque style, a form which had been engendered by the establishment. Knox Free Presbyterian Church, Perth (now St. Paul's United), built in 1854, was a case in point (V-26). In style it was a masons' version of the picturesque, as were its immediate ecclesiastical predecessors in the town of Perth: St. Andrew's Church of Scotland (1832) and St. John's Roman Catholic (1848).

That the citizens of Perth should build in such a style was perfectly comprehensible, but why there were, or why it was ever thought there should be, churches of the Disruption in Canada was harder to understand. The Free Church movement was an upheaval within the Established Church of Scotland, arising out of a purely national matter—the settlement of ministers in parishes by appointment rather than by congregational call. The restriction in congregational liberty, real or imagined, which obtained in Scotland (where the Presbyterian Church was established by law) had no bearing on the Church of Scotland in Canada, since it was not, and never had been, established here. Nevertheless, popular reaction to the cry of freedom in the 1840's was so strong that a portion of the Presbyterian Church in Upper Canada withdrew from association with the Church of Scotland, to become the Free Presbyterian Church.

The Church of Scotland in Upper Canada had dedicated its houses of worship to the glory of God and St. Andrew, St. John or, more rarely, to St. Columba, the ancient national patrons. The Free Church, eager to emphasize its complete divorce from clerical control, eschewed the saints generally, and named their places of worship after the reformers. Thus the Free Presbyterians of

*V-27: The dappled light of a hundred years falls caressingly on Knox gallery stair.*

138

Perth, Canada West, who had withdrawn from the Auld Kirk congregation of St. Andrew's, named their unpretentious wooden church Knox. Nine years later they rebuilt in stone with pinnacles and battlements and lancet windows, the symbolic panoply of the remote feudal aristocrats whose right of jurisdiction in church affairs they had been at such pains to deny. Knox Church was reoriented internally in 1877, and its windows reglazed with a restraint too seldom exercised in that age of ebullience (V-27).

If the Romantic movement had fluttered the Presbyterian dovecots by inadvertently encouraging a retro-feudalism, its effect within the body of the Church of England was both more generally controversial and more architecturally important. This was to be expected; Oxford presented a far more likely setting for the resuscitation of mediaeval piety than did the General Assembly of the Church of Scotland, the chapels and gatehouses of Cambridge a nearer road to the Pointed style than the chill Classicism of Adam's Edinburgh. The influence of the Oxford revival of the spirit reached Upper Canada, through the medium of her concerned clergy, nearly a decade in advance of the architectural teachings of the Cambridge University Camden Society. The Cambridge enthusiasts for a return to Gothic form had to train their missionary-architects and craftsmen in the grammar of the new architectural mediaevalism after converting them to its philosophy, whereas the Oxford clergy, seeking to revive Gothic piety by publishing *Tracts for the Times*, had but to fire the crusading zeal of missionaries already in the field.

In 1841—the year which was to see the publication of John Henry Newman's controversial *Tract 90*—the first Tractarian church in Canada West was built on the Niagara escarpment at Jordan. St. John's, Jordan, was not in itself a controversial building. The clear reasonable light of everyday shone through its diaper-latticed lancet windows (V-28) on an auditory church. The most die-hard low-churchman could sit in his high-backed pew and harken to a sermon preached from an elevated pulpit, having heard the lesson read from the lesser elevation of its matching reading desk. On the other hand the high-churchman—released from his chrysalis of reasoned Georgian thought—could contemplate with satisfaction the decent liturgical organization of the new building. He had entered by a central processional aisle (V-29). A direct vista led from the entrance porch—under the flat Perpendicular supporting arches (V-30) of the gallery, between rows of Gothic-panelled bench ends—directly to the altar itself, set against the east wall, protected by a semicircular rail, and flanked on either side by a pulpit (V-31) and reading desk. St. John's, Jordan was not yet, however, a truly Gothic Revival church, for its Pointedness was admittedly blunt and its neo-mediaevalism still of the picturesque kind.

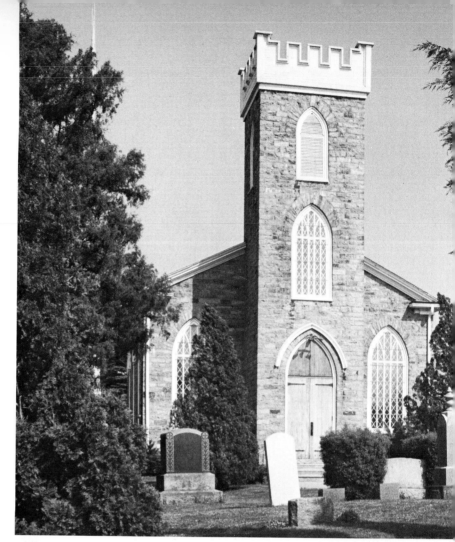

V-28: Tractarianism entered Ontario in St. John's, Jordan (V-28 top left). Special benches set at right angles to the general seating (V-29 bottom left) accommodated the choir, thus freeing the gallery above Howard's reeded Perpendicular arches (V-30 right) for parishioners. Pointed Gothic panels ornamented the bench ends, pulpit (V-31 bottom right) and reading desk.

*V-32: Ryerse Memorial Church
remembers the faith of its
pioneers in reverent grace.*

The vestry records of St. John's, Jordan, did not of course contain the name of the designer of the church (who was probably John George Howard) but did note that the stonemasons responsible were Andrew Dalrymple and Newton Perry. In 1846 it was further recorded that Robert Haines, carpenter, "was to finish all inside work," including the pews. But he was not entrusted with the construction of the pulpit, reading desk, and altar rail, which were to be executed by a "Mr. Springer." The fact that no mention was made of an altar-table would seem to suggest that one had been provided when the church was opened for worship in 1842. Certainly the parish gratefully acknowledged at that time receipt, from the Society for Promoting Christian Knowledge, of two finely bound books—a Bible and a Prayer Book—to be placed on the altar, according to the post-Restoration usage of the Church of England.

St. John's altar has been replaced, but the original must have been very like the handsome Regency walnut altar-tables still in use in Vittoria (III-19) and in the Memorial Church in Port Ryerse. Throughout the Regency period in Upper Canada—which lasted in some areas well into the reign of Queen Victoria—altar-tables were tables indeed. The altar-table in Port Ryerse is of the late Regency type, supported by piers with Gothic lance-headed pseudo-panels inscribed on every face of their shafts—the workmanship obviously that of the craftsman who had already made a similar table for Christ Church, Vittoria shortly after 1845. The whole church, built in memory of Colonel Samuel Ryerse, was anachronistic in 1869. But as a memorial to the bygone day of the Loyalist pioneers, amid whose graves it was set, the little board-and-batten essay in the picturesque was ideal (V-32). It was an utterly appropriate monument to a way of life which took serious things lightly, with a tolerance and charm sorely missing from interdenominational relations in mid-nineteenth-century Canada West.

# VI
# Gothic

*For precept must be upon precept, precept upon precept; line upon line, line upon line; here a little, and there a little.*

*Isaiah* xxviii: *10*

The watershed of neo-mediaevalism can with confidence be pegged at 1841. On one side of the boundary dateline all was picturesque romanticism, fantasy and fun. On the other lay the country of Mister Valiant-for-Truth, architecturally speaking (VI-1), and all because a young professor in a remote college published his first lectures and a number of zealous undergraduates in a larger and older institution founded a journal. The professor was Augustus Welby Northmore Pugin, the indefatigable genius of the Gothic Revival, who had designed furniture for Windsor Castle at the age of fifteen. He called his exposition of mediaeval building *The True Principles of Pointed or Christian Architecture*. The students in question were members of the Cambridge Camden Society, who had banded together to study the Middle Ages and who now undertook to keep Anglican architecture on the rails by monthly instalments of *The Ecclesiologist*.

The year 1841 was to be remembered in Toronto, Canada West, for other reasons—for events which, however, owed a great deal to the same climate of mid-nineteenth-century soul-searching retrospection which had moved the English to re-examine their national church and its places of worship.

In December 1841 the Roman Catholic see of Kingson was divided into two more workable units—the western portion becoming the diocese of Toronto. Michael Power, the newly created bishop, was given his choice of location, and selected the rapidly expanding town of Toronto although it had at that date only one Roman Catholic parish church to serve the needs of its large, predominantly Irish, communion. Bishop Power purchased attractive land on the outskirts of the town from Peter McCutcheon McGill and began to raise money to build his cathedral.

Since the Gothic Revival style was regarded as "too English" by the Church of Rome, the building might not have been designed in that fashion at all had not the chief benefactor, John Elmsley, already come to subscribe to Pugin's beliefs. As a former Anglican, Elmsley was perfectly prepared to build a cathedral in the Decorated English Gothic style (VI-2) once it had been endorsed as aesthetically sound by *The Ecclesiologist*. It had seemed, to the anxious conscience of the architecturally converted Camden Society, that in the richly ornate buildings of the thirteenth and fourteenth centuries lay the only pointedness one could actually trust. It was Puginesque, compartmentalized, crawling with detail, all of which could be interpreted symbolically to demonstrate the sacramentality of its conception. An important point in 1841.

But did remote colonial Canada West have an architect mentally and morally worthy to embark on such a building? It had the very man. William Thomas had arrived, on cue as it were, from Leamington Spa, in April 1841, with his helpmate and their interesting family. His design ability was being demonstrated daily

*VI-1: Pointed Christian architecture, 1845. St. Paul's, London, Canada West (below), St. Michael's Cathedral, Toronto (opposite).*

in the plans and elevations for the Commercial Bank to be erected in the Classical style on King Street. His moral worth would have to be taken on trust; he was a newcomer in their midst. However, mid-Victorian Toronto felt that a quiver filled with eight well-behaved children argued a suitable devotion to hearth and home as well as an incentive to industry and sobriety.

The children had certainly kept their father busy during the month-long Atlantic crossing. Poor Mrs. Thomas had been seasick the whole way from Liverpool to New York and her husband's journal of the crossing reads as a daily chronicle of minor mishaps. Once terra firma had been reached, Thomas had had leisure to look about him, and to record on his journey from New York to Toronto: "the places of worship very neatly built with some pretense to classic Architecture in brick and stone, scarcely any Gothic used in this country. Houses of wood with the Roman orders."

William Thomas was to be the leading exponent of the Decorated style in Canada West. One would like to know what induced him, at the age of forty-one, to abandon an extensive and presumably interesting practice in Birmingham and Leamington Spa for the chancy patronage of the Colonies. It was not for want of friends at court. His younger brother, John Thomas, had shaken off the dust of his Birmingham stonemason's trade to become a sculptor and designer of stained glass in the Barry-Pugin team at Westminster.

The determination to practise architecture as he saw fit may have compelled William Thomas to cross the Atlantic. Incredible as it now seems, it is just possible that he had fallen foul of the Ecclesiologists' arbitrary rule. He may have had the temerity to design in the Gothic style for non-conformists—a proceeding which they could not condone—or to have shown an all too obdurate adherence to Classicism. More than likely the sudden appearance on his Birmingham horizon of Pugin and George Gilbert Scott—both armed with church commissions—before his own St. Matthew, Lister Street was quite finished, led him to believe that Birmingham was architecturally over-populated.

At any rate, Thomas came to Toronto in 1841. He retained a *pied-à-terre* in Leamington Spa until he had published his pattern book, *Designs for Monuments and Chimney Pieces*, in 1843, however; the connotations of Lansdowne Crescent were more reassuring to a publisher firing off a text than were those of Church Street, Toronto. On the other hand, Toronto was further removed from the Ecclesiologists and Mr. Thomas was making the most of that distance. He was building a Gothic church for the United Presbyterians. Situated on the south-east corner of Bay and Richmond Streets, the church (long since demolished) was in the Pointed style, with a Perpendicular tower topped by an octagonal lantern.

Thomas was sophisticated, versatile, hard-working and pleasant. He was, moreover, a good designer, and was a friend of Charles Barry—then at work on that plum of early-nineteenth-century commissions, the new Palace of Westminster in London. Commissions followed as the night the day. By 1845 Thomas had two major church projects in hand—St. Michael's Cathedral for Michael Power, and St. Paul's (VI-3), London for the Reverend Benjamin Cronyn. And, by April 1848, he had one decidedly out-of-hand, the commission for Christ's Church, Hamilton.

On Ash Wednesday 1844 St. Paul's Church, London had been burned out. William Thomas had spent the Lenten season designing its replacement, a neat brick parish church with a handsome Decorated bell tower. He had worked with such despatch that the cornerstone could be laid by John Strachan, Bishop of Toronto, on St. John the Baptist Day. On Ash Wednesday 1845 the new St. Paul's was opened for service, and in 1857, when the Reverend Benjamin Cronyn was elected the first bishop of the new Anglican diocese of Huron, it became a cathedral. Eight years later the bells in the tower were ringing the alarm for a Fenian raid, forcibly reminding the older ladies of 1837, when moulding bullets had been their regular Sabbath occupation.

St. Michael's Cathedral began, *en fête*, 7 April 1845, with an excavation party. An ox was roasted whole to cheer the parish volunteers digging under the direction of John Harper, contractor for the masonry, brickwork and carpentry. Ishmael Iredale was engaged to roof the building, and John Craig bespoken for the painting. Craig assigned the window sashes to the painstaking care of his young apprentice, Michael O'Connor, the only Roman Catholic in his employ. The Cathedral (VI-4) was dedicated 29 September 1848.

By that time William Thomas had become entangled in the convoluted affairs of the building committee of Christ's Church, Hamilton. On 2 April 1848 the committee had recorded in part: "The expenses for the past year have been augmented by an expenditure of £ 50 for plans and specifications of the proposed enlargement of the present and ultimate erection of a parish church on the scale adequate to the growing importance of the city." Thomas had taken them at their word and had, for his fifty pounds, designed them a Decorated Gothic church of which even the Ecclesiologists would have approved. Expressly designed for the Anglican liturgy, it was to be built in stone, and embellished with carving and stained glass designed by the architect's brother, John Thomas in England.

This task complete, Thomas journeyed to Hamilton with his drawings. The building committee thought them perfectly splendid. And now would Mr. Thomas please arrange to chop them up so that the stone chancel and the first two bays of the Gothic nave could be added immediately to their existing church—Robert Wetherell's Classic wooden structure? Whereupon the amiable Mr. Thomas, on the crest of a fine flood of Welsh rage, told them what he thought of such a proceeding. He explained to them at length that one did not make a mockery of a fine building when one had outgrown it. At the end of his impassioned dissertation he realized with despair that his complacent audience had not understood a word of it. The "growing importance" of Hamilton would be enhanced, in their eyes, by the ludicrous patchwork they proposed. So Mr. Thomas, mindful of the eight children in his Gothic house in Toronto, gritted his teeth and built on the addition, sending his eldest son, William T. Thomas, to act as clerk of works while he himself concentrated on new commissions. The important city of Hamilton ridiculed its Anglicans for the patchwork of Christ's Church, calling it the "humpback church."

His pride lacerated, William Thomas then took his original plan for Christ's Church to the Presbyterians. He was met with gratifying enthusiasm. He had a position to restore in that city and so had they, and together, in 1853, they built St. Andrew's (now called St. Paul's) on James Street. It was to be William Thomas' finest church and, mercifully, the least altered of all his buildings.

In the February 1856 issue of *The Canadian Journal of Industry, Science and Art* St. Andrew's Church, Hamilton was described thus:

"This building now erecting from the designs of William Thomas, Esq., Architect, was commenced in 1854. The design is in the Early Decorated Style of English Gothic Architecture, and is being constructed wholly of stone. The tower is of what is styled bush hammered and rubbed work, and the flanks and west end walling of rock work. The windows in the flank walls are of three lights and those in the end recess of four lights each of rich and varied tracery. They will be glazed with tinted glass in ornamental quarries, arranged in geometrical figures. The roof is open to the apex, with arched principals having tracery points in the compartments, and with ceiling ribs and bordered panels.

"The tower, with double buttresses at the angles, already presents a bold and massive effect. The spire with clustering pinnacles at the tower parapet, will be of cut-stone, and from its details, as shown in the beautifully executed chromo-lithographic view which has been forwarded to us it will have a very striking appearance when completed. Its only fault is, that from the richness of the tower and spire the body of the building looks plain by contrast. The entire height will be one hundred and eighty-five feet and the whole will be completed this summer. It is worthy of special note that this will we believe, be the first stone spire erected in Upper Canada."

The unknown journalist was quite right; it *was* the first stone

*VI-3: William Thomas railed Ontario's St. Paul's in London (opposite) with a row of little cast-iron beavers, and set a jovial king at the west door of St. Michael's (VI-4 below).*

149

spire in Upper Canada—the pinnacle of nostalgia, achieved by an architect from the stone-spired heart of England. It was also destined to be the only one (VI-5).

Internally all of William Thomas' churches were designed with sobriety leavened by rich decoration in the best traditions of neo-mediaevalism. But just as some congregations were more ornament-prone, so in like degree were they given to constant change. St. Paul's, London was enlarged and re-enlarged, and in the process its Pointed Gothic flavour evaporated, leaving fleeting glimpses of the Decorated style in memorials and the cheerful checkers of Minton tile in the narthex (VI-6). The tall oak pulpit from which Bishop Cronyn used to declaim was removed bodily to a chapel erected in his memory in the third quarter of the nineteenth century.

The hand which removed St. Paul's pulpit was soon at work on the fabric of St. Michael's, Toronto. Langley & Burke, a firm of earnest Goths of the second dispensation, which followed the precepts of John Ruskin, were called in by Bishop Lynch to complete the cathedral bell tower and renovate the thirty-year-old interior (VI-7). They bunged clerestory windows into the Thomas triforium arches with the laudable intention of admitting both the light of day and the light of serious scholarship. This change necessitated the construction of dormers which, when Langley had done fretting them, set the whole composition back into the picturesque or pre-Gothic Revival school of design. The upper stages of the bell tower and the spire show the mature Langley in better form.

Bishop Lynch had made an effort to keep the completion of the building within the Thomas firm but the drawings supplied had not been inspiring. Cyrus and William T. Thomas, who followed their father's profession with unequal steps, had moved the design office to Montreal after his death in 1860. Cyrus had then gone off to greener fields in Chicago, leaving his younger brother to despatch plans for dull, derivative buildings all over Eastern Canada until 1892.

While William Thomas' sons were diminishing his architectural reputation through the confusion of identity, Hugh Vallance, grandson of one of his master-builders, was keeping it splendidly alive. Vallance, who practised in Montreal, deepened the chancel of St. Paul's (St. Andrew's), Hamilton with such sympathetic skill that it is still the best Decorated Gothic Revival church in Ontario (VI-8). He reset the strongly textured panelling farther back in the new space designed to contain the choir, and provided stylistically correct ends for the benches. Under protest he added couchant lions—the one discordant note—to the chancel ribs. Otherwise the interior (VI-9) stands now as it was designed by William Thomas with the distant assistance of his sculptor

*VI-5 opposite: The lithograph by William Thomas of St. Andrew's (St. Paul's), Hamilton hangs in the vestry of the church.*

*VI-6 and 7: Two Gothic requisites — Minton tile-work underfoot, St. Paul's London (VI-6 below) and crockets wherever possible overhead, St. Michael's, Toronto, (VI-7 above).*

*VI-8: Sumptuous solemnity clothes the Gothic
interior of St. Paul's, Hamilton (VI-8 left). The
deep brown carving of pulpit and gallery (VI-9
above), picked out with salmon, blue and gold, had
to pass inspection by John Thomas, designer to the
Queen, as well as the weekly review by captious
critics in the pews (VI-10 right).*

brother, John Thomas, stained-glass designer to the Queen.

St. Paul's, Hamilton survived unaltered because the Presbyterians had plunged recklessly into colossal debt to build it. Furthermore, the congregation was rent in two in 1871 by a controversial minister, the Reverend Robert Burnett, who withdrew with his supporters to the old church, taking the name of St. Andrew with him. The reduced congregation sadly sold their fine church to the Park Street Baptists, who had outgrown their own premises. The Baptists could not keep up the payments either. Finally, in 1873, the Presbyterians, by then reunited, disposed of their old frame church to a group of German Roman Catholics, bought back their beloved extravagance with the proceeds, and rededicated it to St. Paul. They were thereafter too poor during the critical years to alter the building (VI-10). A blessing indeed! The very worst enemies of elderly architecture are affluence and fire, and it is sometimes difficult to decide which of the two does the greater damage.

The Anglicans of Toronto had no doubt on that score on the dismal morning of 7 April 1849. St. James' Cathedral had just been gutted by fire for the second time in ten years. Nor was that the sum of their distress. The major portion of the business district had burned with it. How could they rebuild St. James'?

The vestry met, and almost immediately split over intention. One group was in favour of shoring up the stone shell for a third lease on life. The other was in favour of boldly embarking on a new building, to which end they proposed giving out the King Street frontage of the churchyard on leasehold for shops. The only point of complete agreement reached was that John Howard should be asked to draw up rules for a design competition for the new cathedral.

The ground rules worked out by Howard and recorded in the vestry minutes were generally explicit. There was to be a tower to front the west, to house ten bells, and to be topped by a spire. The church was to be in the Gothic or Early English style—of white brick with cut-stone dressing and a rubblestone foundation. Seating was required for eighteen hundred to two thousand persons, "including the aisles." The body of the church and a portion of the tower was to be finished immediately. The drawings were to be "executed with care and tinted a pale colour with sepia, elevation shaded with same, sections of stonework with pale India ink . . . to one eighth inch scale." Provision was to be made for the installation of hot air furnaces and, understandably, for a fireproof vault for communion plate, books and papers. Finally there were to be three prizes offered. The successful architect was to receive seventy-five pounds if he was not afterwards employed to superintend the building. The building committee had thoughtfully appointed as a design jury the arch-enemies John George Howard

*VI-11: St. James' Cathedral, 1854, (VI-11 below) introduced the Early English style to the Toronto scene, in a manner infinitely gratifying to Bishop Strachan (VI-12 left). Removal of disfiguring galleries freed the vertical movement of arcade and clerestory (VI-13 right). The mid-Victorian font (VI-14 below left) now stands in the narthex.*

St. James' Cathedral.

and Thomas Young, with Thomas Johnson to serve as buffer between them.

Drawings were received from eleven architects—Cumberland, Thomas, K. Tully, and J. Tully, all of Toronto; Smith, Ostell and Lafevre, all of Montreal; Wheeler of Hartford, Connecticut; and Wills, Pearson and Otis from farther afield. On 12 September 1849 John Howard recorded in his office journal, "Mr. Young and Johnson awarded the premiums according to their own wishes but contrary to what I consider just."

Just or not, the jury had awarded the first prize to Frederick William Cumberland, a bright young man who had come out in 1847 from a good London office to be engineer for the County of York, Canada West, and who had, while serving in that capacity, designed Canada's display for the Great Exhibition of 1851. They gave the second premium to John Ostell, and the third to Kivas Tully.

Despite the jury's verdict "Smith" was called up from Montreal to "explain his plan" to the building committee, and Cumberland was asked to prepare a plan "as large as Mr. Smith's" so that the two might be compared. Mr. Smith's plan was

*VI-15 left: St. James-the-Less, Toronto.*

*VI-16 right: St. Paul's, Bloor Street, now Maurice Cody Hall.*

adopted, and by October he was at work on a borrowed drawing board in John Howard's office. The building committee did not see fit to record the next move, by which their right hand dismissed Smith while their left re-employed Cumberland. But it was accomplished. On 9 January 1850, Mr. Cumberland was ordered to stake out the ground for the new St. James' (VI-11). It was to be entirely new.

Frederick William Cumberland won the contest over Ostell and Tully—and hands down over Thomas—because he was a new Goth, a convinced ecclesiologist conversant with the whole vocabulary of the new style, a sincere churchman who had been brought to believe that the Early English style was the purest and truest expression of Christian building. The Cambridge Camden Society had arrived at that conclusion at least two years before Cumberland left England and had been heartily advocating it ever since. The Society, purged of its pro-Roman tone by the shock of John Henry Newman's conversion, had changed its name to The Ecclesiological Society and had shed its old allegiance to the Decorated or Middle Pointed style at the same time.

Meanwhile, John Ruskin, a new arbiter, had emerged from Dulwich to lead the elect to the pure fountains of taste. Ruskin had just published his vastly influential work *The Seven Lamps of Architecture*, in 1849. In it he restated in cajoling prose some of the views that the Ecclesiologists had been propounding for years, but he advanced far beyond their frontiers in other areas. Every copy of *The Ecclesiologist* and *The Builder* reaching Henry Rowsell's Toronto bookshop thereafter quoted the new oracle, or made favourable comment on a brick church (All Saints, Margaret Street) being built according to *all* the rules by William Butterfield near the British Museum. Brick was in. Early English was the only style for true churchmen. And John Strachan, Bishop of Toronto (VI-12), was very happy. St. James' would be true and beautiful and altogether superior to Cronyn's Decorated St. Paul's, London, that triumphant centre of the Low Church party in Canada West.

Frederick William Cumberland built the cathedral in discreet partnership with Thomas Ridout—a fellow engineer and one of the many scions of a large important Toronto connection. The architects fulfilled the letter of the contract requirements, building immediately the main body of a pleasing Early English church and the lower stages of its bell tower. Thomas had designed his Toronto cathedral, St. Michael's, with a nave arcade and a solid triforium under a pitched roof, omitting the clerestory which would have required expensive aisle roofs. Cumberland's St. James' had a nave arcade and clerestory but omitted the triforium gallery stage (VI-13). Sufficient onto the day were the galleries he had to install.

Dr. Eric Ross Arthur, in *No Mean City*, has dealt faithfully with the internal problems of St. James', as well as with Cumberland's other major works, all of which were concentrated in Toronto. They need not be reconsidered here, but mention must be made of one of them: a church attributed to Cumberland and his major design partner William Storm—the chapel of St. James-the-Less in St. James' cemetery, Toronto.

William G. Storm was a nearly-native product. Five years younger than Cumberland, he had been born in Yorkshire in 1826, the son of Thomas Storm, a building contractor who brought his family to Upper Canada in 1830. Young William studied architecture along with William Thomas' sons in their father's office, and seems to have travelled with them on educational trips to Europe. In 1850 he was enticed, with a promise of partnership, into the offices of Cumberland and Ridout, so that he might draw up the new cathedral for them. Storm learned the lesson well; when, later on, he and Cumberland won the competition for a new university building he set off at once for England to fetch a couple of draftsmen to do the tedious bits. He brought back George and Edward Radford who had learned all that needed to be known about Gothic detail (VI-14) under Pugin's careful guidance. Two years later the Chapel of St. James-the-Less was designed in the offices of Cumberland and Storm, and like many products of busy architectural firms, there were several opinions as to its authorship.

The chapel was a delightful building, nestling on its site with all of the artless charm of a little mediaeval church which had grown quietly in a remote English rural parish (VI-15). Many of its choicest details, as well as its massing of forms, were to appear again two years later in the winning designs for St. Pauls', Yorkville submitted by the Radford brothers, on their own, in the competition of 1860. Neither St. James-the-Less nor St. Paul's was the least bit Early English. They were Decorated and decorative, and whatever Ruskin and the Ecclesiologists might have thought Pugin would have been pleased with them.

In point of fact, the Ecclesiologists would have concurred in every choice the Radfords made (VI-16). The arbiters had been not unmindful of the cultural darkness known to pervade the Colonies, and had carefully selected, for copying abroad, three English churches—all equally unsuitable for Moosonee, Alice Springs or Rawalpindi. The churches, St. Michael's, Long Stanton; All Saints, Teversham; and St. Mary's, Arnold—all within easy reach of Cambridge and thus well known to the critics—were stout little stone buildings whose steeply pitched roofs plunged down to deep eaves over low aisle walls. All had minimal decoration in the Early English taste, and all were—within the limits of the newly elaborated ritual—functional. The edict was published in *The Ecclesiologist* and thereafter one stream of Gothic building in Canada

West ran obediently in the approved channel, while two others elected to follow divergent courses. The approved school of architectural thought, which tended to hover around seats of government, first appeared in Toronto in the 1850's, when that city was briefly capital of the United Province of Canada.

While the draftsmen were at work on plans for St. James-the-Less in Cumberland's office, Thomas Fuller, another recently arrived English architect, was drawing up an even more correct church to be built near Colonel Denison's estate, Bellevue, well beyond the western town limits. Thomas Fuller had studied and practised architecture in his native Bath and in London, and had come to Canada by way of Antigua where he had supervised a cathedral being built to his designs in 1851. Shortly after his arrival in Toronto, Fuller had formed a partnership with Chilion Jones, architect of that city, grandson of Ephriam Jones of Prescott, and thus kin to half the old Family Compact.

The partners' first commission, St. Stephen's-in-the-Fields, Toronto (VI-17) was designed circumspectly in the manner of St. Michael's, Long Stanton as published in *The Ecclesiologist*. It rose in a strong wedge from a broad base solidly buttressed to a charming open bell cote, but the wedge was of the isosceles variety of 1858, not the equilateral form of 1230, and the iron work of the chancel cresting was frankly frivolous.

From such a promising beginning one would expect success to attend the firm of Fuller and Jones. It followed quickly. In 1859 the partners won the competition for the new Houses of Parliament to be built in Bytown, the chosen capital of Canada. By 1866 Charles Baillairgé had been appointed to the team to make it properly Canadian, Bytown had become Ottawa (VI-18), and Thomas Fuller was designing the church of St. Alban-the-Martyr on Daly Avenue to house the devotions of the civil service.

*VI-17: Polychromatic masonry.*
*St. Stephen's-in-the-Fields, 1858.*

But the luck ran out. St. Stephen's-in-the-Fields had burned in 1865, and its shell was enlarged and aggressively improved by other hands. The distinguished high-Victorian Houses of Parliament — still standing when Fuller died in 1898 — were destroyed by fire in 1917.

St. Alban-the-Martyr, on the other hand, had had a history of trouble from the beginning. Quicksand had been discovered during the excavation, and the design had had to be modified. But Fuller was not available for consultation; he was on his way to Albany, having, with Augustus Laver, submitted the prize-winning entry in competition for the new capital of New York State. Chilion Jones had sunk without a trace into the Department of Public Works. So St. Alban-the-Martyr was eventually completed by a younger architect, King Arnoldi, in the spirit of Fuller — and of St. Michael's, Long Stanton — in 1877. The interior of St. Alban's — which in its heyday contained among its communicants seven cabinet ministers, headed by Sir John A. Macdonald — was seriously rendered in late-Victorian transitional style in the manner made popular by the English ecclesiologists, Butterfield and Eastlake.

The Ecclesiological movement, like a skein of wild geese, kept changing leaders in full flight, and thus renewing its youthful zeal,

for a very long time. This was true in Ontario also. Thus a number of small country churches in the Ottawa Valley and the Upper St. Lawrence basin proclaimed, by their strongly textured stonework, steeply pitched roofs, sloping buttresses, and gabled aisle windows, the widespread influence of the official architects of Ottawa and their numerous masons and master-builders. One of the most charming of these churches is St. John the Baptist, Lyn (VI-19), built in 1860 when that community was giving Brockville serious commercial competition in the County of Leeds. Another is St. Paul's, Almonte, in nearby Lanark, which was erected, so its vestry minutes record, by the United Church of England and Ireland in 1863. The entry further noted that the plan of the church in Lyn had been adopted for its construction.

While the churches of Almonte and Lyn relate stylistically to the known works of Fuller and his follower Arnoldi, there was another contender in the Department of Public Works who was designing in the English-country-church idiom. This was Thomas Seaton Scott, late of Montreal, who had been commissioned in 1867 to design a chapel-of-ease for the Governor-General. The Government of Canada had been successfully implanted in Ottawa, but the Governor-General was housed in a suburb, New Edinburgh or Mackay's Bush. St. Bartholomew, New Edinburgh

*VI-18 opposite: Official Gothic, 1867; open bell cote, St. Alban-the-Martyr, Ottawa.*

*VI-19 bottom: St. John the Baptist, Lyn, rural Early English.*

*VI-20 right: The Vice-regal pew, St. Bartholomew's, Rockcliffe.*

*VI-21 and 22 opposite: Ecclesiastical twins—St. Mark's, Barriefield (VI-21 above) and St. George's, Trenton (VI-22 below).*

was a charming, low-walled stone church with a steeply pitched roof and a timber porch set prettily—if unsymbolically—toward the early morning light on the east flank wall. Memorial brasses accumulated on the white plaster walls above its chastely carved Gothic benches and the armorial bearings of many Governors-General have come to line the corbel-table below the trusses of Scott's open timber roof (VI-20).

Twenty years earlier citizens at the other end of the Rideau Canal system had watched with fascination an open timber roof going up above the stonework of the new church in Barriefield (VI-21). Open timber construction in a church roof was something of a marvel in the Kingston area in 1845, but to Alfred Brunel, the designer of the building, the stark reality of engineering was quite simply the way of life. For as long as he could remember his father and his grandfather had been inventing everything from stocking-frames to steamboats during their more restful moments between bridge building and railway tunnelling. In fact, Isambard Kingdom Brunel's *Great Britain*, the largest iron steamship then afloat and the first to use a screw propeller, was making her first Atlantic crossing while his son was building St. Mark's. Alfred Brunel designed another church for the Anglicans, St. George's— a twin for St. Mark's—in Trenton (VI-22), and then went on to a career of blameless anonymity as City Engineer in Toronto.

The open timber roof in pre-Confederation Ontario, when found in close conjunction with low aisle walls, clearly proclaims an ecclesiologically sound Anglican church. In conjunction with a higher wall and larger windows, it can mean a number of different things.

A vaulted ceiling, on the other hand, was the all-but-exclusive choice of the Church of Rome for its buildings in Canada West. The vaulting was generally quadripartite in form, following—afar off, in wood and plaster—the masonry construction of thirteenth-century England and France. Given an Irish cleric and an English or Irish architect, the church vaulting would be Early English in style. If the architect were Irish and the priest an archaeologically-minded Jesuit fresh from France, the vaulting would likely be Rayonnant—the French way of saying the same thing. Unfortunately these early essays in plaster vaulting were all fragilely susceptible to sudden climatic change and the attendant vagaries of early-nineteenth-century heating systems. Father Point's plaster vaulting of 1845 at L'Assomption, Sandwich had to be completely rebuilt in 1903.

The interiors of nearly all the major Roman Catholic churches of Ontario built before 1860 have been recast several times. There are, however, at least two handsome interiors which have retained their pre-Confederation character: St. Mary's, Hamilton and the third church of St. Andrew, St. Andrews West in Stormont County.

In 1856 the little wooden church of St. Mary on Mulberry Street in Hamilton suddenly found itself a cathedral. Bishop Farrell, appointed to the new diocese of Hamilton, was still considering proposals for rebuilding it in 1859 when the church burned. The building programme was stepped up, and in 1860 the Bishop laid the cornerstone of a red brick Gothic church designed, according to old accounts, by "the late Mr. Kartum who died before the building was completed." Nothing whatsoever seems to be known about the unfortunate Kartum or his plans. The original galleries, constructed by carpenter O'Brien, were removed in 1870. But the main altar, the heart and soul of the building, designed by Zepherin Perrault of Montreal (VI-23) and built by Mr. Cloohey, is still there.

In 1862 Bishop Farrell, while on a journey to France, purchased statues of the Virgin Mary and St. Joseph. The return voyage was so rough that some cargo had to be shipped over the side. St. Joseph was sacrificed to the angry sea but Our Lady was brought safely to Hamilton and stands today under the central fretted pinnacle of the retable designed by Zepherin Perrault who, as a *menuisier* and sculptor of Montreal, Canada East, had had considerable exposure to the intricacies of Gothic Revival decoration.

The Montreal architects who employed him made it their business to be *au courant* with the state of both English and French

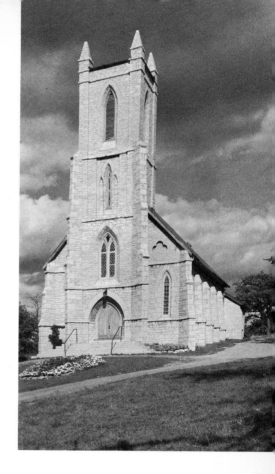

architecture and to add to their reference store such publications as dealt with it. And although monographs by Lassus and Viollet-le-Duc on the Parisian restoration of Notre Dame and the Sainte Chapelle might not actually come into the hands of craftsmen like Perrault, the vocabulary of the French Gothic filtered through to them, and they used it to beautify altars, pulpits, bosses and benches in Roman Catholic churches all over Canada West.

In 1857 the Reverend John Hay, parish priest of St. Andrews West, Stormont County, recorded minutes concerning the building of his new church. The building committee accepted the tender whereby Alan Grant agreed to build the church according to plans furnished by John Power, architect, of Kingston, "for the sum of £3800 to be finished by May 1861." The church was to be of good sound stone with a "rockwork finish." It was to be 115' × 55' with a bell tower and spire. Grant could not find the necessary financial backing, however, so the contract was taken over by James Matthews of Montreal. By November 1860 tinners from Montreal were at work on the roof. Once the roof was secure, the carpenters, under William Birch of Kingston, "boarded up the doors and windows and went away for the winter."

Father Hay forestalled future defections of this kind by purchasing four stoves and seven coal scuttles before signing a contract with Zepherin Perrault in 1861. Perrault had furnished plans for "plastering and finishing the interior, erecting galleries and altars in the same style as the cathedral [St. Mary's] in Hamilton." Father Hay donated the six hundred dollars required for a handsome main altar with tall pinnacles and a central figure of St. Andrew carved in wood. He then persuaded John Macdonell, a lumberman of Bytown, to pay for a side altar to St. John, promising him future burial beneath it. The statue of St. John (VI-24) is one of Perrault's finest works, and the sculptor was so pleased with it that he decided to donate the other side altar himself.

Zepherin Perrault seems to have belonged to a Montreal branch of the Perraults of St. Jean-Port-Joli, a family of carvers and sculptors of whom the best known was Chrysostome Perrault who died in 1829.

John Power, the architect of St. Andrew's, came from a line of builders. Born in Colyton, Devon, he emigrated in 1846 to Kingston, Canada West, where he practised, for a time, in partnership with Edward Horsey. In 1890, now in partnership with his sons Joseph and Thomas, Power enlarged St. George's Cathedral, Kingston. And when St. George's burned nine years later the Power firm rebuilt it. In the early 1860's, when his church in St. Andrews West was nearing completion, John Power designed a remarkable Gothic church for the Congregationalists of Kingston

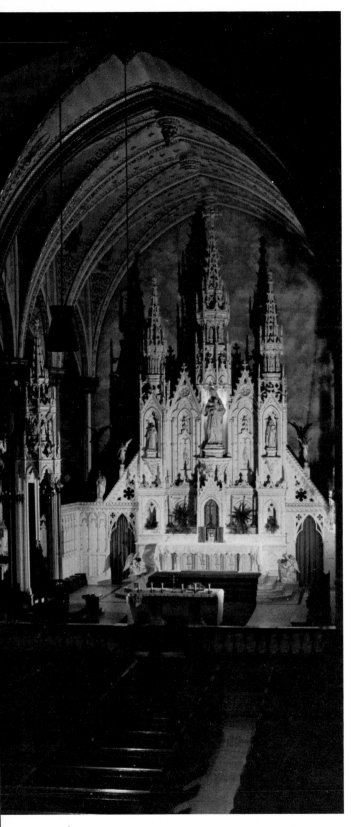

*VI-23:* Veni Creator Spiritus.
*High altar, St. Mary's, Hamilton,*
*designed by Zepherin Perrault*
*in 1850.*

(VI-25). As far as he was concerned, the Gothic style was not reserved for any one denomination.

There were architects, however, who preferred to design for a
single denomination—usually the communion to which the architect himself belonged. The designer was then completely conversant with the liturgy of the church, aware of its peculiar spatial
needs, and entirely in sympathy with its architectural aspirations.
Such was the background of the Church of Our Lady of the Immaculate Conception, Guelph. Designed in 1863 by Joseph Connolly, a recent arrival from Limerick, the church was a-building
from 1876 to 1926—very good going in Gothic terms. Cologne
Cathedral, on which the Guelph church is locally believed to have
been modelled, was begun in 1275 and not completed until 1880.
When Our Lady, Guelph was being planned, the vast German
Cathedral was impressively in the news. Work was once more going forward on the twin towers of Cologne, the plans for which
had been mislaid for several centuries. There does not seem to
have been any other reason for associating Connolly's Guelph
church with Cologne—of which Sir Banister Fletcher wrote in *A
History of Architecture on the Comparative Method*, "Cologne Cathedral
. . . is a conspicuous instance of the adaptation of the details of a
style, without having assimilated the spirit that created it." Our
Lady of the Immaculate Conception, Guelph, on the other hand,
was *French* Gothic in style—and very good French Gothic at that.
It had a rose window over the west door, a chevet of chapels encircling the chancel, a slim decorative flèche pointing heavenward
above the crossing—all in the manner of thirteenth-century France
(le Style Ogival Rayonnant). Joseph Connolly, straight from the
busy architectural office of McCarthy of Dublin, had assimilated
the style very well on his travels. So well, indeed, that his Guelph
church, although designed in the manner of Pierre de Montreuil
(who built the Sainte Chapelle for St. Louis IX of France) had no
need to be like any building but itself.(VI-26).

Between 1870 and 1890 Connolly designed a number of buildings for the Roman Catholic Church, among which were the
churches of St. Mary, Bathurst Street and the second church of St.
Paul, Power Street, in Toronto. He also designed one cathedral
for them, St. Peter's, London, and enlarged a second, St. Mary's,
Kingston. But in none of his later buildings did he equal his work
at Guelph.

Guelph was founded on rock, the building material of the
Gothic period and of the Gothic Revival. As early as 1857 a local
architect, David Allan, was designing a house of worship for the
Presbyterians of the Church of Scotland in that style. He was assisted in this pious endeavour by William Hay, an Edinburgh architect recently arrived in Toronto. The church that came off
their drawing boards was described by James Croil, in a report

*VI-24 and 25: Perrault's finest
sculpture (VI-24 opposite), the statue
above St. John's altar in a church
designed by John Power who also
planned First Congregational,
Kingston (VI-25 below).*

*VI-26 overleaf: Our Lady of the
Immaculate Conception, Guelph,
designed in 1863 by Joseph
Connolly, completed in 1926.*

167

entitled *The Church of Scotland in Canada in 1866*, as "of freestone surmounted by a fine spire and occupies a commanding site. Adjoining it is the manse, a handsome stone building." Croil gives the cost as being four thousand, five hundred pounds. The church building accounts of 1850 recorded an optimistic two thousand, six hundred and sixty-nine pounds, of which one thousand, four hundred and thirty-four went to the masons, five hundred and fifty-eight to the carpenters, and seventy-five to the architects. The church, inevitably dedicated to St. Andrew, still occupies the site—rendered somewhat less commanding by a snarl of service wires emanating from a pole transformer fixed to the only good viewing point (VI-27). Internally the church has been diminished less. Original Gothic brackets support the gallery, from which the choir has been wafted to sit in the communion place under the Early English moulded arches of the pulpit screen. Gothic panelling stands behind the comfortable sofa on which the minister sits him down (VI-28), visually oppressed now by the weight of organ pipes over his head.

David Allan was a member of St. Andrew's session, and as such he has the distinction of being the only architect in Ontario to be commemorated (VI-29) in a church of his designing. His church or his family seem to have conveniently forgotten the part played by William Hay in the enterprise.

William Hay deserves better of posterity. His contribution to church building in Ontario was considerable. Although few of his own churches remain, the elusive Aberdonian formed a link between the London office of the prolific George Gilbert Scott, who built some three hundred and twenty-six churches at home and abroad, and that of Henry Langley, who eventually had over seventy Ontario churches to his credit.

Born in Cruden, Aberdeenshire, in 1818, William Hay received his early architectural training from John Henderson of Edinburgh. In the early 1840's he joined the London office of George Gilbert Scott who was then working in partnership with William Moffat. They sent young William Hay to St. John's, Newfoundland in 1848, to act as clerk of works on Scott's cathedral. After four years of supervising and designing government projects in Newfoundland and Nova Scotia, Hay betook himself to Toronto, where his first major commissions were the workhouse and the hospital.

Hay's practice grew. By 1855 he was supervising the building of the hospital and designing three churches and a college: Gould Street Presbyterian (VI-30); St. Basil's Church in St. Michael's College, for the Roman Catholic diocese of Toronto; and St. George's Church (VI-31), for the Anglicans of Newcastle. Assistance was urgently necessary, and it appeared in the person of Henry Langley—enthusiastic, diligent, with some drawing experi-

168

FOY · POUR · DEVOIR

*VI-27: Hydro wires destroy the
impact of much Ontario architecture.
St. Andrew's, Guelph (VI-27 above),
designed by David Allan and William
Hay, has handsome Gothic detailing
on its pulpit (VI-28 right) and the
Allan coat-of-arms in one of its
stained-glass windows (VI-29).*

*VI-30 opposite page: Broach
spires and asymmetrical balance
distinguished Hay's interpretation of Early English, in Gould
Street Presbyterian Church, Toronto.*

170

ence behind him in the Toronto Academy—just nineteen years old, and eager to sign on for a seven-year apprenticeship.

Hay designed St. Basil's and St. George's as asymmetrical compositions. The bell tower, set at one side, in line with the liturgical west end, was buttressed in a plain Early English style, given two louvered lancet openings on each face of the bell chamber, and crowned with a graceful broach spire. Matching lancet openings were grouped together to form the major east and west windows. Paired lancets were designed to light the flank walls. Both churches were designed with open timber ceilings (VI-32); Hay had learned, from Scott and Moffat, to pay no attention to the Ecclesiologists' ban on building in the English parish church style for non-conformists—a practical attitude which he in turn inculcated in his apprentice.

St. George's, Newcastle was altered somewhat by that same apprentice twenty years later. A half-timbered porch was built out from the tower base, and the lancets in either gable wall were removed in favour of larger windows of an indeterminately Pointed style. St. Basil's has suffered more drastic treatment. Its "Protestant" timbering has been hidden by plaster vaulting, and several cubits have been added to its stature at either end, necessitating the complete rebuilding of chancel, tower, and principal façade.

In 1857 Hay had collaborated with David Allan on St. Andrew's, Guelph. In the following year he designed two interesting chapels, one in board-and-batten (VI-33) for the garrison in Toronto (demolished long ago), the other, in brick, for Trinity College (never built). He may also have designed the unusual Presbyterian church seen in London by James Croil in 1861 and described by him as octagonal on the outside and having a Greek cross form within. In 1864 the inventive and restless Hay left Canada to roam about, building here and there until 1872, when he finally settled down in Edinburgh and addressed himself to the task of restoring St. Giles. His most successful Canadian work was the training of Henry Langley.

The Henry Langley repertoire ranged from orphanages to railway stations—with time out to plan an official residence for a Lieutenant-Governor. In forty-four years of practice he designed over seventy churches and either altered, enlarged or completed many more. Spires were his speciality, spires designed with great verve and ebullience. However, masonry gusto tends to be expensive, so Langley, with his partners and satellites, worked out a number of pleasing variations on three or four useful church plans which could be scaled up or down, simplified or enriched to taste: A side tower for the Anglicans in Port Hope; central for the Georgetown Baptists. Single lancet windows in St. Thomas; triple for St. Patrick's, Toronto. Change the gable window on the

NORTH ELEVATION
SCALE 8 FEET TO AN INCH

171

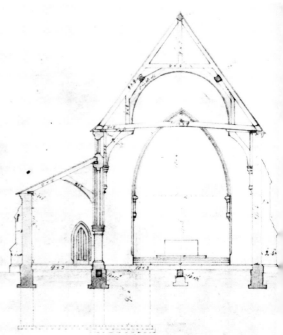

*VI-31: St. George's, Newcastle, 1854, retains its broach spire (VI-31 left) and open timber roof (VI-32 above). Hay's romantic essay in wood for the Toronto Garrison (VI-33 top right) was replaced by a more urban building.*

*VI-34: High Victorian style was highly coloured with polychromatic masonry, as in St. Peter's, Carlton St., Toronto (right below) and with bright stained glass, St. George's, Newcastle (far right below).*

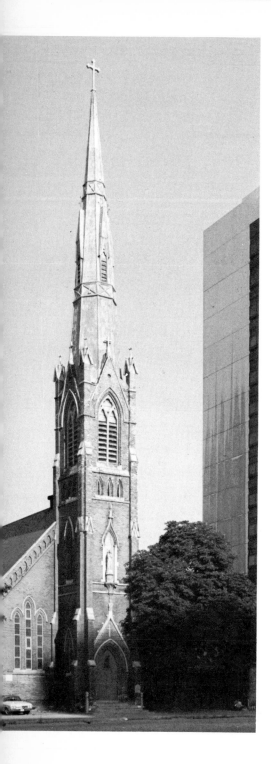

*VI-35: St. Patrick's, Toronto, now Korean Roman Catholic, was still reminiscent of Hay's work.*

Whitby plan and send it off to Stratford, and for the church on a lower budget use William Hay's spire.

Immediately on emerging full-fledged from Hay's office in 1862, Henry Langley formed a partnership with Thomas Gundry, an architect recently arrived in Toronto from England. The first church commission the partners received was more instructive than challenging. They were asked to rebuild St. Stephen's-in-the-Fields, severely damaged by fire in 1865. It was a useful digression into the polychromatic vein—something that had not come Langley's way in Hay's office—and before the year was out Messrs. Gundry and Langley were designing a church of their own in the colourful style (VI-34). This was St. Peter's Anglican Church, Carlton Street, which C. Pelham Mulvaney, in *Toronto Past and Present Until 1882*, described thus: "St. Peter's Church, corner of Carlton and Bleeker Streets is *bijou* rendering of first-pointed Gothic, with clerestory windows and elaborately decorated chancel. It is one of the prettiest churches on the east side of the city."

Mulvaney cannot have been well read in the works of Ruskin nor particularly *au fait* with the designs of William Butterfield which were appearing in all the architectural journals, or he would have known that the juxtaposition of highly coloured materials had come to be regarded as mediaevalism's true expression. Fuller's St. Stephen's-in-the-Fields had been a polychromatic composition of red brick, with grey stone dressing. The "constructional colouration"—as the Ecclesiologists would have put it—of St. Peter's was less expensive. Langley used red and white brick from the Don Valley for his Butterfieldian building.

Henry Langley's third church commission, All Saints, Whitby, drawn up in 1865 and completed several years later, was a more cautious essay in the Hay tradition—a St. George's, Newcastle in stone, with its tower switched to the other side. The following year, 1866, marked Langley's maturity as an architect. His design for the bell chamber and spire of St. Michael's Cathedral, Toronto, was full blown, high-Victorian Gothic—as bedecked with crockets as his florid lettering. From then on Gundry and Langley tailored their Neo-Gothic more freely to the site and to the congregational climate of their clients.

In 1869, the year in which Thomas Gundry died, the firm built a plain brick Baptist church in Georgetown and a large clerestoried stone church for the Anglicans of Guelph who had become disenchanted with their unfinished but very interesting Romanesque building. It was both too early and too late for the Romanesque style in Ontario. Henry Langley—who shared George Gilbert Scott's gift for judging such matters—gave them just the Gothic they wanted. Free from all tutelage, Langley—with his finger on the pulse of public taste and an eye on the architectural journals—began cautiously to introduce Continental touches here and there in his neo-mediaeval building. French crocketed gables, lace-edged louvers, and a tendency to bits of wrought iron on ridges and finials were characteristic of his buildings in the early seventies—the unpartnered years of increasing popularity before the spate of hackneyed commissions.

St. Patrick's, William Street (VI-35), built in 1870 to serve the needs of Toronto's growing Irish population, was one of the most pleasing of Langley's smaller city churches of this period. His most interesting and uncharacteristic town church was St. James' Methodist (VI-36), a board-and-batten, Swiss-rural-Gothic confection in Parry Sound.

The major Langley commission, in the hiatus between his association with Thomas Gundry and his later partnership with his nephew, Edmund Burke, was his design for Metropolitan Church, Toronto (VI-37). It was described by the worthy Dr. Mulvaney at some length: "The Metropolitan Church, which we may well regard as the cathedral of Methodism, is a monument to the energy, magnetism and culture of the late Reverend Morley Punshon. . . . No church in Toronto has such great advantages of position. . . . The handsome grounds of this church form one of the finest open spaces in this city, and to a great city such open spaces, environed with metal fences of adequate dignity are an architectural necessity. . . . The entire building is of white brick, with abundant cut

*VI-36: St. James', Parry Sound.*
*Langley's Swiss embroidery on the*
*Gothic theme, no longer standing.*

*VI-37: Metropolitan Methodist, Toronto, is Henry Langley's cathedral style.*

stone dressing. It is a modernized form of the French thirteenth century Gothic, and consists of nave, transepts and choir."

In the portions deleted from the foregoing quotation Dr. Mulvaney had managed to describe Metropolitan's neighbour, St. James' Cathedral, as a basilica—which it is not—and to assign credit for the design of Metropolitan itself to another architect, William Storm. There may have been slight reason for connecting Storm with Metropolitan. The Storms were Methodists, and Thomas Storm had been a pillar of the Richmond Street Chapel long before his son William became an architect. Langley may have had to suffer some supervision by William Storm, but Metropolitan, as it was before the disastrous fire of 1926, was indubitably the masterpiece of Henry Langley—mid-Victorian Toronto industry celebrated in yellow brick.

Industry was not, of course, the sole preserve of the industrialists, or even of the industrial workers, nor was mid-Victorian piety uniformly expressed in material terms. Peace, quiet and simplicity were never far to seek in Victorian Ontario.

# VII
# *Plain*

*... and Jacob was a plain man ....*
*Genesis* xxv: *27*

There were, in Upper Canada, several religious groups which scarcely noticed that the Gothic style had been revived. To the Society of Friends, the Mennonites, the Amish, the Moravian Brethren, the United Brethren in Christ, the followers of Gaiwiio and the Children of Peace, the battle for the Pointed, or Christian, style was of no moment. Believing, as they all did, that the temple of God was not made with hands but was built within the heart of mankind, each sect regarded itself as an elect people which must stand aside from worldly pursuits to witness to that belief. The several codes to which these denominations subscribed had, by placing particular emphasis on simplicity, industry, discipline, and conformity to rule, provided a post-Reformation alternative to the conventual life. Their places of worship were naturally distinguished by an austerity consistent with the sober self-denial of their daily walk and conversation. They all rejected the "steeple house" and the temple in favour of the meetinghouse (VII-1). All, that is, except the Old Order Amish who rejected the meetinghouse as well, meeting in their own houses in the manner of the very early Church.

The Society of Friends, often called Quakers, was early in the field. Some Friends came into Upper Canada with the Loyalists from New Jersey, New York and Pennsylvania following the American Revolution. True to their principle of non-violence, the Friends had remained neutral during the war but had suffered confiscation of property and physical violence for refusing to participate as revolutionaries. A few had been goaded into taking up arms against their tormenters and had been disowned by the Friends in consequence. When these militant ex-Quakers joined the Loyalist migration into Upper Canada, a number of their relatives who were still *bona fide* members of the Society came with them. They settled in Niagara and along the Bay of Quinte, moving farther inland to other locations when some of their co-religionists came to join them.

The Yonge Street Meeting was founded by Timothy Rogers who left Vergennes, Vermont in 1797 because he believed that a link was needed between the Friends already established in Pelham Township in the Niagara District, and those in the Johnstown District at Westlake in Hallowell Township. Rogers applied for land some thirty or forty miles north from York and made the happy discovery that two Friends from Philadelphia, Isaac Phillips and Samuel Lundy, had already secured land nearby. From this small nucleus the community grew, meeting first in the Rogers' house and then in a small log building on their land.

By 1807 the Yonge Street Meeting had advanced from a Preparative Meeting, the smallest unit of communal worship among

*VII-2: Calm simplicity enfolded
the Society of Friends (VII-2 above).
Austere trim surrounds the doors
(VII-3 right) and the sliding
panels which allow for open or
segregated meeting (VII-4 opposite).
Yonge Street Meeting, Newmarket, 1811.*

180

VII-5: Plan of Sparta meetinghouse. Railed benches were
occupied by elder Friends.

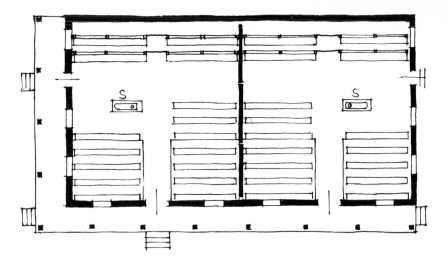

the Friends, to the status of a Monthly Meeting with supervisory duties to several Preparative Meetings in the area. A new and larger place of meeting was required, and subscriptions were taken to build it on the two acres of land donated by Asa and Mary Rogers for the purpose. The proposed building was to be thirty-five feet by seventy feet, but because the projected cost of $1,750 was prohibitive, the dimensions were cut to thirty feet by sixty feet.

Early descriptions of the building fail to give an exact idea of its appearance. Observers generally described it as being a large meetinghouse, of the "usual Quaker type." The board-and-batten siding now in place (VII-2) was anything but usual in 1811 when the Newmarket meetinghouse is believed to have been built. Then, and for many years thereafter, the common siding in Upper Canada was horizontal weather-boarding, the medium of long usage in New England and longer still in the old English counties of Kent and Sussex. Presumably the Newmarket meetinghouse was re-sided, if not actually rebuilt, in the second half of the nineteenth century, when builders had assimilated the vertical emphasis of the Gothic style (VII-3).

The timeless, functional directness of the Quaker meeting-house plan and the traditional lack of adornment to the structure, alike make it difficult to pinpoint a building date. Moreover there is a dearth of documentary evidence. The very nature of the Society of Friends, that of a true democracy, which dictated the spatial organization of their meetinghouse, made the recording of statistics regarding it virtually unnecessary. All business pertaining to the group was decided in open meeting; everyone knew what decision had been taken, and just when and how new meeting-houses were to be built. It must have seemed redundant to them to write it all down.

The Friends sat on plain benches in a rectangular room di-

VII-6: The old meetinghouse at Pine Orchard, built in 1821 (demolished).

vided centrally by a partition with easily movable panels (VII-4). The two chambers thus created were entered by separate doors – the women's meeting on the left, the men's meeting on the right. Similar benches, placed on raised or stepped platforms facing the meetings were intended for the elders and ministers among them (VII-5). Their elevated position, a gesture of respect freely granted by their fellows, was principally designed to assure that the meeting would be able to see and hear them when the spirit moved them to address it. The movable wall panels were raised to the open position for First Day and Fourth Day meetings for shared worship. They were closed when the men and women wished to meet separately to discuss discipline or business which was peculiarly their province. All of the early Quaker meetinghouses still standing in Ontario have had a door cut through the central partition wall at a later date, when the rules were relaxed to allow families to sit together for the open meeting.

The Friends' settlement in York prospered and expanded. New meetings were established. There was a placid group at Pine Orchard whose meetinghouse, built in 1821, was archetypical in form and sobriety (VII-6). And there was a group of stormy petrels at Sharon, whose structures were to be very, very different.

Slight modifications of style crept into the traditional buildings as time went on. A second meetinghouse, built by the Friends at Coldstream, in Lobo Township, in 1859, was a simple rendition of the customary form in brick, but the rail along its raised dais was supported by baluster-turned posts (VII-7) of a mildly Italianate cast.

Six years later the Yarmouth Meeting in Elgin County decided to build a new and larger meetinghouse in the grove beside their burial ground at Sparta. Their old meetinghouse was filled with sorrowful memories of the grim morning in 1838 when Joshua Gillam Doan, son of Jonathan Doan, the first Quaker to settle in

VII-7: Turned rail on elders' bench, Coldstream, 1859.

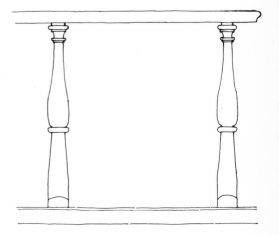

Yarmouth, was buried. Joshua Doan, imbued from childhood with the Friends' philosophy of equality and freedom, had been so far carried away by the emotional tide of reform that he had abandoned the sect's equally strong tenet of nonviolence. He had joined enthusiastically in the ill-fated Mackenzie Rebellion, only to be captured, imprisoned in the courthouse in London, and executed. Thereafter Joshua's pacific brother Israel had been granted permission to bury his body at Sparta. The Friends, mourning him doubly as a member fallen from their high code of conduct and as a comrade who had met an untimely death, gathered in large numbers in the old meetinghouse – their united thoughts directed by Sarah Wright Haight, their principal minister.

The new Sparta meetinghouse, sited handsomely in a grove of trees well back from a quiet country road and constructed to the familiar pattern, is quietly but unmistakably Greek (VII-8). The frieze board below the deeply projecting roof cornice was made deeper than of old and the interior trim surrounding all doors and window openings was "eared" – that is, the architrave was projected slightly beyond the jambs in the Classical manner. The Doric repose of the grey and white interior (VII-9) has been further enlivened by the presence of scarlet-bound hymn books and a remarkable box stove laden with opulent iron fruit.

The Spartan Friends fared better than the Athenians in Upper Canada. No trace remains of the Quaker meetinghouse at Farmersville (now Athens) in Leeds county. The Athens Meeting split over the Hicksite controversy which divided North American Quaker thought in 1829. And, like many another small community, the Athens Meeting dwindled and died out.

An earlier split of cyclonic velocity had riven the peace of the York County Friends. In 1807 the Yonge Street Monthly Meeting "allowed a Meeting for Worship" at Sharon in Gwillimbury Township. Called the Queen Street Meeting, it was established under the guidance of a committee composed of Samuel Lundy, Charles Chapman, Isaac Phillips, Reuben Burr, Nathaniel Pierson and Obadiah Griffin. Land for the meetinghouse was given by David Wilson, a Sharon Friend, in 1810, and a building was put up quickly.

The craftsmen engaged in the building of these meetinghouses were usually Friends themselves. Two of the best builders in York County, Ebenezer Doan, a master-builder from Bucks County, Pennsylvania, and Rowland Burr, son of Reuben Burr, a New Jersey Friend, belonged to the Yonge Street Meeting in its infancy. Rowland Burr "married-out" of the Society with a vengeance in 1819; he was disowned by the Friends because his alliance with Hester L'Amoroux of Scarborough was solemnized by the Reverend John Strachan at St. James'. (Burr may have started out with the idea of despoiling the Egyptians – he was building the

*VII-8 and 9 opposite: Sparta awaits the Spirit in cool green shade (VII-8 top), its Classic calm warmed by a Normandale stove (VII-9 bottom).*

VII-10: Sharon Temple of the Children of Peace (VII-10 left), the most remarkable place of worship in Upper Canada, was built with consummate skill (VII-11 above) by Ebenezer Doan, whose brother John made the Ark (VII-12 right). The meetinghouse (VII-13 below) has been demolished, but David Wilson's study, which stood between it and the Temple, remains.

Grange in York for D'Arcy Boulton at the time – but he ended up by joining them.) Ebenezer Doan left the Friends with David Wilson in 1812, when that worthy became the prophet of a new religious group, the Children of Peace.

David Wilson's checkered career had encompassed both joinery and sailoring, and had led him as far afield as China before bringing him to Upper Canada in 1800. On the strength of a single year's schooling he had decided to become a teacher and it was in that capacity that he appeared among the Friends in Sharon. Much struck by their faith in the guiding care of the inner light of the spirit, Wilson abandoned his Presbyterian adherence to join with them. But he grew restless in the peaceful meetings. He longed for more colourful ceremonials. The more he meditated on it, the more certain he became that he had been selected to lead the people on a more joyous path than the Friends' discipline permitted.

One by one the Friends seceded from the Queen Street Meeting to join David Wilson's group, until in 1825 it was decided to abandon the meetinghouse to the new sect. The Quaker remnant retreated to the Yonge Street Meeting, and the triumphant Children of Peace set in train an ambitious building programme.

The religious observances of the Children of Peace required two theatres of operation, a meetinghouse for services of regular occurrence – modelled on the Quaker form, to which they had all been accustomed, and a temple (VII-10) for festivals ritually celebrated with feasting, illumination and song. Wilson enlisted Ebenezer Doan to help him, and together they planned a temple which would symbolize in every timber the tenets of their new creed. They produced a monument to the joiner's skill which was unique in Upper Canada.

Sharon Temple was square in plan, rising in three tiers from a sixty-by-sixty-foot base to a twelve-by-twelve-foot lantern. Each tier was illumined by tall windows and adorned with little pinnacle lanterns at each corner. Turned and reeded half-columns flanked each of the four identical entrance doorways centred in the quadruplicate façades of the ground storey (VII-11). Matching reeded quarter-columns below reeded friezes were used to finish the corners of all three storeys. The little lanterns were similarly treated, minute reeded pilasters replacing the columns at their corners.

The second storey, or music chamber, was supported internally by a continuous arcade on twelve turned columns about a square open space, each column being named for one of the apostles. A smaller square, defined by the four columns which supported the lantern (VII-12) contained the Ark – a model in black walnut of the lowest storey of the temple itself. The Ark, which was the work of John Doan, brother of the master-builder, held a tiny table on which the Bible was placed.

On the festival seasons of springtime and harvest the Children of Peace rejoiced. They illuminated their temple by affixing a candle to the gazing bar of every window pane. At some point in the ensuing ritual a choir of remarkably level-headed young ladies, robed in flowing white gowns and singing as they came, descended the break-neck Jacob's ladder from the choir loft in the second storey, with lighted candles in their hands. On high days the choral contribution was backed up by a silver band. After 1843, when the new meetinghouse was built (VII-13), the choir was accompanied by a fine organ.

Ebenezer Doan turned his temple design inside out for the meetinghouse, running the arcade around the outside to compliment David Wilson's delightful little study, set demurely between the meetinghouse and the temple. The extraordinary builder completed the complex by constructing a cylindrical privy.

The Children of Peace bemusedly followed their remarkable prophet to the end. But after his death in 1866 the stricken sect deteriorated rapidly. The meetinghouse fell into disuse and was demolished, though the temple has fortunately been preserved by the York Pioneer and Historical Society who house in its hauntingly beautiful worship space a somewhat incongruous collection of bygones.

While the Children of Peace were silently erecting their elaborate temple a dedicated group was engaged in building a modest meetinghouse near the Sour Springs in Brant County. This was the Upper Cayuga Longhouse (VII-14) in which the Creator was

*VII-14: The Upper Cayuga Longhouse built by followers of the Old Way.*

to be worshipped in the Old Way, the way expounded long ago by the great leader, Deganawidah, in the old homeland below the Great Lakes.

The observance of traditional worship, which had declined under the bludgeoning of European invasion, had been revived. In 1800, Ganioda'yo (Handsome Lake), half brother of the Seneca Chief, Cornplanter, had had a vision. In it the Giver of Power had instructed him to exhort the people to return to the old ceremonies and to live uprightly respecting the ancient laws. The Gaiwiio (the good message of Handsome Lake) urged the believers to listen to the inner light of conscience, to be temperate in thought and behaviour, to avoid strong drink, and at all times to be considerate of each other and of strangers.

The longhouse plan achieved by the followers of Handsome Lake derived from traditional Iroquoian form, with modifications borrowed from the Society of Friends, the sect which had encouraged Handsome Lake in his mission of reform.

The Upper Cayuga Longhouse near the Sour Springs in Ontario differs from its prototype, the Seneca Longhouse at Cold Springs, New York, in the placing of the entrance doorways. The Cold Springs doors — one for men and one for women — are set, Quaker-fashion, near either end of one wall. In the Sour Springs Longhouse the entrances are in opposite walls, diagonally opposite to each other, so that the men and women enter their respective seating areas in a manner more closely resembling the ancient Iroquoian pattern (VII-15). In both buildings the speaker's bench occupies the centre of the long axis of the room, with a stove — replacing the traditional fire — at either end. The Sour Springs stoves were handsomely cast in the Greek taste, the end plates decorated with the anthemion or palmette within a lyre — an appropriate symbol when it is recalled that the Iroquoian religious philosophy has been likened to that of ancient Greece. The Sour Springs Longhouse, like the Quaker meetinghouse at Newmarket, shows evidence of some rebuilding in Ontario's Gothic Revival period; its gable ends were finished with board-and-batten siding and the attic lighted by a mildly Gothic window.

The Cayugan followers of Deganawidah were prepared to make a slight concession to the fashionable architectural style. The Moravian Delaware on the Thames — called "nephews" by the Iroquois — were not so disposed. Their meetinghouse at New Fairfield on the south bank of the river, completed in 1845, was a quietly elegant Neo-Classic building. It was a conservative design, but their difficult history had made them cautious. The building was seen and commended, in 1845, by Colonel Bonnycastle who wrote of the New Fairfield community in *Canada and the Canadians*: "Their spiritual and temporal concerns are under the supervision of the brethren at Bethlehem, the principal settlement of the

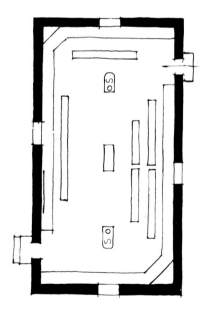

*VII-15: Plan of longhouse according to arrangement devised by Handsome Lake*

190

Moravian fraternity in the United States; and they have a neat chapel and school, conducted with the decorum and good results for which that sect are noted."

The neat chapel was the third Moravian meetinghouse built by the Delaware in the County of Kent – the second on the New Fairfield site. Their first Canadian place of worship, a handsome two-storeyed structure (VII-16) built on the north bank of the Thames in 1793, had been burned by American troops under General Harrison, after the Battle of Thamesville in 1813. A long history of persecution, of fleeing from place to place as each peaceful refuge was over-run, had convinced the Delaware of the futility of trying to explain to riotous soldiery that they had been pacifist Moravian Brethren for well over half a century.

The Delaware had first encountered missionary Moravian Brethren in Pennsylvania. In 1772, in an effort to escape wars, both European and Indian, the tribe had moved from their traditional lands along the Delaware to Ohio, where they established themselves in three industrious communities. Captured during the American Revolution by belligerent Wyandots who haled them along Lake Erie, one group sought refuge for a time with the British at Detroit. After the war they returned for a season to their old location, but then emigrated to Upper Canada, settling briefly near Amherstburg. In 1793, they received a Crown grant of fifty-one thousand acres on the Thomas. There they joyfully began to build Fairfield, a village of forty neat log cabins and two schools, centred about a steep-roofed meetinghouse. Their joy was short-lived; the village was completely destroyed and their lands laid waste in 1813.

After the war the Delaware, who with their Moravian missionaries had fled for safety to Burlington Heights, returned to the Thames and built New Fairfield, across the river from their devastated village. A simple log meetinghouse served them there until the early 1840's when they began to build the present structure (VII-17). In 1902 the Moravian missionaries withdrew, and the congregation of New Fairfield (VII-1) joined with the Methodist Church, later entering, with that body, into the United Church of Canada as the pastoral charge of Moraviantown.

The Society of Friends, the People of the Longhouse, and the Moravian Brethren are, in their several ways, "plain" people, but when the term is used the average Ontarian immediately thinks "Mennonite." This is, in itself, a tribute to the quiet piety, sober industry, and endurance displayed by the Canadian followers of Menno Simons in a materialistic world. It is also, of course, due in part to the distinctive dress of some Mennonites and to their reluctance to have anything whatsoever to do with the internal combustion engine.

The Mennonite sect was founded in Holland in 1536 by

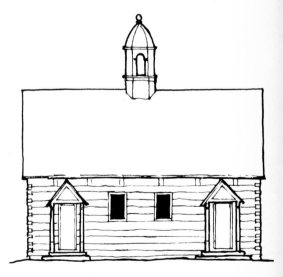

VII-16: *Moravian meetinghouse, built by the Delaware on the Thames in 1793.*

Menno Simons, a priest from Freisland, in protest against a politically minded church. The Mennonites, in common with the Society of Friends, believe in meeting together for silent prayer, in spontaneous sermons without a text, in marrying within the sect, and in sobriety and uniformity of costume as a means of curbing vanity and worldliness. Unlike the Quakers, the Mennonites shared with the Moravians the custom of appointing bishops (without territorial sees), fathers of the church, to administer the rites of baptism and the Lord's Supper. And, as was the custom in episcopal systems, the role of women was a distinctly subordinate one.

Mennonite settlers coming into Upper Canada in the wake of the Loyalists in 1786 located in the Niagara District in the counties of Lincoln and Welland. In 1799 Joseph Schoerg and Samuel Betzner walked up from Pennsylvania to spy out territory for a larger migration. They bespoke the vast acreage along the Grand River known as the Beasley Tract, and plodded patiently home again to collect their families, friends and neighbours for the final trek.

The careful Mennonites were just beginning to feel at home on their new lands when they discovered to their horror that a mortgage of twenty thousand dollars — a vast sum at that time — stood against Richard Beasley's holdings. Schoerg walked back to Pennsylvania again, accompanied on this pilgrimage by Samuel Bricker. None of Schoerg's connections was able to assist him, however, and he returned to Canada disconsolate. But Bricker

*VII-17 opposite: New Fairfield (Moraviantown United Church).*

*VII-18 left: A moulded cornice relieves the austerity of the early Mennonite meetinghouse at Elmira.*

tackled his wife's family, the Ebys, with better results. A joint-stock company was formed by the Mennonites in Pennsylvania, the money raised, and the Beasley mortgage purchased. In 1807 an additional forty-three thousand acres in Woolwich Township was purchased, and after the Napoleonic war, Mennonites from Holland, Germany and Russia flocked out to join them. Additional German settlers of other denominational affiliations settled near them as well, ensuring a continuing German character for the County of Waterloo.

The familiar Mennonite meetinghouse of Waterloo (VII-18) was a low one-storey, or storey-and-a-half, timber structure framed by skilled brethren in sturdy simplicity. It was weatherboarded, provided with panelled doors – two in one side and one in the gable end – and with a generous number of small-paned windows. It was painted white inside and out, and furnished with rows of unpainted pine benches. A long, light timber fixed above head height over the central aisle and fitted at regular intervals with wooden pegs was designed to hold the sober, wide-brimmed hats of the male congregation during the worship services.

The austere, Conservative, or Martin Mennonites, exacted a like austerity from their horses, tethered row upon row to hitching chains in sun, wind, rain and snow without even a sermon to distract them (VII-19). The less rigorous Old Order brethren, mercifully regarding their beasts, constructed lengthy carriage-sheds behind their meetinghouses, and in time the meetinghouses of this persuasion became a degree less plain. A photograph in the Meredith Collection, Public Archives of Canada, of a meetinghouse in York County (VII-20) illustrates the gradual change.

In 1807 the first Mennonite settlers had made their way into Markham Township, taking up land near the Quaker settlement, and had begun, almost imperceptibly, to modify their attitude toward the customs and amenities enjoyed by their neighbours.

*VII-19: A later example of an ageless style near Wallenstein, Waterloo.*

Mennonite meetinghouses in the counties of York and Ontario tended to be in brick – a sensible selection on clay lands – and these plain people began gradually to adopt the use of oil lamps, window shades, and carriage sheds, in the manner of the Society of Friends living near them. In time the carriage sheds disappeared from the meetinghouse yard at Altona in Pickering Township (VII-21), as the Mennonite brethren slowly accepted the mobility of the automobile.

Over the years there had come to be six distinct divisions of Mennonites in Ontario, with a number of subdivisions within at least two of the groups. These were: the Amish, the Conservative Mennonites – the Martin, the Old Order, the Markham; the Mennonite Brethren, the United Missionary, and the Sterling Avenue Mennonites. Some groups, like the Amish and the Martin Mennonites, retain the plain dress and avoid higher education and mechanization. Their meetinghouses remain totally conservative in consequence. Other groups, interested in missionary activity and wider personal horizons, advocate freedom to pursue learning in many fields.

An earlier splinter group had broken off from the mainstream of Mennonite thought in the closing years of the eighteenth century to become the United Brethren in Christ. The sect, founded in Frederick City, Maryland in 1800 by Martin Boehm, a Mennonite from Pennsylvania, and Philip Otterbein, pastor of a Dutch Reformed congregation in Baltimore, gained adherence from both denominations. Some of the Brethren eventually migrated to Upper Canada, settling in the Grand River Basin in the counties of Perth and Waterloo. Their places of worship, like those of the more lenient orders of Mennonites, tended to be church-like in form, architecturally indistinguishable from the simple ecclesiastical buildings of other evangelical denominations. They believed – in common with the Mennonites and all other sects derived di-

*VII-20: Mennonite meeting- ,
house, Markham, built
1850, photographed 1933.*

*VII-21 right: Altona Mennonite
meetinghouse.*

VII-22: "An Anabaptist is a thing I am not a member of," wrote eight-year-old Marjorie Flemming. The builders of Freeport Church of the Brethren in Christ (VII-22 right), who decked its windows with Tudor labels were Anabaptists, but the hand, pointing eternally heavenward (VII-23 below), was Lutheran.

rectly or indirectly from Anabaptist theology – in administering baptism to adults on profession of faith, but – again like the Mennonite body as a whole – they did not have a hard-and-fast rule on the method of administering it. The original Mennonite method of baptism had been by pouring water on the head of the initiate, but some groups had come to believe that total immersion was the true form practised by the early Church and that this should be accomplished by a single immersion, backwards, as opposed to the practice of the German Pietist Church of the Brethren, sometimes called Dunkers, who practised a triple immersion in a forward position in symbolic homage to the Trinity.

The meetinghouse built by the Church of the Brethren in Christ at Freeport (VII-22) in Waterloo in 1861 has been moved for preservation to Doon Pioneer Village. It was always eclectic in design, (VII-23) and its custodians have increased its catholicity by affixing an admonishing metal hand (from the steeple of St. Paul's Lutheran Church, Bridgeport) to the top of its little belfry.

The Freeport builders themselves had swerved toward the neo-mediaeval position sufficiently to place heavily moulded Tudor labels over the windows. Moving back to the conservative middle road, they had set a Georgian belfry on its roof ridge. Then, letting the pendulum of taste carry them to the other stylistic node, they had carried a heavily projecting cornice across the gabled face of the little building to form a pediment in the more comfortable Greek style. It was a riotously exotic expression for plain people, whose progenitors had reacted, one and all, against the elaboration of ritual, decoration, colour and carving – the whole panoply of the Gothic and Renaissance worlds. There had been no occasion for them to fear the Greeks.

# VIII
# Greek

*There were certain Greeks among them ....*
*John* XII: *20*

Architectural style based on the Greek orders, Doric, Ionic and Corinthian, had been brought back for a curtain call in early-nineteenth-century Europe. The Greek wars for liberation had built up the required emotional steam pressure. The developing discipline of archeology had replenished the vocabulary, and Napoleon had put on the show. In North America the Classical Revival in architecture was closely identified with the young Republic – so closely in fact that it was never accorded more than a tepid reception in British North America (VIII-1). Yet, oddly enough, the first true Greek Doric portico to appear in Upper Canada was designed by James Cooper for St. Andrew's Presbyterian Church, Niagara-on-the-Lake, built in 1831 to replace an earlier church destroyed when the Americans burned the town in December 1813.

The Niagara Presbyterians had had to save carefully for rather a long time to amass money enough to rebuild. Every family in the congregation had lost home, business premises and gear in the war; shelter had to be their first consideration. And though compensation was forthcoming from the government for domestic loss, it was not available for their church. Official reasoning on the subject was a trifle difficult to follow. The Reverend John Burns had surrendered his church, on request, to Dr. A.S. Thom, the garrison staff-surgeon, for use as a hospital in 1812. It had then occurred to the military that the tall church tower made a useful observation point for scanning activity on the hostile bank of the Niagara River. The War Losses Commission argued that because the church was serving in a military capacity at the time of its destruction by the enemy no compensation was due to the congregation for its loss. Compensation of four hundred pounds was eventually paid in 1837 by a legislature become nervously aware, on the eve of the Mackenzie Rebellion, that it would be well to placate the principal residents on the Niagara frontier.

In the meantime, the Presbyterians of Niagara had worked out their own financial salvation. Their church building fund, established in 1819, was sufficiently subscribed ten years later to warrant a request to the Glasgow Colonial Society for a settled minister. Robert McGill of Ayr was ordained by the Glasgow Presbytery for the Niagara charge in 1829. On 6 April 1830 McGill reported to the Glasgow Society that he had some eight hundred and thirty-one parishioners, that they had raised four hundred pounds, and that a friend in Montreal had promised an additional one hundred pounds toward building the Niagara church (VIII-2).

On 31 May 1831 the cornerstone of "St. Andrew's Church of the Established Church of Scotland at Niagara" was laid in the presence of the 79th Regiment, the Cameronians, who played "national music." The pipes were skirling for an elegant church which

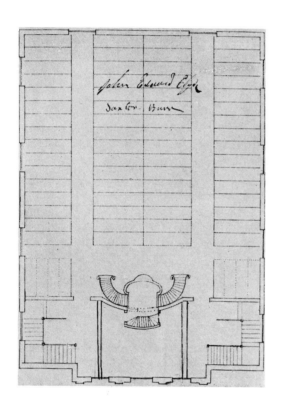

VIII-2 *right: St. Andrew's Church of Scotland, Niagara-on-the-Lake, 1831.*

VIII-3 *above: Plan of St. Andrew's, corrected by the Reverend Robert McGill.*

was to rise under the guiding care of James Edward Clyde and Saxton Burr, builders, who had contracted, for twelve hundred pounds, to follow the plans and specifications pieced together by the building committee under the direction of James Cooper, a respected member of the congregation. Following "Cooper's plan" (which was still in existence in 1938 when St. Andrew's was restored by Dr. Eric Arthur) was not an easy task. A number of pattern books had been consulted for the drawings; a number of divergent opinions were apparent in the alterations made to the drawings before the contract was let; and a number of omissions can be noted in the finished work.

The plan, side elevation, and section of a Georgian church had been derived from *Rudiments of Architecture* published by Asher Benjamin of Massachusetts in 1820. But while Asher Benjamin had relied on earlier sources, including those published by two Scots, James Gibbs and Peter Nicholson, he had not personally encountered the fearsome self-consequence of a Presbyterian minister of the Established Kirk. In the plan for St. Andrew's, Niagara the pulpit was placed with its back to the principal entrance façade — reversing the Benjaminian organization of space, a disposition which allowed the congregation to enter by any one of the three doors in the face of the building but gave ministerial access directly to the rear pulpit stair. It was not enough. Heavy pen lines, drawn slightly askew on the plan (VIII-3), and an amendment to the specifications mark the direct intervention of the Reverend Robert McGill, who did not propose to allow everyone to enter by *his* door in the easy-going North American manner. Since the new partition walls defining his private antechamber would block public access by all three doors shown on the original plan, the entrance front had to be reorganized. The broad central bay of slight projection, in the style of Asher Benjamin, was scrapped, and a flat façade more Classic in character built as a background for Cooper's Doric portico. Nor was the egalitarian simplicity of the three matching Greek doors allowed to stand; Mr. McGill's central doorway was given the additional dignity of a round-headed fan-transom in the old style.

James Cooper had obviously had trouble over his design for the façade from the outset. He had drawn a Doric temple for Niagara (VIII-4), but before the contractors signed the drawing, a second sheet (cut to fit neatly around the apex of the pediment) had been pasted to his Theseion, giving it a Doric-columned, three-storeyed steeple taken directly from a Peter Nicholson publication (III-6). No further alterations to the drawing or amendments to the specifications seem to have been made, but somehow or other, the Nicholson spire underwent a metamorphosis whereby it became a two-storeyed structure of North American Ionic cast.

Presumably it was necessary economy which telescoped the

*VIII-4 left: Cooper's drawing
of a Doric temple fitted
with a Nicholson steeple.*

*VIII-5 below: The lingering
benediction of Georgian serenity.*

spire, and which invaded the interior, deciding that the columns supporting the gallery should not be fluted as specified, although they were constructed without bases (VIII-5), after the true Doric fashion. There was quite possibly a division of opinion between members of the building committee, of which John Young was chairman, or among the trustees of St. Andrew's, of whom Andrew Heron, William Clarke, Jared Stocking, William Street Servos, and Robert Hamilton were probably the most contentious. Many of these gentlemen were of United Empire Loyalist stock, with several North American generations behind them. Others had emigrated directly from Scotland and had maintained close ties with a familial network of landed proprietors in and around Edinburgh and Glasgow where the Greek Revival style was in full spate.

Peter Nicholson was still busily churning out builders' pattern books at his architectural school in Newcastle-on-Tyne when St. Andrew's, Niagara was being built, but he had come from East Lothian, by way of training in Edinburgh and London, to practise in Glasgow and Ayeshire a little over a decade earlier. The Clarkes, Kerrs and Hamiltons were familiar with his works, and so was the Reverend Robert McGill.

It may have been the chairman of the building committee, John Young himself, whose preference for the Ionic Order set the spire on St. Andrew's. Certainly the pulpit, built in 1840 with money bequeathed by Young for the express purpose, was ornamented with Ionic columns handsomely carved by John Davidson who, it should be noted, kept a copy of Nicholson's *Carpenter's Assistant* for ready reference.

The vicissitudes of James Cooper's Doric temple did not cease with the alterations by the original builders. In 1854 a tornado struck, severely damaging the spire, roof, and rear gable wall. The congregation commissioned Kivas Tully of Toronto to repair their church, and after considerable argument allowed him to change the shape of the after-portion from a gable to a hipped roof. In the process of rebuilding, Tully had the wall taken down a depth of four feet and rebuilt, altering the ceiling from a semi-elliptical vault to a flat plane, and omitting the cornice which originally finished the interior. In order to better accommodate the new hipped portion, Tully raised the roof height, changing the pitch of the raking cornices on Cooper's Doric pediment in the process, and thereby contriving to make St. Andrew's less Greek and more Georgian than its builders had intended. Tully may also have been responsible for the sunburst centred in the tympanum of the pediment. Certainly the laurel wreath drawn on the elevation in that position, if it was ever installed, would have been diminished by the increased roof pitch.

Little is known about James Cooper beyond the fact that he

204

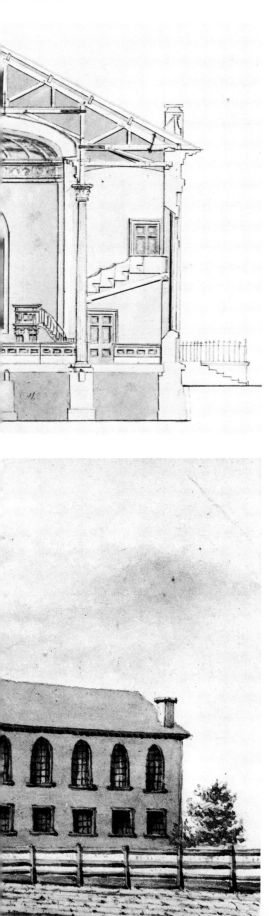

*VIII-6 top left: Sectional drawing of St. James', York, 1831, by Thomas Rogers, now in the Cathedral archives.*

*VIII-7 and 8: Rogers' ill-fated churches, St. James', York (VIII-7 above), burned in 1839, and St. George's, Kingston (VIII-8 bottom left), marred in the making.*

was recorded as a member in good standing on the Reverend Robert McGill's communion role in 1829 – with the cautionary parenthetic information that his wife was a "nonconformist, possibly a Baptist (?)" He was still resident in Niagara in 1833 when he became an elder of St. Andrew's, although he had, in March 1831, submitted plans and specifications for a new market building in York, a commission for which he received twenty-five pounds. Cooper's estimated cost of six thousand pounds for the market was considered to be too expensive, so two members of the building committee, Dr. W.W. Baldwin and James Grant Chewett, devised a simpler building – which eventually cost the taxpayers of York well over nine thousand pounds.

Three months later, Chewett, having somehow shaken off the worthy Dr. Baldwin, was well launched on an even more expensive project, the supervision of a new St. James' in Toronto for Archdeacon Strachan. It was to be built of hammer-dressed Kingston limestone – one hundred and forty feet long, eighty feet wide, and forty-one feet from ground line to cornice. Outside it was to be soberly Greek with Doric pilasters and a rather strange monumental plinth, or tower base, with an inset clock. The specifications did not make provision for any superstructure on the tower base, and certainly none was built. Those same specifications (as published in Robertson's *Landmarks*) – did, however, require the columns supporting the gallery, and the group of four on which the pulpit was placed, to be Ionic. The manuscript copy (in the archives of St. James' Cathedral), signed by both J.G. Chewett and John Richey, the builder, in 1831, specified that the Corinthian Order was to be employed as shown on the drawings (VIII-6). Moreover, the contract between the churchwardens and John Lacey, the joiner, for pews, gallery fronts and chancel panelling in black walnut, specified that the Corinthian capitals were to be carved in the same wood.

Having gone all out for carved walnut, the parishioners of St. James' had had to forgo stained glass. James Craig, master-painter on the job, had decorated the chancel window for them, but the effect was not particularly happy. Anna Brownell Jameson, an art critic of international reputation, writing of St. James' in 1833, noted: "The interior of the Episcopal Church here is rather elegant with the exception of a huge window of painted glass which cost five hundred pounds and is in a vile, tawdry taste."

The elegant St. James' of 1831 bore on its cornerstone sundry information which concluded with the words, "James G. Chewett, Architect. John Richey, Builder." Unfortunately the penultimate statement was not quite true. Chewett signed the specifications as "architect for the time being appointed" – the clerk of works. The drawing (VIII-7), which called for a fluted conical spire rising

*VIII-9: Design for chapel from Nicholson's* Principles of Architecture.

from a ring of Corinthian columns in the style of Nash, bore the signature of T. Rogers.

Posterity has not been kind to Thomas Rogers who comes into Upper Canadian view, plans in hand for a new St. George's at Kingston, in 1825. His presumed training and his place of origin have alike been forgotten. His buildings have been attributed to other men.

Rogers fared little better at the hands of his contemporaries. The building committee of St. George's pared away the Ionic portico from his design and lost the tower portion of it, causing the masons, Robert Mathers and Andrew Lauder, to put up a severe old-fashioned Georgian building with an awkward bell tower in eight ill-proportioned stages (VIII-8). And thus it stood from 1826 until 1840 – a constant source of irritation to its designer.

Presumably in the belief that parochial lack of appreciation was confined to Kingston, Rogers sent his fashionable Regency plan for a Corinthian St. James' to Archdeacon Strachan in 1831. Again the building committee mutilated his Classical Revival façade, by instructing Chewett to omit the spire and the encircling colonnade. Furthermore, they added insult to Rogers' injury by cutting Chewett's name on the cornerstone.

Meanwhile the much-tried Rogers was busy in Kingston, surveying new streets, collecting the dog tax, and supervising the building of a general hospital to the designs of Wells and Thompson of Montreal. The hospital, completed by 1833, had exhausted the budget; it could not be equipped for patients, and so remained empty, waiting its destiny. It was eventually altered, in 1841, to house the Legislative Assembly of the United Province of Canada.

Thomas Rogers was not asked to convert the building, nor did he win the competition for the Kingston city hall; both plums went to George Browne, the government architect from Quebec. Rogers, who had acquired a local reputation for being difficult, took to drink and was dismissed from his municipal duties for "infirmities" just when the vestry of St. George's had finally decided to resuscitate his design.

Poor Thomas Rogers. An architect who could not manage the collection of the dog tax was unlikely to be entrusted with the aggrandizement of a major church. The commission was placed in the reliable hands of one of the other architects practising in Kingston's heyday – either William Coverdale or George Browne. The surviving detailing of the 1840-46 front of St. George's cathedral looks very like Browne's work on the city hall. It could be said with equal truth that much of it looks very like the design for a chapel published by James Gibbs and later reproduced several times by Peter Nicholson (VIII-9). But after twenty years of

*VIII-10: A Canadian descendant of Nicholson's chapel. St. George's, Kingston, photographed in 1862, before the addition of transepts, chancel and dome.*

struggle with architects and builders to achieve a handsome church, the Anglicans of Kingston were not inclined to quibble about sources.

Buckingham, in *Canada, Nova Scotia, New Brunswick*, published in 1843, wrote of Kingston: "The Episcopal church here being under repair, and having a new spire making for it, the persons to whom this work was entrusted, contracted with the penitentiary to quarry and dress the stone required for the purpose, which they furnished according to order; but the working masons employed in the reparation of the church refused to use the stone, because it was quarried and dressed by convicts, to the detriment of the free and honest labourers; and accordingly it was all rejected to the loss of course of one or both of the contracting parties."

The loss must have been considerable. The second St. George's was being lengthened by a bay which had to be a massive structure capable of supporting the stone bell tower above it. The architect, an experienced designer of some skill, cleared away the naive ineptitude of 1826 and gave St. George's a dignified Classical façade (VIII-10) with a handsome Tuscan portico – which coincided more nearly with Rogers' intention. The pilasters of the source book's cylindrical bell chamber were replaced by the more vigorous movement of attached Corinthian columns, and the entablature given a bolder profile. Round-headed niches set between the principal entrance and the flanking Tuscan pilasters, clean-cut mouldings on the secondary doors, and bracketed sills below the windows – all were composed with a lively sense of the visual aridity of undiluted Kingston limestone, whether the stone-dressers were bond or free.

In 1862 St. George's became a cathedral. In 1891 it was greatly enlarged. And on New Year's Day in 1899 it was gutted by fire. During the fire the inimical strength of that same Kingston limestone and the workmanship of the masons of 1826 and 1840 proved their worth. The bell tower stood firm while its bell crashed to ruin through the lesser dome. Behind the brave façade and within the original walls the cathedral was rebuilt under the immediate supervision of the architect of the 1891 addition, Joseph Power.

The limestone walls of Rogers' St. James' withstood their trial by fire too, and that on the very eve of becoming a cathedral. When it burned, on 5 January 1839, the parishioners collected the insurance and, shunning the expensive Chewett, sought out John Ewart, the Scots builder-architect, to reconstruct it for them.

British architects and builders were thicker on the ground in Toronto in 1839 than they had been while it was still little York. John Ewart, John Richey and Robert Petch had all come to Upper Canada before 1822. Richard Woodsworth was in York by 1830. John George Howard had immigrated in 1832, Joseph

Sheard in 1833; and Thomas Young was busily drawing the townscape for publication by 1835. James Grant Chewett represented local talent, and Dr. Baldwin was eternally helpful in his triple capacity as doctor, lawyer and amateur architect. One day perhaps it will be revealed whether it was Thomas Rogers or one of these others who thumbed through his copy of Nicholson to devise Zion for the Reverend John Roaf's flock, which was worshipping in Toronto after the manner approved by the Congregational Union of England and Wales.

The Congregationalists built their Doric Zion (VIII-11) on the north-east corner of Adelaide and Bay Streets, covering its brick walls with sparkling white plaster dashed with marble dust and scored to represent ashlar blocks. The design (in the archives of the United Church) followed the patternbook, line for line, but the builder departed from it at the apex of its pediment. The resultant gawky bell chamber impressed the Congregationalists less and less, once the graceful battlemented towers of Lane's Holy Trinity and the octagonal lantern of Thomas' United Presbyterian Church had come to share the Bay Street skyline with it. When Zion burned in 1855, igniting some of the shingles on the firehall roof in the conflagration, it was replaced by a towered church in the Italianate style designed by William Thomas.

Derivatives of the Gibbs-Nicholson Greek chapel were still being built in Toronto as late as 1848. In that year the Baptists be-

*VIII-11: Many-towered Toronto, from the muddy intersection of Bay and Adelaide Streets, before the fire of 1855. A water-colour in the archives of the United Church of Canada.*

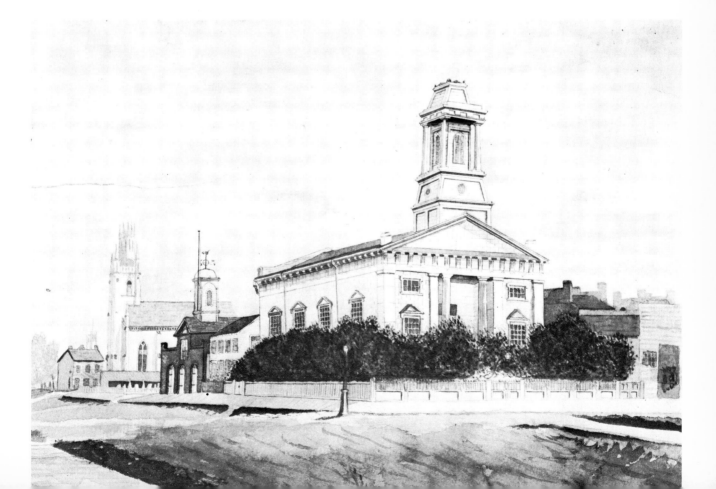

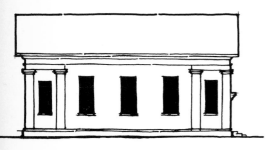

*VIII-12: Bond Street Baptist Church, Toronto, 1848 (top).*

*VIII-13: Vittoria Baptist, 1851 (above left).*

gan to break ground for a new church on Bond Street. Their designer had worked out an ambitious T-shaped building (VIII-12) for them, with ample space for a baptistry. The exterior was austerely Doric, with plain, bold entablatures supported on strongly articulated pilasters. The façade retained the recessed Egypto-Greek umbrage of the Nicholson prototype, but dispensed with the Doric columns in antis which graced Zion Congregational.

A Baptist church was built in the simplified Doric Revival style (VIII-13) in Vittoria three years later. Crisply stated in brick by its original builders, it had a deep architrave with a heavily projecting cornice and end bays defined by paired pilasters. Its classic form has been obscured by later alterations, however.

The stripped-down Greek temple shape – a long rectilinear block, with one of its pedimented gable ends serving as the principal façade – had been the favourite form for Methodist chapels since Upper Canada had come into existence. A simple timber example of the basic type had been built by Robert Petch in 1818, on the corner of King and Jordan Streets, for the Methodists of York. By 1832 it had been outgrown and Petch had then built a larger edition of it in brick on the south-east corner of Newgate and Toronto Streets. It was a dull building, but its author – flown with the scale of the commission – had set his initials at either end of the pediment.

English Methodists, coming into Toronto in strength in the second quarter of the nineteenth century, were less pleased with the Newgate chapel. They did not think highly of its design, and they were deeply suspicious of the soundness of the "American"

210

*VIII-14: Wesleyan Doric. Richmond Street Chapel, Toronto, 1844.*

doctrine being preached within its walls. Dissension rent Toronto Methodism. The English faction withdrew to premises on George Street, and when they had gathered sufficient funds they commissioned one of their number to design a chapel to be built on Richmond Street. Interpreting his instructions to mean that English adherence was to be expressed in the form as well as in the name of the new chapel, Richard Woodsworth used John Wesley's City Road Chapel in London as his model, modifying its late-eighteenth-century detail to suit the taste of 1844.

Woodsworth, a master-builder in Yorkshire, had emigrated to York in 1830, by which time the whole Methodist connection to the uttermost boundaries of Upper Canada was aware that Wesley's London chapel had been given a Doric portico in 1815 by the Reverend Joseph Benson. Woodsworth's Richmond Street portico was to be twice the size of Benson's, and Roman Doric rather than Regency Greek, but the chapel (VIII-14) was demonstrably akin to the published engravings of Wesley's chapel, so all was well.

Meanwhile, the Greek Revival as a style for Church of England edifices, was being viewed with mixed feelings by the Canadian hierarchy. John Strachan, whose fine Classic St. James' burned in 1839 just before his consecration as bishop, set out to inspect the new diocese of Toronto in 1840. His remarks on the unfinished garrison church at Penetanguishene (VIII-15) were not encouraging. "It requires some alteration on the outside to make it look more like an English church," he wrote. Captain Moberley, the naval commandant, and Colonel Keating, military comman-

VIII-15: *The serviceable Greek face (left) of St. James-on-the-Lines was altered (VIII-16 above) to please Bishop Strachan. A processional aisle of military width marches to a chancel (VIII-17 right) brave with scarlet, blue and gold.*

212

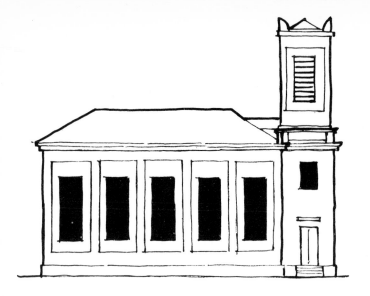

*VIII-18: Conjectural restoration of Thomas Young's Holy Trinity, Streetsville, 1844.*

der of the garrison, did not see anything amiss with their joint design, but recognizing the superior right of the Bishop to order church matters, they gave directions for a stylistic about-face. The engineers fell to work with a will, and contrived to camouflage the overt Greekery of St. James-on-the-Lines sufficiently to escape censure in Archdeacon Bethune's report of 1847 (VIII-16). Bethune was moved to write that St. James, Penetanguishene was in a "very respectable condition," which can be interpreted to mean that it had been Gothicized within and had acquired both an adequate chancel and a fanciful belfry, and that Bethune's own special area of architectural insistence, the central processional aisle, had been more than adequately met (VIII-17). The central aisle of this St. James was designed to accommodate soldiers marching in four abreast.

Archdeacon Bethune, on his rounds, had noted of Trinity Church, Streetsville that it was "built of brick, and a neat and capacious edifice in the Grecian style, the tower however, as yet being incomplete." In some respects it still is.

Wishing to separate Streetsville from Springfield-on-the-Credit as a parish, Bishop Strachan wrote the Bishop of Glasgow in 1841, asking him to send a suitable priest. Reverend Robert Jackson MacGeorge arrived in Toronto 9 September 1841, and by the following March he had John George Howard at work on plans for his Streetsville church. Howard's estimated cost of a thousand pounds for a Gothic church was exactly double the amount the building committee was prepared to expend. Worse still, the committee denied all responsibility for the commission and, brushing aside the threatened lawsuit, procured plans for a simple Greek Revival building (VIII-18) from Howard's rival, Thomas Young. When it became known that Young carried his plans in the official procession at the laying of the cornerstone, 6 September 1844, Howard's fury rose to such apoplectic heights that his doctor had to apply leeches to his temples as an antidote to frustrated ambition. The rivalry which probably began over the commission to design Kings College, ceased only when Thomas Young died in 1853.

Twenty-three years after the architect's death the tower of Holy Trinity was heightened, a chancel built, and the gallery removed. The windows were Gothicized in the closing years of the nineteenth century. The permastone patch on the tower base was the gift of the twentieth.

The battle of the styles – Greek versus Goth, Howard versus Young – was just nicely underway when the Wesleyan Methodists decided to try again to build a chapel in Vienna. Their previous attempt had been interrupted by the more immediate conflicts of the Mackenzie Rebellion. Accordingly, on 22 February 1845, at the Conference of the Malahide Circuit, with the Reverend William Ryerson, the western member of that reigning dynasty of Methodist clergymen, as chairman, it was resolved: "It is deemed expedient to build a chapel in Vienna for the Wesleyan Methodist Church in Canada ... a subscription having been presented before the Quarterly Conference for that purpose, amounting to sterling one hundred and fifty pounds currency."

The money was expended on building a carpenter's-Greek chapel (VIII-19), but the rival claims of the Georgian and Gothic styles were not completely excluded from it; the chapel had

*VIII-19: Minimal Doric, Vienna, Elgin County, 1845.*

*VIII-20: Conservation—Fisherville Church, Black Creek Pioneer Village.*

*VIII-21: Conversion—a former Methodist church, Galt, bedecked with a purple tympanum and a "Colonial" door by the Cambridge Lions Club.*

round-headed windows with Gothic glazing bars. The Viennese Methodists were large-minded in these matters, as was fitting in a preaching circuit which comprised Vienna, Gravesend, and Copenhagen – with Port Burwell thrown in to remind the incumbent that he was still in Elgin County, Canada West.

A little cautious Gothicism had begun to impinge on the Classic statement of rural Presbyterianism as well. In 1856 the builders of Fisherville Church – now sitting with an air of pleased surprise (VII-20) in Black Creek Pioneer Village – placed a pointed arch above the panelling behind its rigidly Classical pulpit. Externally the builders'-Greek tradition was maintained in the pedimented trim on windows and door pleasantly spaced in its harled wall.

The Presbyterians might have a nostalgic inclination to the Doric as the style dominant in Edinburgh, but it remained for the Methodists to close the chapter on the Greek Revival in Ontario. They had begun it in utter simplicity at Hay Bay when Upper Canada was still a part of the colony of Quebec. They finished it in academic correctness with a Doric portico in Galt (VIII-21) on the eve of Confederation.

# IX
# *Italianate*

*... They of Italy salute you.*
*Hebrews* XIII: *24*

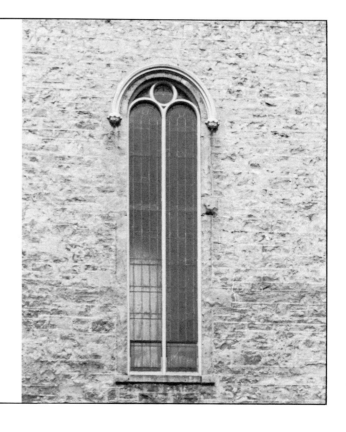

For those who wished to be neither Goth nor Greek there were alternative forms of architecture, hoary with the traditions of centuries of worship. A courageous advocate of the wider view wrote to the editor of *The Builder* in a letter published 7 September 1850. In it he remarked: "To maintain that Gothic Architecture is essentially Christian architecture is preposterous.... [It] did not even generally prevail at any period in the history of Christianity.... The great mass of Christian churches have been Roman, Byzantine, Lombard, Norman, Moorish, Italian or Classical."

The doughty British advocate of the boundless horizon was not concerned with non-Christian places of worship which, had he elected to enumerate them, had employed an even wider range of style. Builders in pre-Confederation Ontario tended to toy with Norman and Italianate (IX-1) styles and with a hybrid form which they were pleased to call Lombard and which was, as often as not, more nearly German Romanesque. Perhaps they had the heyday of the Holy Roman Empire in mind, but it seems unlikely. A number of them were simply following the well-established path of common building sense which had found the rounded arch, the barrel vault and the dome to be of great utility in containing assembly space within a skin of brick or of any aggregate medium. It was a very long way from the barrel-vaulted temple storehouse of Ramesses II at Thebes to St. Thomas' Church, Shanty Bay, but they were both built of mud.

The mud walls of St. Thomas' were rising slowly when Bishop Strachan first saw them in June 1840, but hopes were entertained of the church being roofed and rough-cast before the winter. The roof, when in place, would project protectively, providing the deep eaves so necessary to the life of mud walls in Upper Canada. The tower of St. Thomas', completed a little later, was strengthened by tall framing timbers, infilled with mud brick, buttressed, and rough-cast against the weather. Its pyramidal roof, of correspondingly deep projection, was supported visually by curved brackets. All openings were round-headed – the windows and doors deeply recessed – with no external trim save boldly stated sills (IX-2).

The building is believed to have been designed by Edward O'Brien, a gentleman-farmer from Cork whose father, Captain Lucius O'Brien, had served in the Royal Artillery and who had doubtless had his perceptions sharpened by the excellent drawing classes at Woolwich. Draftsmanship continued in the O'Brien posterity. Lucius O'Brien, second son of the designer of St. Thomas', Shanty Bay, was to be an artist of distinction in late-nineteenth-century Ontario.

Legend has it that Edward O'Brien followed the style of his native parish church in his design for St. Thomas'. In so far as the

*IX-2: St. Thomas' mud-walled church, Shanty Bay.*

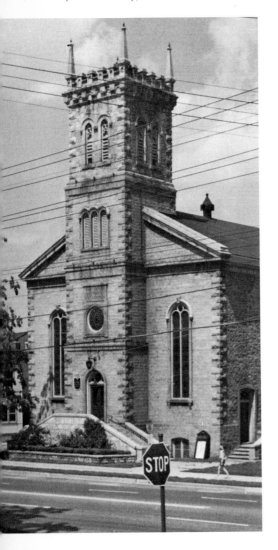

church could be called Norman, perhaps he did. The bracketed roof derived from Northern Italy, but since both the Italianate romantic style and twelfth-century Norman stem from Romanesque building, which in turn grew out of Roman engineering practice, one is at liberty to decide whether St. Thomas', Shanty Bay is Anglo-Irish-Norman, Romantic Italianate or practical Simcoe pioneer.

If the mud brick of York and Simcoe had made round-headed windows a necessity in Shanty Bay, the like could not be said of Guelph limestone. It was mid-nineteenth-century taste – veering in the wake of Ruskin's *Stones of Venice* published in 1850-51 – which decreed that the Wesleyan Methodists of Guelph might place Italianate windows in their new chapel.

An article published in the Methodist oracle, *The Christian Guardian*, 12 March 1856, announced that the Wesleyans of Guelph had decided to keep their old church and to build a new one beside it. The new building was in "cut stone, 85′ × 55′, not yet finished, and requires a tower to complete it." But it was already an ornament to the town (IX-3). The designer of the church, M. Hutchinson Clark, a builder-architect who had an office on Hughson Street in Hamilton, wrote indignantly to the trustees, 26 November 1855, complaining comprehensively of the masonry executed by Messrs. Freeman and Hartley in the body of the building. He did not care for Holt and Robinson's carpentry either, but conceded that the carpenters were young and would improve with direction. He could have taken pardonable exception to the aggressive texture of the upper storey of the tower, whose knobby cornice accorded ill with the arid Classicism of the pediment below. It still has the look of different hands at work at a later date when more money had been found.

No such hybrid structure, locally concocted from Venetian Gothic and outmoded Greek, would please Archdeacon Palmer and his building committee when they set out to build a church a few blocks away on St. George's Square in 1851. They had gone straight to William Thomas of Toronto for the latest thing from antiquity. They found him bubbling over with exciting ideas and impressions, having just returned from an extended holiday in England where he had been a fascinated frequenter of the Great Exhibition in the Crystal Palace. There he had seen works submitted by all the leading architects and engineers then practising in Europe. The beautifully executed creations of their busy brains ran the whole gamut from the most daringly functional to the ridiculously grandiose, and contrived on the way to revive every known style of architecture with eclectic impartiality. It was now permissible to model one's designs on monuments built from the time of Alfred the Great to the reign of James I, from Charlemagne to Louis XV – or, having crossed the Alps with Frederick

Barbarossa – to borrow from the Medici. From the welter of possibility William Thomas elected to follow the Normans (IX-4) who had gone out from Caen to build solidly and extensively from England to Sicily.

Thus it was that the Anglicans found themselves building, on St. George's Square in Guelph, a Norman church derived from Southwell Minster. Their efforts lacked conviction, for they had never been completely won over to either zigzag mouldings or to an altar rail supported by rounded arches set on stout little spiral-twist columns. They went on nibbling away at completion of their church in a desultory way, but when their architect died, on Christmas day 1860, interest in the project died with him. Thirteen years later the churchwardens of St. George's demolished the still-unfinished Norman church, bought another site, and in 1873 built a fine, fashionable Gothic church on it, to the designs of the all-Ontario favourite, Henry Langley.

The Romanesque churches of William Thomas were not fated to endure. Two splendid examples in Toronto – photographed by O. Thompson in 1868, and described in *Toronto in the Camera* as being "in the Lombardian style" – were demolished to make way for commercial buildings. They were the second Zion Congregational Church, built in 1856 to replace the first destroyed by fire in 1855, and Cooke's Church, erected on the corner of Queen and

*IX-4: The most elaborate Romanesque or "Lombard" church in mid-Victorian Ontario.*

*IX-5: Zion Chapel, Bay and Adelaide Streets, Toronto, 1856.*

ZION CHAPEL
ADELAIDE St TORONTO
Wm Thomas Architect
Printed in Colours by Maclear & Co King St Toronto

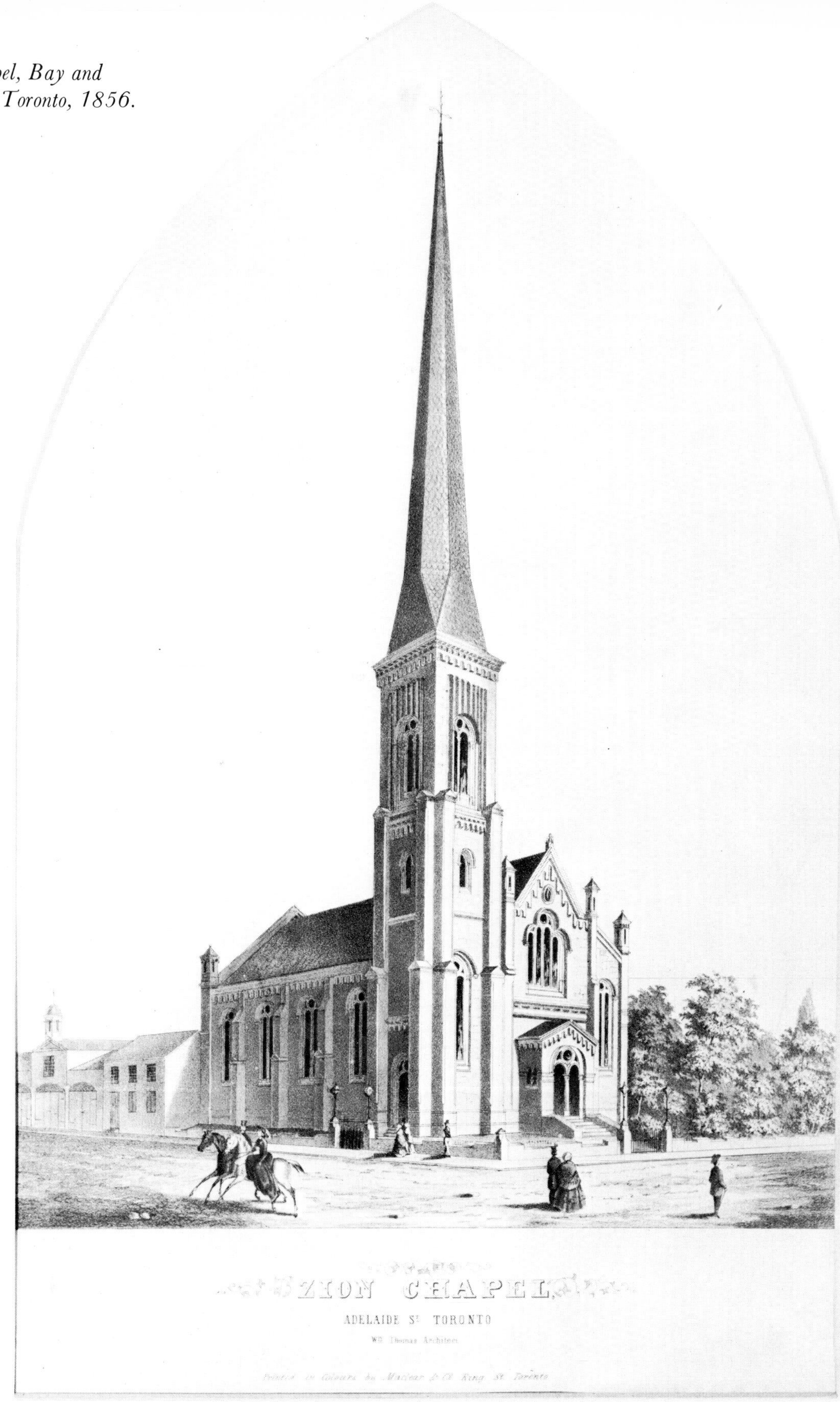

Mutual Streets in 1857 by Presbyterians from Ulster. Zion was the more Lombardian of Thomas' two Romanesque churches, when Thompson saw it, because it had lost its towering spire (IX-5) to a violent windstorm in 1862. Thereafter it wore a row of rather commonplace little battlements and four harmless pinnacles above the channelled texturing of its bell chamber. Both churches had the approved Pisan Gothic tracery in their round-headed windows, but Cooke's Presbyterian Church, with its twin towers (IX-6) and spattering of little bull's eye windows, was the more boldly Norman in character.

During the decade which followed his emigration to Canada in 1841, William Thomas had made a number of journeys home to England. Some of his Atlantic crossings were business trips, but on several occasions he had taken his student sons, William and Cyrus, and his articled apprentice, William Storm, with him on study expeditions to look at both old and new buildings in England and France. In his designs for St. Andrew's Presbyterian Church, built in 1875 at the corner of King and Simcoe Streets, for the leading Presbyterian congregation of Toronto, William Storm gave ample evidence that the apprentice had shared Thomas' enthusiasm for the massive dignity (IX-7) of the Norman style. The body of St. Andrew's was early Norman French from its triple-arched entrance to its rose window. Only in the flank tower was any concession made to the other partner in the "auld al-

*IX-6 above: Cooke's Presbyterian Church from* Toronto in the Camera.

*IX-7 below left: The crow-stepped gables of St. Andrew's, King Street, Toronto, are gone. The bartizans (below right) remain.*

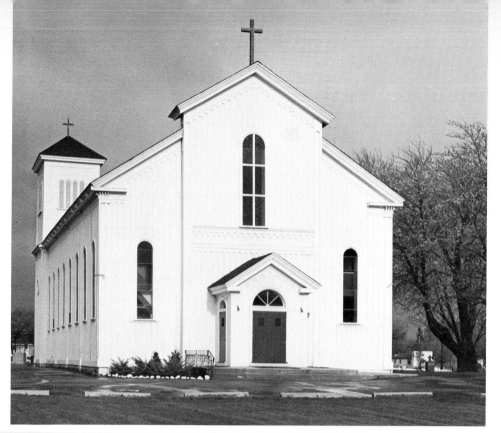

liance." There Storm had enlivened his skyline with the whimsical silhouette of crow-stepped gables flanked by conical roofed bartizans – the corner turrets by which late Victorians had identified the Scottish Baronial style.

C. Pelham Mulvaney, in *Toronto Past and Present Until 1882*, went on about St. Andrew's at great length. Midway through his description, Dr. Mulvaney remarked: "The richness of the elaborately wreathed and sculptured moulding over the main entrance, and the interlacing mullions of the window tracery, are worthy of special remark. The stone used in the construction of this beautiful church is mainly Georgetown rubblestone, with facings of Ohio stone, in contrast with which is the occasional introduction of the reddish brown freestone found in the neighbourhood of Queenston Heights. The colour of the stonework will be improved and harmonized by the mellowing influence of time. At the main entrance are handsome columns of finely polished red granite smooth and glittering as a mirror. These are from the Bay of Fundy. . . ."

Since the mellowing influence of time in downtown Toronto was heavily laden with coal smoke, the fine carving has been somewhat obscured, but the sturdy towers of St. Andrew's still stand impressive guard for the right to worship in the commercial heart of a great city. Equally impressive in twin-towered integrity is the carpenter's-Romanesque church of St. Joseph, Corunna.

*IX-8 and 9 opposite: Gabled St. Joseph's faces the St. Clair River (IX-8 top); its towered German Romanesque apse (IX-9 bottom) faces toward Corunna.*

*IX-10 below: Two saints—two towers. Reconstruction of St. Simon and St. Jude, Belle River.*

*IX-11: The Rhineland Romanesque shell of St. Francis Xavier, Carlsruhe (top opposite page) contains a startlingly handsome interior (above). The stacked corbels of its crossing arches, unremarkable in Istanbul, are decidedly exotic in Bruce County.*

The Roman Catholic parish of Corunna was founded on the St. Clair River in 1862 and shortly thereafter the church began to take form, designed by a builder-architect of great sensitivity who handled his simple medium with consummate skill. Board-and-batten cladding in his hands became a texture of elegant blind arcading, gracefully varied on the west front (IX-8) by a band of richer texture above the entrance porch, and deepened at the angles of the building to form defining pilasters – bracketed under the eaves. Access to the churchyard moved with the years from the riverfront inland (IX-9). The highway from Sarnia now passes close behind the beautiful curve of the semicircular apse, flanked in the Frankish Romanesque manner by pyramidal-roofed twin bell towers.

Three other churches in the area display a degree of kinship with this building – St. John, Sombra, a pretty little wooden chapel down-river from Corunna; the more ambitious brick church of St. Simon and St. Jude in Belle River on Lake St. Clair; and St. Francis Xavier, Carlsruhe, in Bruce.

St. Simon and St. Jude, Belle River, was designed, in 1868, as a Tuscan basilica – aisled and clerestoried – with paired round-headed windows in its flank walls and a wheel window over the porch. The verges of the gables on roof and porch were fitted with neatly scalloped boards and open-work finial crosses. Matching verge boards ran down the aisle roofs from the nave gable to Lombardic towerlets (IX-10) decorated with deeply channelled brick arcading and bracketed eaves. On one side, forward from the principal façade, now stands a more Gothic tower – a difference of parish opinion made permanent in red Chatham brick.

The Romanesque style, as revived and built in the 1850's, continued to be popular with Roman Catholic congregations in the Lake Huron area until the turn of the century, by which time it had, in fact, become so outmoded elsewhere that it was due shortly to be reworked and re-revived as a new architectural expression.

The parishioners of St. Francis Xavier, Carlsruhe, Bruce County, preferred that their Romanesque be traditional. Thus in 1873 their designer was free to compose for them a white brick basilica (IX-11) of impressive scale and suitably Germanic derivation. He piled up the masses of brick masonry – gabled nave, semi-cylindrical apse, and supporting transepts – in the eleventh-century Rhenish-Dutch manner and crowned the crossing with an octagonal cupola shingled after the fashion of nineteenth-century Ontario.

Brick, the medium natural to the Romanesque style, had been employed by the Regular Baptists of Brantford to build a church spiced with Tuscan detail but more conventionally Upper Canadian in form. On 17 February 1857, after "some discussion and

*IX-12: First Baptist, Brantford, restored to its pre-Langley look.*

227

*IX-13 and 14: Two Georgians made over in the Italianate style—St. Alexander's, Sand Point (IX-14 right), and St. Andrew's, Colborne (IX-13 above) which was retrimmed in the Art Nouveau period.*

suggestions," they had adopted plans drawn up for them by John Turner, a Brantford architect. Ten days later they accepted the tender of William Pickering for the carpenters' and joiners' work, at three thousand, four hundred and forty dollars. On 17 April 1857 the building committee (who liked to work backwards) accepted the tender for the brickwork and, after four days' consideration, bought an additional parcel of land so that the site would be large enough to accommodate the building. They cleared away the wreckage of their earlier church, which had burned in January when not quite finished, and still in debt for the destroyed building, set to work on the new. By 1862 it was ready for worship – a substantial Italianate church without (IX-12) and pleasantly appointed within. In his interesting history of the congregation of First Baptist Church, Brantford, published in 1890, T.S. Shenston made this comment: "Burnt down January 12th 1857. Rebuilt 1858. Enlarged at back and disfigured in front, 1887."

A number of centre-towered, slightly Italianate churches are to be found here and there in Ontario. Some of them were built in that style, others were altered to conform to it – a transformation so easily affected when the original church had been Georgian in form that the steps of transition are not always immediately detectable. St. Andrew's Presbyterian Church, Colborne underwent two revisions to arrive at its present appearance (IX-13). The church, as originally built in 1830, was a workmanlike rubblestone structure with fan-transomed, double-sashed windows, returned narrow Georgian eaves, and six panelled doors. A document was found under the pulpit during the Italianate phase of alteration which had been secreted there with just such well-meant tampering in mind. It recorded: "The Church was projected [drawn] by Archibald Fraser builder and architect from Scotland. The pulpit and spire were begun in eighteen and thirty-two and finished in eighteen and thirty-three." The document was signed by four Scots joiners, William Penman, James Aitcheson, Addams Sharp and Thomas Mills – who built the pulpit and finished the interior.

The interior of St. Andrew's, Colborne was recast in the 1870's, the ceiling altered and the building re-roofed, reusing the old timbers. The new roof was given eaves of greater projection supported by paired brackets. At the same time the well-worn double doors were replaced with a pair panelled in the new proportion. St. Andrew's was brought up to date again in 1910, when the Art Nouveau Movement had brought the beauty of the curve back to popular attention. This time loving hands reglazed all character from the windows and then altered the belfry. Its width was reduced and its height increased under a heavily over-hung roof, in the style of Frank Lloyd Wright's earlier period, topped off with a roof comb somewhat reminiscent of a Victorian foot scraper.

*IX-15: Manitoulin Italianate, with knobs on. St. Antony of Padua, Mindemoya.*

229

*IX-16 and 17: The freedom of the Italianate style made it comfortable for rural churches (IX-16 above) and nonconformist denominations (IX-17 opposite).*

The doors and windows of St. Alexander, Sand Point, in Renfrew (IX-14), tell much the same story. St. Alexander was founded under the patronage of John and Alexander Macdonell who had run a fur-trading post, a shop, a hotel and a post office and were still managing anything else that came their way when Sand Point was a declining link in the chain of lumber communities on the upper Ottawa. In 1845 John Macdonell had graciously bestowed a pair of stone holy-water stoups on the white weather-boarded church in his native parish of St. Alexander, Lochiel, in Glengarry County. St. Alexander, Sand Point was a white weather-boarded church too, with a neatly returned Neo-Classic cornice on a roof of Neo-Gothic pitch. In the alterations which overtook it, before Sand Point's economic collapse, St. Alexander was adjusted to the Italianate style. Its new doors were constructed to the late nineteenth-century proportion, with long panels above the lock rail and short panels below it. The tower window was elongated and fitted with Pisan Gothic tracery to match the new belfry. In the general renovation the transom above the central doorway was somehow overlooked and allowed to remain unrepentently Neo-Classic. St. Antony of Padua, Mindemoya (IX-15), built while St. Alexander's was being altered, is more consistently Italianate.

The builders of Milford Methodist Church reversed the treatment, concentrating their Italianate detailing (IX-16) on the entrance doorway. They, of course, were building a new church in 1865, and although its form remained conservatively Georgian, they had altered the proportion of its fan-transomed windows to a vaguely Gothic height.

St. John's Presbyterian Church, Almonte, built in the same year, was a quiet blend of late-Georgian stonework and Pisan Gothic window tracery. But once they were safely atop the tower, out of reach of short-sighted interference from below, the carpenters set up a Lilliputian Gothic village of battlement and pinnacle (IX-17) above the tray-like cornice.

Not all the earlier churches being made over in the Italianate style could be reconciled with a central tower. The Wesleyan Methodists of Bath had proudly announced in *The Christian Guardian* the opening of their new church, 30 September 1849. At that time it was a pleasant late-Georgian chapel with round-headed windows in its flanks and two entrance doorways in the gable wall. In 1861 the Bath Circuit reported to the Methodist Conference, in part: "To the industry and perseverance of Brother Michael Fawcett, we are indebted for the church in Bath. . . . to Brother Clappison for freedom from financial embarrassment. In improving the church the Ladies Aid has expended over two hundred and fifty dollars." Some time after 1861 the debt-free Wesleyans built a tower (IX-18) over one of the entrance doorways and thus at one side of the principal façade. Curved labels

*IX-18 and 19: Round-headed arches inside and out were the order of the Italianate day for the Methodist churches of Bath (IX-18 above left) and Sydney Township (IX-19 above right).*

*IX-20 opposite: Mount Carmel Methodist Episcopal, Troy. The designer's compass was much in use on churches for "the Methodist mountain."*

with elaborately decorative keystones were set over the new entrance doorway and all the reglazed windows in the body of the church, so that they might relate in style to the heavily bracketed cornice which gave importance to the new tower. A less happy structure now obscures the other early doorway, giving access to the furnace.

The hand of the late Victorian improver fell most heavily in church interiors. Convinced that the spirit of holiness rejoiced in stencilled walls, bright stained glass and high gloss varnish, they tore out austere white box pews, spider-framed fan-transoms and tall Neo-Classic pulpits elegantly fashioned in walnut and cherry. All denominations participated in the destructive crusade, which ranged from St. John's, Sandwich in Essex, to St. Andrew's, Williamstown in Glengarry, leaving few churches completely unscathed. The little Wesleyan Methodist chapel built in Sydney Township in 1855, a member of the little group of cobblestone buildings of the Hastings County gravel ridge, was swept and garnished into Italianate conformity with the rest. In so small a building interest was concentrated on the communion place (IX-19) and the pulpit furniture. The round-headed panels of the pulpit front were not only Italianate, they were symbolic — the tables of the law in form if not in content. The multitudinous vase-turnings which adorned the communion rail, the pulpit, and the pulpit chairs symbolized quite simply the late Victorians' love of curved form and their delight in the ingenious products of mechanization.

*IX-21: Carefully chosen stained glass complemented the graceful proportions of Troy's windows.*

Italianate church furnishings were rarely seen in their proper context in Ontario. All too often they were thrust into Georgian or Gothic Revival interiors which had been somewhat ineptly altered to receive them. Where the church and its furnishings had been designed as a coherent composition, the possibilities for grace inherent in the Italianate style can be justly appreciated. The United Church of Canada in Troy, Wentworth County (IX-20), was so designed. Built as Mount Carmel Methodist Episcopal Church in 1873 – when the Niagara Escarpment was still locally known as "the Methodist mountain" – it was on the watershed between the two strains of Methodist influence. To the east, the Methodist churches were largely Wesleyan, Primitive, or Bible Christian, all strongly English in their affiliation. West from Niagara, the Methodist churches of Upper Canada were more likely to be Methodist Episcopal, in connection with the parent American Church of that name.

On 21 October 1872, the Wesleyan Methodists of Troy appointed a committee to raise money for a new church. The committee worked diligently, and before the year was out funds were in hand to buy a new lot, leaving the old churchyard free for continued use as a cemetery. The congregation engaged a Brantford architect to design the new building, and were so happy in their choice that they were later moved to record: "Mr. Mellish has acted honourably in all dealings as a true gentleman." The excellent Mr. Mellish had designed them a church which was unostentatiously Italianate – a towerless, gabled structure composed in strong flat planes and equally strong curved lines, externally expressed in its fenestration and in the contrasting structural colour of patterned brick. The contrasting red and white brick of the façade was supplied by Watt, a Brantford building contractor. All other brick used in constructing the body of the church was made at the west end of the village by Samuel Wood, proprietor of the Troy brickyard.

The Brantford builders enriched the interior of Mount Carmel, Troy, with handsome plaster work. Semicircular plaster labels (IX-21) with oak leaf terminals decoratively framed the heads of the tall windows below a rich cornice. Five foliated ceiling medallions held stout iron hooks from which oil lamps were to hang suspended on iron rods twelve feet in length. The joinery was equally pleasing. Round-ended horizontal panels, alternating with moulded quatrefoils, ornamented the front of the gallery which was supported by cast-iron columns. All was very harmoniously handled, but the installation worthy of special consideration was the pulpit sofa. North American Presbyterians and Methodists alike were given to placing a sofa, rather than a collection of chairs, behind their pulpits, for the accommodation of the incumbent and visiting clergy, but the Troy sofa was in a class by itself

*IX-22: Designed to accommodate clerical broadcloth, the Troy sofa enjoyed a brief holiday in the Sunday School room, as seating for the starched frills of the primary class.*

*IX-23: Built by the Free Presbyterians in 1852, Grace Church was acquired by the Methodists of Niagara-on-the-Lake in 1875.*

(IX-22). Designed for the shallow apse in which it sits, it was entrusted to John Roelofson, cabinetmaker of Troy, who was apparently so accustomed to carve walnut and to button velvet for Victorian drawing rooms that he provided a Pompadour sofa for the clergy of the Beverley Circuit.

A number of other examples of the gabled Italianate church in textured or patterned brick, which had appeared along the limestone ridge of the Niagara escarpment, can be presumed to have inspired the builders of Troy. Grace United Church, Niagara-on-the-Lake, the farthest outpost of the group, was also the earliest. It was built by the Free Kirk Presbyterians in 1852, the year in which William Thomas – the pioneer of the Lombard style in Upper Canada – was designing Brock's Monument for Queenston. Grace Church (IX-23) was sold to the Methodists in 1875 after the union of the Presbyterian Churches in Canada. Now, amid the claims of St. Andrew, St. Mark and St. Vincent de Paul for architectural recognition in Niagara-on-the-Lake, the reticent charms of Grace tend to be slighted.

A little-known and highly important place of worship in the Italianate style stood for many years on Richmond Street just east of Victoria in downtown Toronto. This was the Richmond Street Synagogue, constructed in 1875 for the Hebrew community of Toronto, which had been formed in 1856 but which had not hitherto enjoyed a place of congregation designed for that purpose (IX-24). An article in a defunct Toronto newspaper – *The Leader*, published on the opening day, 20 January 1876, recorded in part: "The new building, prepared according to plans by Messrs. Stewart and

Strickland of this city, is 33 feet front by 63 feet in depth. There is a high stone basement which places the body of the building at a considerable elevation, the main door being reached by a number of easy steps. The body of the building is of red brick finished in white. The basement contains a schoolroom and lodge room, in which is built a vault for the preservation of valuable documents. The main building has a vestibule cut off in front, over which is a gallery, where sit the female portion of the congregation. In the midst of the main room is a reading desk upon a raised platform, and the seats are placed around facing it, except toward the Ark, which is at the extreme end facing the doorway. Over the Ark is placed a painting representing the Tables of Stone on which the Law was delivered to Moses on Mount Sinai. Before the Ark is drawn the veil, and on the right is a small desk from which the sermon was yesterday delivered. The seats, though plain are comfortable, and the building is of such size as to meet all of the requirements of the congregation."

Earlier on the writer had noted the building and property costs as amounting to twelve thousand dollars and added: "Towards this amount the Christians have given five hundred dollars, the Jews of Montreal one thousand dollars and the sum has been raised to six thousand dollars by the Jews here.... The president and officers of the congregation are: President; Mr. J. Green, Treasurer; Alex Miller, Secretary; Isaac Davis; Mark Kassel, and L. Walters Trustees; Mark Solomon, Chairman of the Building Committee; L. Cohen Acting Reader and Conductor of the Choir and Music."

The major emigration of Jews from Europe to Ontario lay in the future. On the chilly day in 1876 when the Richmond Street Synagogue was opened, the principal Hebrew congregation in Canada was to be found in Montreal. Small groups of Jewish people had come into Upper Canada from the days of the Loyalists on, but they were too far removed from their kindred and their established places of worship, and they tended to drift away again. The names of two Jews appeared on the list of Loyalists settling in the old Eastern District, and the land grants assigned to them were shown on Patrick McNiff's map of 1794 inscribed with the names of Samuel Moses and Meyer Solomon. Their names are lonely on that map amid the Cryslers, Casselmans, Schwerdfegers, Van Allens, Macdonells, MacDonalds, Camerons and Grants with which it was so thickly set. Oral tradition in Dundas County has it that one of them, firm in his faith, sold his land grant and sought out the company of his co-religionists in Montreal, while the other, finding it increasingly difficult to worship alone, quietly joined the Reverend Samuel Schwerdfeger's Lutheran congregation.

The path of the Dundas Lutherans in the early years had been

*IX-24: The first synagogue in Ontario, erected on Richmond Street in Toronto in 1875.*

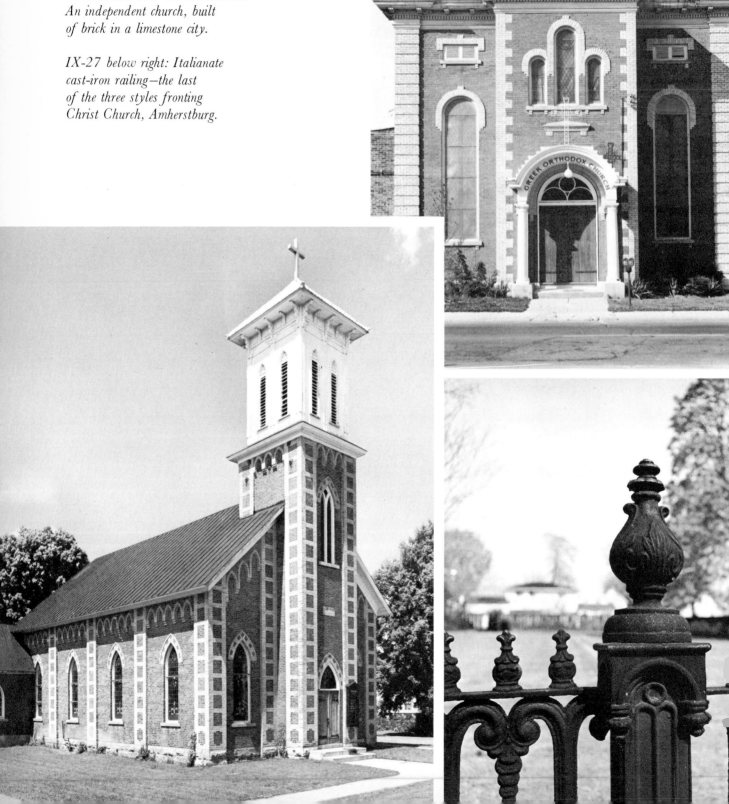

*IX-25 below: Brackets and corbels and patterned brick encase the Lutherans of Morrisburg.*

*IX-26 right: Baptist, Christian Scientist and now Greek Orthodox. An independent church, built of brick in a limestone city.*

*IX-27 below right: Italianate cast-iron railing—the last of the three styles fronting Christ Church, Amherstburg.*

fraught with dissension which had tried their faith too, but those shoals were long safely passed when the charms of patterned brick were revealed to them. St. Paul's Evangelical Lutheran Church, built in Morrisburg in 1875, was frankly eclectic (IX-25). Up the sides of nave and tower climbed laddered pilasters in red and white brick joined at the top by an arcaded Gothic frieze. When a bell became possible they housed it in a Tuscan tempietta set nonchalantly on top of the Gothic tower.

The importance of wearing a cheerful ecclesiastic countenance was even more forthrightly stated three years later in Kingston when the little Baptist church of 1845 on Johnson Street was given the imposing false front (IX-26) with which it now welcomes a Greek Orthodox congregation. The designer who effected the transformation may have been John Power. The religious body which veneered the church with brick and ordered the new look is believed to have been composed of Christian Scientists. The church has thus contained the faith of many people worshipping one God in several ways. Power's façade expressed the building's purpose better even than he perhaps intended. It is at once dignified and uninhibited — an eclectic selection of Baroque, Georgian and Norman detail stylishly blended to the inarticulate taste of the many.

# X
# *Vernacular*

*I am debtor both to the Greek and to the Barbarians; both to the wise and to the unwise.*

*Romans* I: *14*

Form and style in the early vernacular churches of Upper Canada followed the dictates of necessity rather than the unanimous choice of the worshippers. This was to be as true of settlement along the pre-Cambrian shield and the north shore of Lake Superior as it had been along the northern shores of the St. Lawrence, Lake Ontario, and Lake Erie, two generations earlier (X-1). Log was always the first medium of construction. Great seasoned tree trunks were squared with a broad axe, cornered carefully, and set alternately to compensate for the natural taper from butt to tip. The building form would vary a little, however, as the frontier was inched back.

The earliest log meetinghouses were square in plan, built by militiamen accustomed to the construction of block houses, and the fortress aspect of the early places of worship was intensified by enforced economy in the scale and number of the windows. They were adequate but not beautiful structures, yet when economy was of primary consideration the square plan was ideal, and was to be employed for brick chapels as well. March Street Baptist Church (X-2) was built in York in 1832 to the square plan, as were two small cottage-roofed Methodist chapels for outlying congregations, one on Asquith Avenue in Yorkville in 1840, the other on Queen Street West in 1841 when York had become Toronto.

Because they failed to satisfy the architectural yearnings of their congregations, the little square buildings were either replaced as soon as was humanly possible or were altered out of all recognition. (The Yorkville Chapel later became a very small medical school and then an equally small house.) As a result of population dispersal and economic recession a few retained much of their original character, however.

A good example of the blockhouse school of Ontario church architecture is still to be found near Maxville in Glengarry County, having served out a second term of usefulness as a community hall. Athol Congregational Chapel (X-3) was built in 1837 in the eighteenth concession of the Indian Lands, by Scots from Perthshire who had been taking up land in the area since 1815.

The Indian Lands, a narrow strip running up the western side of Glengarry County from the St. Lawrence to the Prescott boundary, had been reserved for a band of the Loyalist Six Nations who preferred to live on Cornwall Island or across the St. Lawrence around the old mission at St. Regis, Quebec. Settlers coming into the area thereafter acquired lands on leasehold from the band through their agent. In the second decade of the nineteenth century the Indian Agent, worn down by constant bargaining (which had to be translated from Iroquois to English to Gaelic and back again) persuaded the government to allow the Cornwall Island band to sell the reserved portion of Glengarry to the leaseholders.

At this point the Congregationalists of Athol began to cut

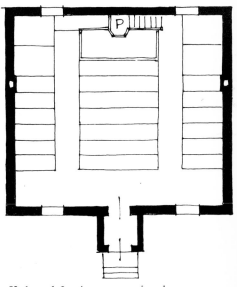

*X-1 and 2: Anonymous hands glazed St. James' Presbyterian, Kemptville (X-1 opposite) with uninhibited charm, and set lancet windows in March Street Baptist (X-2 above) to dignify its simple cottage plan.*

timber for their chapel. They already had a minister, the Reverend William McKillican, who had come to them in 1817, and they had been formally organized as a congregation since 1823. They built a sturdy, square, planked-log structure with three windows in both its southern and northern faces – and two in the west. An entrance doorway was centred in the east wall, and a shingled hipped roof crowned the edifice. The interior was austerely and functionally disposed, serving the diminishing needs of a congregation that gradually transferred its allegiance to a daughter congregation in the railway village which had grown up nearby. In 1920 the old church was sold to the Presbyterians for use as a community and church hall.

The Athol Congregationalists had had two tenurial hurdles to get over before they could build their chapel. One, the problem of reserved Indian Land, had been local; the other, which was province-wide, had been solved by legislation passed in 1829 and entitled *An Act for Religious Societies Therein Named*. The Act stated in part: "It is enacted that whenever any religious congregation or society of Presbyterians, Lutherans, Calvinists, Methodists, Congregationalists, Independents, Anabaptists, Quakers, Mennonists, Tunkers, Moravians shall have occasion to take a conveyance of land for the site of a church, meetinghouse or chapel or a burying ground it shall and may be lawful for them to appoint trustees to whom and their successors . . . the requisite land for all or any of the purposes aforesaid (not exceeding five acres for any one congregation) may be conveyed . . . ." (The Churches of England, Scotland and and Rome, of course, already enjoyed this privilege.) Not a wildly exciting document, one would have said, but the immediate result of its passing was an acceleration in church building by the named religious groups. Some of them had built places of worship before the passage of the Act, but all had had to

*X-3 and 4: Athol Congregational, 1837 (X-3 below) and Providence Church, 1834 (X-4 top opposite) were pioneer churches of the receding frontier.*

depend on an awkward tenure whereby the deed for the land on which their building stood was held personally by the clergyman or a member of the congregation. When the landholder died the church property passed to his heirs who were not necessarily either members of the sect or even residents of the country. With the passage of the Act of 1829 it had become possible for the sparsely settled members of several denominations, by appointing representatives to a joint board of trustees, to build a community church. Providence Church, which rose in 1834 – the first chapel to be

*X-5 and 6: Beaver Dams, 1832.*

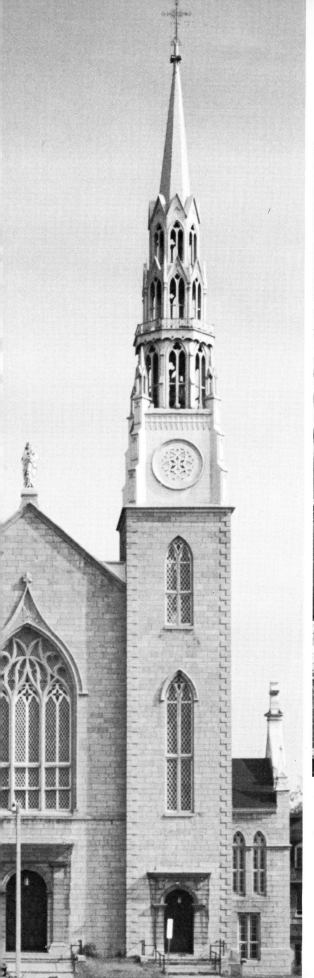

X-7: The designation "Basilica" clung to Notre Dame, Ottawa (X-7 centre), begun in that form in 1841. Altered stonework at gallery level (X-8 far left top) marks the change of stylistic direction to Gothic in 1844. The chief glories of Notre Dame are the golden Madonna (X-9 far left bottom), carved by Cordonna, and the Victorian opulence of the interior (X-10 above).

built in Kitley Township (X-4) – was such an ecumenical structure. It has been removed for safekeeping from Leeds to Upper Canada Village.

The later builders of log churches abandoned the square plan along with the designation "meetinghouse." The ensuing church might not provide greater accommodation than of old, but it would certainly be rectangular in plan, with its principal entrance set in one gable wall. In early examples the gables were weather-boarded and the doorway was dignified with the best joinery the artisans could command. It was possible to read into such simple buildings a tenuous Greek Revival inspiration, a resemblance which moved a little nearer to historic precedent when post-and-beam construction was employed – as was the intention advertised in 1831 by the Methodists of "Beaver Dams by Thorold."

Hiram Swayze's advertisement stated that the chapel was to be forty by fifty feet with a gallery in one end and on each side (X-5). The walls were to be of brick twenty feet high (actually timber-framed, and infilled with soft brick), and they were to be weather-boarded. When Egerton Ryerson, that determined fighter for mass education, came to minister at Beaver Dams in 1832 he spoke to the assembly from a tall pulpit which enabled him to see easily into a gallery supported handsomely by turned Tuscan columns. In 1879 the auditorium was converted to a single-storey height by the simple expedient of ceiling in the central space at the level of the gallery floor (X-6). It seemed good to the building committee to leave the gallery area undisturbed – slumbering peacefully in the hope of future restoration.

While Egerton Ryerson was still preaching in the comparative obscurity of Beaver Dams, the Roman Catholic flock of Father Cannon in Bytown-on-the-Ottawa was building a modest wooden chapel. None of these conditions was to be of long duration. Ryerson went on to prominence in the political and pedagogical life of Upper Canada; Bytown was chosen to become the national capital; and Notre Dame (X-7) was destined for long years of architectural growth which began in 1839 when Father Cannon received the plans for a new church. It was Father Cannon's intention to build the Church of Notre Dame as a stone basilica in the Classical manner then in high favour with Baillairgé, Browne, Gavreau, and Hacker, the leading architects practising in the archdiocese of Quebec. Furthermore, Father Cannon had, close at hand, excellent builder-masons who had worked on the fabric of Notre Dame in Montreal, under the supervision of Thomas MacKay and John Redpath, with whom they had moved on to build the locks at Bytown.

In 1841 the building contract for Notre Dame was given to Antoine Robillard and for three years the handsome ashlar walls

*X-11: Split-fan vaulting in wood, designed by Bouillon for the chapel of Sacred Heart Convent, Ottawa.*

of a Classic church grew slowly up to a usable single-storey height (X-8). Its three round-headed doorways were contained between Tuscan pilasters supporting bold, severe entablatures, a classical restatement of the Baroque interpretation of the Roman triumphal arch. A few windows from this stage of the construction remain *in situ*, their Regency glazing set in squat rectangular openings defined by monolithic sills and shallow cambered arches.

In 1844 pastoral control was assumed by the Oblate Fathers who, having assimilated the fashionable idea that the Pointed style was the correct wear for Christian churches, proceeded to build the main portion of Notre Dame in a somewhat archaic Regency version of it. It was in this second stage of its building life – while it was still a steep-roofed, galleried church with two incomplete west towers – that Notre Dame became the cathedral of the new Roman Catholic diocese of Ottawa. Monseigneur Joseph-Eugène Guigues, Provincial of the Oblates of Mary Immaculate, was consecrated Bishop of Ottawa, 30 July 1848. Ten years later Bishop Guigues had the satisfaction of seeing the cathedral silhouette enhanced by the erection of square bell chambers crowned by soaring, staged, octagonal spires. In 1862 a choir was built at the east end, improving the proportion of the building, and three years later the western façade was completed when the gilded Madonna was set above the apex of the west gable wall (X-9), the gift of the raftsmen of the Ottawa in homage to their special benefactress.

The first Roman Catholic Bishop of Ottawa had established the external aspect of Notre Dame; the second concentrated his attention on the interior (X-10). Consecrated to his high office in 1874, Bishop Duhamel had craftsmen at work on the cathedral by 1878, and again expert craftsmen were there ready to hand – just off the job at the Parliament Buildings. Furthermore he had, in Canon Bouillon, the diocesan architect, a designer of interior space whose skill in handling the rich *passé* palate of early Gothic ornament was equalled only by the immensity of his proposed budgets. Poor Canon Bouillon was not given the thirty-five million dollars necessary to raise on the Ottawa his dream church, Nova Sancta Sophia, which was to be finer than Justinian's on the Bosphorus and larger than St. Peter's in Rome. Instead he was allowed to alter Notre Dame, behind its Regency Gothic façade, and to set Philippe Parizeau to work carving a rich triforium above the chancel stalls. The triforium niches were destined to hold thirty statues of prophets, evangelists, saints and martyrs carved to life scale by Louis-Philippe Hébert.

The interior of Notre Dame was a marvellous kaleidoscope of Victorian texture and colour. But Canon Bouillon's most interesting structural composition, which employed split-fan vaulting (X-11), was once to be found in the 1888 chapel of the convent of Our

*X-12 and 13: Wesley Church, Camden Township (above), most charming of the eighteen Saul churches, was pleasantly furnished (below) in vernacular Gothic style.*

Lady of the Sacred Heart in Ottawa. The wooden fan vaulting was salvaged by the National Capital Commission when the convent was demolished in 1972.

While the contractors and stonemasons who had built the Bytown locks were setting to work on government projects in the new capital at Ottawa, similar groups were moving out from the building recession settling over Kingston, one of the old capitals, at the other end of the Rideau Canal. The stonemasons who had worked for Kingston architects in the 1840's set up on their own as master-builders in the adjacent counties of Hastings, Lennox and Addington in the 1850's, and their apprentices carried on their building practices until the end of the nineteenth century.

The most prolific firm of builder-masons operating in the area was that of the Saul brothers of Camden East who, with auxiliary assistance from sons, nephews and cousins, built some eighteen stone churches in Hastings, Lennox and Addington in the latter half of the nineteenth century. They were ably seconded in a number of their better efforts by Miles Storms, a joiner from the nearby hamlet of Moscow. The Saul-Storms churches were distinguished, as a group, by the uniformly high quality of their stonework and by the handsome treatment of late Regency glaz-

ing in windows and overdoors. In Wesley Church, Camden Township (X-12), built by the Sauls in 1863, the mason-builders managed to increase the apparent scale of the little church by setting on the gable a minute bell cote of monumental derivation topped by a spirelet and weathervane. The Methodists of Camden thus acquired the dignity of a belfry which prohibited the expensive purchase of a bell.

The interior of Wesley Church, carried out presumably by the joiner who embroidered its eaves with curvaceous brackets, was more sedately Gothic in treatment (X-13). Later hands diluted the sobriety of the gallery face by installing a band of garlanded pressed-sheet metal between the rail and the caps of the supporting columns.

When the Sauls and Miles Storms came to build in Colebrook (X-14) in 1874, the shape of overdoors had changed; the camber of the mid-century had given way to level horizontal lintels. But Storms was still making Regency glazing bars for the windows. A decade later, St. Andrew's Presbyterian Church, Camden East, although still constructed in the Saul tradition of stonework, was glazed (X-15) in a vernacular Gothic style in which its designer contrived, by an unorthodox treatment of the components, to

*X-14 and 15: Regency glazing enhanced Colebrook (X-14 left), but a more robust vernacular prevailed in Camden East Presbyterian (X-15 below).*

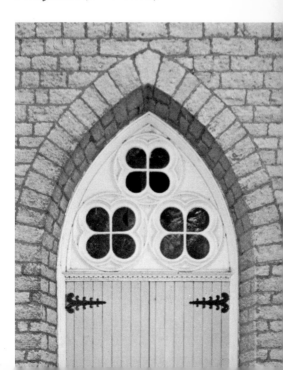

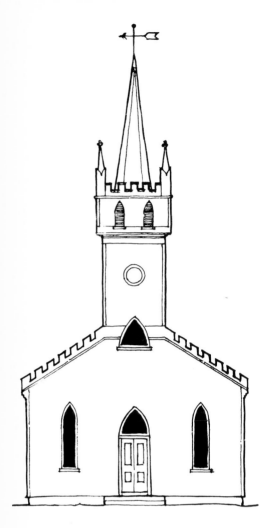

maintain the Regency tradition of Lennox and Addington picturesque.

The natural informality of wood lent itself more readily than did brick or stone to picturesque intricacies at the hands of Upper Canadian builders. Unfortunately, however, the twiddly bits came off even more easily than they went on, so that builders'-Regency churches tended to become less and less picturesque over the years. A number of such amendments can be seen in a small group of weather-boarded churches of great charm which are to be found in and around Grafton, Colborne and Vernonville in Northumberland County.

The joiners of Northumberland had proven their skill a generation earlier in the domestic field with a number of pleasing houses in the Neo-Classic style, of which the best-known example was, perhaps, the Barnum House in Grafton. One would expect a builder's-Regency church such as St. Andrew's, Grafton (well within the orbit of the designer-builder, William Grieve of Cobourg) to be both interesting in form and meticulous in detail, and one is not disappointed. The lively silhouette of the building triumphantly evaded major alterations which destroyed the elegant proportions of its windows and door, so that the conjectural reconstruction of its façade (X-16) is still possible.

St. Andrew's, Grafton was completed in 1844. In the following year the Anglican parish of Colborne began construction of a markedly similar but somewhat less baronial church. However, when the joiners packed their tools away in 1845 they were unlikely to have left Trinity's octagonal tower-lantern without a suit-

*X-16 and 17: Northumberland churches in the Regency style of William Grieve—St. Andrew's Presbyterian, Grafton (X-16 above) and Holy Trinity, Colborne (X-17 right).*

able complement of flanking pinnacles. And while the stained-glass window which lights the bell-ringers' stage of the tower today (X-17) is a pleasing eccentricity, the original builder, William Grieve, can neither be credited nor blamed for it. The window migrated from the chancel (X-18) to its present position when the altar-place was enlarged (X-19) to conform to later notions of ecclesiological propriety.

St. Andrew's, Vernonville, on the other hand, suffered from a few obvious accretions: ventilating sections in the lower sash of the windows, and little battlemented sheds on either side of the tower base. The late building date of 1862, still fairly legible on the characteristic frame of its painted clock face, places St. Andrew's near the outer periphery of Grieve's influence. St. Andrew's, Grafton, has lost its would-be clock and the dial of Trinity, Colborne has been painted out, but St. Andrew's, Vernonville (X-20) still patiently proclaims the appointed hour to be half past two, although the only wasps presently concerned are the winged variety.

In simple buildings the vertical movement of the true Gothic Revival became visible as board-and-batten siding. Vertical siding, when used in conjunction with rolling scrolls and drip-pendant verge boards, was picturesque by intention, and fully exploited the joiners' skill. It was this aspect of the medium which decided the mechanics of Bath to employ it on the remarkable building (X-21) which came to be known as the Layer Cake Church. Dr. Burleigh, in his *History of the Buildings of Bath*, points out that the joiners' intention in 1850 was to furnish themselves with a Mechanics Institute when they employed Abraham Harris,

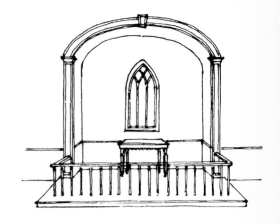

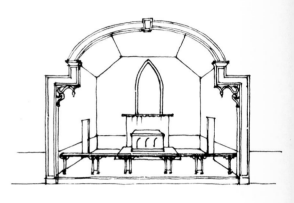

*X-18 and 19 above: The altar place, Holy Trinity, Colborne. Before (top), and after (X-19) Archdeacon Bethune's visitation.*

*X-20 left: Vernonville, 2:30 p.m., A.D. 1862.*

*X-21: The Layer Cake Church, Bath (X-21 above), built as a Mechanics' Institute and now a Senior Citizens' Club, briefly housed the stratified devotions (X-22 opposite) of Presbyterians below and Anglicans above.*

one of their number, to construct the building for them. But economic recession overtook Bath when the town refused to countenance the noise and smoke necessarily attached to railways. The mechanics could not pay, so Harris took a lien on the building. He seems then to have searched for suitable tenants and found a congregation of homeless Presbyterians who were prepared to be either Italianate or Gothic as the landlord chose (X-22). The ground floor was accordingly fitted up for them, the Masonic Lodge took over the second storey, and all went merrily on until Harris fell on evil times and ran up a large bill with the local doctor before dying. The building was then deeded by Harris' widow to Dr. Roderick Kennedy who, when *he* died, left it to the Anglicans with the stipulation that the Presbyterians were to be allowed to continue in occupation of the ground floor during such time as they agreed to pay for half of the upkeep of the building. The Anglicans used the upper floor as a parish hall, and on several occasions, when their church was undergoing intensive repairs, they used the Layer Cake for services as well. Thus the old Mechanics Institute lived on in Bath, as a surprising example of layered, picturesque tolerance, until the advent of Church Union in 1925. The Presbyterians then moved out to join with the Methodists who naturally refused to make any contribution to the repair of the old building. The Layer Cake Church mouldered for a time but has recently been acquired by the Millhaven Women's Institute, for use as a Senior Citizens' Centre. The lower layer of the Bath building was faintly Italianate about its door, while Knox Church, Port Carling (X-23), as wilfully picturesque in its way as the Bath Layer Cake, was Italianate – or rather Swiss Alpine – from the beginning.

Regency picturesque character or detailing, when found in rural churches of the 1860's, usually occurs in areas of late settlement. Specific detailing can, in some instances, be traced to an earlier, admired source building. Thus the criss-cross glazing bars, heavy mullions and redundant gallery panels in the windows of St. John's Anglican Church, Ida (X-24) built in Cavan Township in the upper reaches of Durham in 1866, derived from Kivas Tully's work on St. Mark's, Port Hope. The townships of Cavan in Durham, South Monaghan in Northumberland, and North Monaghan in Peterborough were settled in the second decade of the nineteenth century under Peter Robinson's scheme which brought many emigrants from Ireland to Upper Canada. Reverend Samuel Armour of Maghera, County Derry, Ireland, first Rector of St. John's, selected a commanding hilltop site for the Church of England and Ireland in the Canadian Cavan. As he gazed over the sweeping prospect of the drumlins of Durham, Samuel Armour – moved to recollection of the opening lines of Tennyson's "Oenone" – bestowed upon his hilltop the name of Ida,

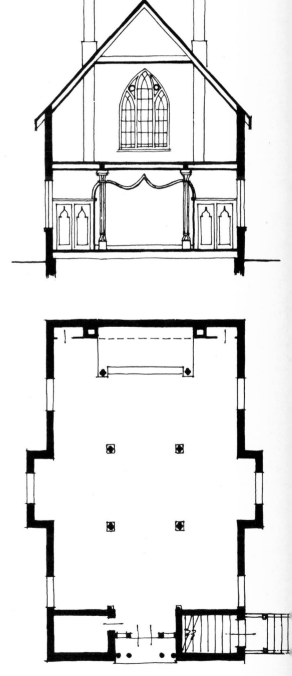

*X-23 below: Muskoka picturesque. Knox Presbyterian, Port Carling.*

*X-24 bottom left: St. John's, Ida, 1866.*

*X-25 top left: South Monaghan Presbyterian.*

for it seemed to him that here, in truth, lay a vale "lovelier than all the valleys of the Ionian hills."

The Ulster Presbyterians of South Monaghan, applying themselves with their accustomed industry to the tasks of raising a suitable church, were able, by 1863, to afford a commodious edifice buttressed and pinnacled in brick (X-25). The pleasing pattern of glass and the fine form of the drip labels which graced South Monaghan Presbyterian forecast the more ambitious detailing (X-26) which would be executed under Thomas Johnson's direction on St. Paul's, Bowmanville eight years later.

While the Presbyterians of South Monaghan were buttressing their church, the Free Presbyterians of Merrickville were buttressing their pulpit. Knox Presbyterian Church, Merrickville was a delightful blend of picturesque Gothic and Classic in red brick. It was neatly finished by 1861 but for the tower, which had been carried up a few courses above the roof ridge, capped and left to the mercy of future congregations. The company then assembled proposed to expend their resources on the appointments of the interior. The focal point in the visual organization of Upper Canadian Presbyterian church interiors continued, throughout the nineteenth century, to be the pulpit from which the Scriptures were to be expounded at some length every Sabbath. The communion-place – of greater spiritual significance but less frequent use – was in any case closely associated with it, so that interest could be concentrated in a relatively small area. Knox, Merrickville is fortunate in that it has retained not only the picturesque Gothic pulpit (buttressed to withstand emphatic discourse) but has kept as well the crocketed screen (X-27) behind it. The Upper Canadian attached pulpit screen was a vestigial survival from a more picturesque past.

The Free Presbyterians of Athol, building their brick church defiantly on a hilltop (so that the Church of Scotland congregation, from which they had just parted with a degree of acrimony, must need see it) felt that they need not indulge in the expense of pulpit screens. Their minister, the Reverend Daniel Gordon, was picturesque enough already. Gordon, a fiery, eloquent Free Kirk Scot from Perthshire, arrived in the unsuspecting township of Kenyon in 1853 and thereafter became something of a local legend. Elderly parishioners of Athol used to recall long, languorous summer Sunday afternoons when weary harvesters, unaccustomed to sitting all day, were inclined to fall into an uneasy slumber as soon as the Reverend Daniel launched into his sermon. Ministerial response was unpredictable. The minister, casting an eye over his nodding congregation, might shake them out of their coma by announcing that wheat was selling at ten dollars a bushel on the open market, and when he had their startled attention, point out with merciless exactness the future reserved for the followers of Mammon. He might, on

*X-26: Johnson's dolphins cavort engagingly around the windows of St. Paul's, Bowmanville.*

255

*X-29 and 30: Bold Gothic mouldings (X-29 right) define the bracket (designed to support a Presbyterian baptismal basin) affixed to the pulpit of St. Andrew's, Gananoque. Similar detailing (X-30 far right) decorated the gallery rail.*

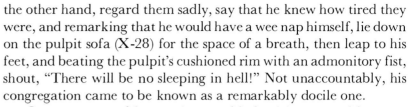

*X-27 and 28: Shedding sounding-boards, separate entrances and screens, the mid-Victorian Presbyterian pulpit (X-27 far left) abated not one jot of its authority. The colourful first incumbent of Gordon Presbyterian Church in Athol (X-28 left) lives on in several early-twentieth-century Canadian novels by his son, Ralph Connor.*

the other hand, regard them sadly, say that he knew how tired they were, and remarking that he would have a wee nap himself, lie down on the pulpit sofa (X-28) for the space of a breath, then leap to his feet, and beating the pulpit's cushioned rim with an admonitory fist, shout, "There will be no sleeping in hell!" Not unaccountably, his congregation came to be known as a remarkably docile one.

On one memorable occasion an elderly visitor, seated between two of his sons on a front bench in Gordon's church was seen to lean rather heavily toward one of them as the sermon moved to its end. The young man, placing an arm about his father, held him upright until the end of the homily and then, to everyone's surprise, both sons remained seated with their father while the congregation stood for prayer. When the minister descended from his place of authority to rebuke such unseemly conduct, he discovered, to his infinite discomfiture, that the old man was dead.

Sedate St. Andrew's, Gananoque was never called upon to witness such *outré* behaviour. When lumber magnate John Mac-Donald gave Gananoque its first wooden church building in 1830, a town meeting was called to decide which denomination it should be. Presbyterianism won the vote, and a minister was called. After several decades of amicably sharing a number of premises with Methodists of several varieties, the Presbyterians were assisted in building a stone church, in 1853, by their early patron whose business had been flourishing. The stone church was enlarged and improved several times thereafter, acquiring its spire in 1875, the gallery in 1877, and transepts in 1887. The pulpit (X-29) would seem to belong to the same period of installation as the gallery front, for both were constructed in the serious vernacular Gothic idiom (X-30). The mouldings were boldly cut by Mitchell and Wilson's joiners and applied with some knowledge of their stylistic derivation.

A similarly earnest approach to the problem of designing a Gothic Revival church suitable to its site and to congregational needs activated the builders of First Baptist, Beamsville, when they began to consider building their present church in 1855. It was the third place of worship built in the immediate area by the Baptists in Clinton Township. The first, a log building of domestic scale run up quickly on the lakeshore by the first settlers, was replaced in 1808 by a more ambitious building on land donated for the purpose by Jacob Boehm, a United Empire Loyalist from Sussex, New Jersey. The congregation grew – as congregations were wont to do in mid-nineteenth-century Upper Canada – and a larger building was required. Their builder gave them a church rather than a meetinghouse, nicely composed in brick, with well-placed windows and a lively arcading of little Gothic arches in wood (X-31) below the tower cornices and the raking cornices of the principal façade.

257

*X-31, 32 and 33: Lancet arcading under the eaves (X-31 above) of First Baptist, Beamsville; louvered lancets in a Lutheran belfry in Zurich (X-32 right top); and paired lancet-tracery wherever possible, for the Presbyterians of Maple (X-33, right below), attest adherence to the Pointed style.*

The designers of brick churches, in the Upper Canadian vernacular Gothic employed in First Baptist, Beamsville, and St. Peter's, Zurich, defined the bays of the nave with starkly plain pilasters set at intervals along the flank walls and, as structural supports, on the façades and towers. Cornices might then be embellished by a Gothic arcading in wood, as in Beamsville, or an enriching texture of corbelled brick. St. Peter's Lutheran (X-32), built in Zurich, Huron County in 1861, has rows of pendant crosslets under its eaves and is dignified by a square-based tower. Above the bracketed Italianate cornice of St. Peter's rises an octagonal lantern and soaring bell-cast spire – the hallmark of the nineteenth-century Lutheran church in Ontario.

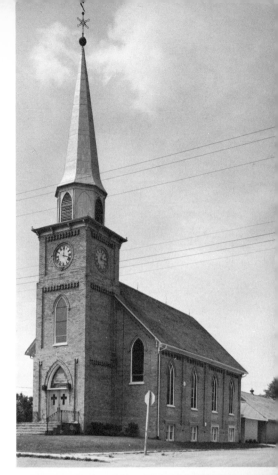

Octagonal spire-lanterns were not built only on Lutheran churches, of course. The shape was very popular with Roman Catholic builders in the Ottawa Valley, and one of the handsomest in central Ontario was erected in 1862 for the Presbyterians of Maple in York County. St. Andrew's, Maple is, in fact, such a splendid example of carpenter's-Gothic (X-33) that one suspects the unrecorded assistance of an architect's plans carried out in excellent joinery by John McDonald, contractor on the site.

Much the same aura of the ghostly presence of an unremembered architect surrounds the harmonious composition of basic Gothic form in white brick which in 1865 became St. Paul's Anglican Church, Clinton (X-34), in Huron County. Sweeping steps, neatly curved about the doorway in the tower base, gave graceful access to the gallery whose arcaded front was shaded by an acorn-tipped, scalloped verge-board in the Italianate style (X-35).

Italianate gabled churches enjoyed (or suffered) as many changes at the hands of vernacular builders in Ontario as the Northern Gothic style had already done. Seemingly most popular in the counties of Lincoln, Simcoe, Wentworth, and York, they ranged in date from Grace Church, Niagara, of 1852, to Annan Methodist, of 1881, farther afield in Grey County.

One of the most architecturally interesting of Ontario's gabled towerless churches now houses the First Reformed Congregation of Hamilton. It was built on the corner of Charlton and Hess Streets in 1882 for a Baptist congregation (possibly to the design of C.W. Mulligan) and was remarkable for having not one but three important gabled façades. The transept faces (X-36) best display the unorthodox designer's skilful use of texture and colour in brickwork. The four fanciful pinnacles with which he flourished each gabled silhouette still attest how excellent was the casting produced by the iron founders of Hamilton.

Two unusual little churches, many miles removed from each other, now shelter under the ecclesiastical umbrella of the United Church of Canada. The originality of these structures lies not in their ornament but in their shape, for both are octagonal in plan.

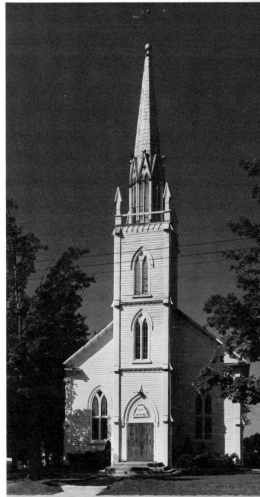

*X-34 and 35: The Gothic staircases (X-34 below) of St. Paul's, Clinton, sweep composedly onward and upward to the gallery (X-35 bottom).*

*X-36 right: A skilful juxtaposition of late-Victorian textures. First Reformed Congregation of Hamilton.*

Speedside United Church (X-37), the earlier of the two, was built in 1855 as the Second Congregationalist Church of Eramosa Township, and as one might anticipate from its proximity to Guelph, it was constructed of stone.

Polygonal churches had been built in Europe from time to time, and the history of polygonal baptistries and chapter houses stretches away into the dawn of the early Christian Church, but the immediate antecedents of both these Upper Canadian octagonal churches were more likely to be found among the post-Reformation polygonal churches of Scotland.

Speedside Church retained its original seating plan (X-38). Dalhousie Mills United Church unfortunately has not, nor does visible evidence remain on which to base such a plan. It is possible, however, to reconstruct, with some degree of accuracy, an impression of its exterior appearance (X-39) in 1869, when the original lantern and spire were still in place and all three entrance doorways opened to admit the Presbyterians of Dalhousie Mills to worship there.

A somewhat more imposing polygonal structure rose some twenty years later in the Methodist camp meeting ground at Grimsby Beach, in Lincoln County (X-40). This was a sixteen-sided marquee, one hundred feet high, designed to serve as a semi-sheltered auditorium for protracted religious experience. It was set in the midst of a village of Methodist summer cottages — a permanent camp meeting place. The temple was altogether marvellous when built, but the days of its glory were cut short by the grim years of the First World War. In the post-war years the building fell into disrepair. The times were out of joint for camp meetings; furthermore, the Methodist Church was engaged in the prolonged discussion with the Presbyterian Church of Canada and the Congregational Church which eventually led to the formation of the United Church of Canada. Neither of the other two contracting parties was camp-meeting prone. The old colourful days were recorded, however. A water-colour drawing (X-41) by U.S. Wright, now in the United Church archives, shows the Grimsby Beach camp meeting ground as it appeared in 1859 when fervent sermons were declaimed from an open rostrum to the faithful, uncomfortably seated on planks in the centre of a pine grove. Among the trees around the concourse area were set little log cabins which provided temporary housing for the several weeks of meetings.

Camp meetings and religious revivals of all sorts added spice and excitement to life in Canada's formative years, as well as providing vehicles for possible spiritual experience of greater moment — but they were seasonal occurrences. The weekly meeting-place for shared worship was of far greater importance in the life of every community and denomination, no matter how simple its form might be, and the basic vernacular church of Ontario was indeed a very simple structure.

X-37 and 38: Speedside United Church (above) built in 1855, has retained its original seating plan (X-38 below).

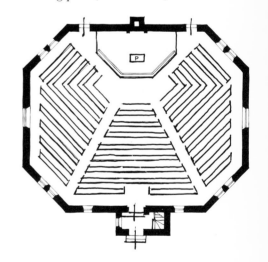

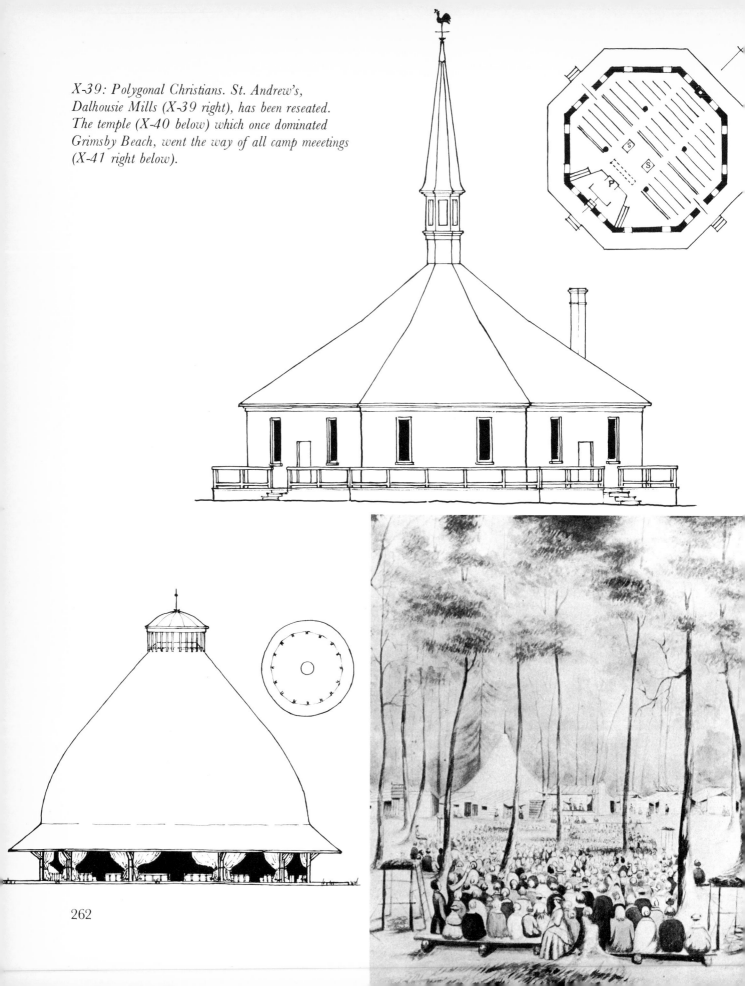

*X-39: Polygonal Christians. St. Andrew's, Dalhousie Mills (X-39 right), has been reseated. The temple (X-40 below) which once dominated Grimsby Beach, went the way of all camp meeetings (X-41 right below).*

The rectangular auditorium or preaching hall, set templewise, was the most adaptable. It could be fashioned from any locally available building material – mud, wood, brick or stone – singly or in combination. It could be furnished simply or with infinite care and elaboration to suit the liturgical, emotional and visual needs of the congregation. Furthermore, with a judicious use of architectural detail it could be brought to within hailing distance, at least, of any fashionable ecclesiastical style. It could, of course, be altered almost as easily, so that early examples no longer show their shining morning faces to the world.

Haldimand Baptist Church, near Wicklow, in Northumberland County, is a case in point (X-42). It proudly proclaims on its re-boarded façade that it was built in 1824. The glazing bars in the flanking windows deny the statement, which – partially substantiated by the pitch of the roof – is in all probability applicable only to the timber framing concealed in its walls. Stone was not so easily changed (although later masons have managed to conceal quantities of fine early stonework under the smears of false tuck-pointing.) So the hands of the false clock face (X-43) in the gable of the little stone community chapel at Dixie, in Peel County, still hopefully stand at eleven o'clock, the hour of prayer in 1837. Its windows were always square-headed, matter-of-fact, and timeless.

The windows of Macville Wesleyan Church (X-44) in York County, invested the little brick box with a degree of late-Georgian elegance which was reinforced by decorative quoins, somewhat outmoded elsewhere by 1857. Tayside Baptist Church, built a year later, was designed by an obstinately Georgian builder too, one who conformed to the pressures of Gothic style just enough to raise the roof pitch and to lengthen the windows (X-45). The length of the upper panels in his otherwise Georgian door also betrays the late date of this Neo-Classic survival in Stormont County.

Regency Gothic whimsy was infinitely adaptable. Its sham feudalism could be applied to the little towerless box churches of Upper Canada with economic ease. Peculiarly suited to wood, it was also susceptible to alteration and addition. St. Luke's Anglican Church (X-46), built in Palermo, Halton County in 1845, has lost its original glazing bars to the blandishments of the traveller in stained glass, and has acquired an inconsequential belfry so that its pristine charm is best evaluated in a restoration drawing.

West Dumfries Wesleyan Chapel, Brant County, retains the elegant spider web of its Regency window muntins, but its original door was replaced by the Italianate school of improvers who installed a turned communion rail and scroll-ended benches in its little inside (X-47). The cobblestone work of the West Dumfries Church walls presents an excellent case study of the craft which had its most comprehensive North American run on the other side

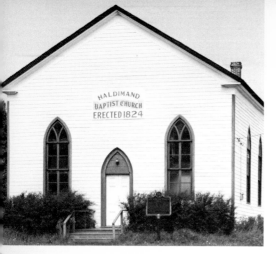

*X-42: Surviving clues — a roof-pitch and a date (X-42 top). Arrested time (X-43 middle). A question of bonding (X-44 bottom).*

of Lake Ontario, from Rochester to Buffalo. It was introduced into Brant County by Levi Boughton, late of Normandale, New York, who settled in Paris, Ontario in 1838. Cobblestone as a building medium has a limited range in Ontario. It is found in Brant County and a small segment of Hastings where suitable stones were kindly deposited by one of the major glaciations.

Dressed fieldstone was the more usual medium for vernacular church building, and was strikingly employed in a number of small interesting churches by builders whose sensitivity seems to have been commensurate with their trade skill. One of the best preserved little fieldstone churches in Ontario is St. Andrew's Presbyterian, Eversley, in York County (X-48), which served the spiritual needs of its surrounding community for little over a decade. It was closed in 1859, when a larger church was built in King, and thereafter it remained as a decorative mortuary chapel in its little churchyard. It was beautifully restored in its later years by Lady Eaton.

The basic vernacular box church form became as nearly Gothic as its nature would admit by the middle of the nineteenth century. The broad lancet form of the window openings, introduced in the Regency Gothic period, was now glazed with larger panes held in position by simple tracery of stronger construction. In its simplest form the building depended, for beauty of statement, on the integrity of its stonework and the pattern of its windows and overdoor. St. Andrew's, Kirkhill, as built by master-mason John Redpath in 1845 was such a church. Redpath went on to Montreal and a more lucrative career as a sugar importer in the West India trade, while St. Andrew's Free Church continued to serve its congregation in undiminished dignity for twenty years. Then the rival Church of Scotland congregation of St. Columba, Kirkhill built a tall spired church on the nearest hill, and some among the congregation of St. Andrew's began to be dissatisfied with the visual impact of their own church. Architectural alterations were not entered upon lightly, however, in the township of Lochiel, so that St. Andrew's was not endowed with its Georgian Revival porch and steeple (X-49) until 1918.

A somewhat similar chain of building circumstance seems to lie behind the present appearance of St. Paul's Evangelical Lutheran Church (X-50), which stands by an extremely dusty country road, south of Neustadt in Grey County. The local mason-builder arranged his material according to a personal or regional preference, concentrating the more highly coloured stone toward the centre of each wall surface and saving great blocks of light greyish stone for an informal quoining. An octagonal lantern and spire in the Ontario Lutheran form was added to this interesting little church some time after the building year, 1874, recorded in Deutsch Gothic lettering on its date stone.

*X-45: Tayside Baptist (X-45 above), a gable of Gothic height above a late Georgian door (left).*

*X-46 below: Diminutive Regency. St. Luke's Anglican, Palermo.*

X-47 above right: West Dumfries Methodist Chapel, Paris Plains.

X-48 above: St. Andrew's Presbyterian, Eversley, York.

X-49 right: St. Andrew's Free Church, Kirkhill, 1845. Porch and steeple, 1918.

Some comparatively early vernacular churches have been so lovingly altered inside and out that only a vestige remains to advise the uninitiated of their true significance. Such is the case with the First Baptist Church in Amherstburg. Its original name-board (X-51) alone reveals that this was one of the earliest churches in Ontario to house the worship of Afro-American Baptists as a free congregation. It was founded by a small community of people who had escaped from slavery in the United States by means of the Underground Railway, which had its main terminal in freedom in Chatham, Ontario.

The importance of Upper Canada's part in the drama of the Underground Railway has entered into Ontario legend. So much so, indeed, that it has become attached to some buildings on whose history it has no bearing whatsoever. One of these is the African Episcopal Church on Wilberforce Street north of Shanty Bay, in Simcoe County. The church was built in an area settled by veterans of the 1812 campaign. Many of them had been members of the Corps of Colour, raised in Niagara, which had served with distinction under Captain Runchey at Queenston and at Stoney Creek. The land granted to the rank-and-file veterans of 1812 seems to have been uniformly poor, whether it was in Simcoe or in Lanark – for service at Beaver Dams or at Waterloo. Its inhospitable nature was all too comparable to the difficult terrain which had been impartially bestowed on Loyalist veterans of all creeds and colours.

Military settlers' first places of worship tended, therefore, to be generally austere. The interior of the African Episcopal Church (X-52) retains to the present the forthright simplicity of accommodation which once confronted the majority of rural Upper Canadian worshippers in all the early meetinghouses in the province. Comfortable pews there undoubtedly were, but there were far more benches of this kind.

Years of painstaking research may one day uncover the names of all the builder-masons or master-joiners who planned the vernacular churches of Upper Canada. Unfortunately when that distant day dawns a great many of the little buildings themselves will have disappeared forever from our view. It is already difficult to determine which minute meetinghouse was in mind when William Tyrell of Weston drew its front and flank elevations, together with a plan of its simple foundations, on a sheet of paper now in the Rare Book section of the Robarts' Library, University of Toronto.

*X-50: St. Paul's Evangelical Lutheran, south of Neustadt.*

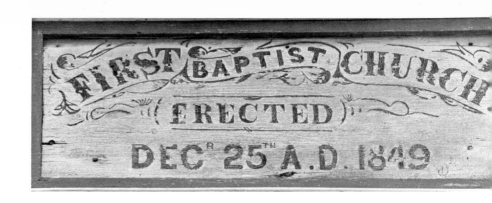

*XX-51 right: Freedom under the crown, Amherstburg.*

*X-52 below: An evocative little double-bench under the windows, for children grown and gone.*

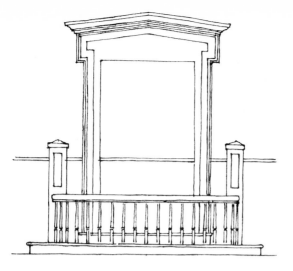

*X-53 top: Eared Greek Revival pulpit screen. Ellis Chapel.*

*X-54 bottom: Pilastered brick, Bethel Presbyterian, Middlesex County.*

*X-55: Ontario vernacular. Georgian, Regency and Gothic detailing, blended to taste and applied to a simple, well-built structure. St. Paul's Presbyterian, Halton County.*

*X-56: Shingles were thicker when the Nelson finial was cut in 1867.*

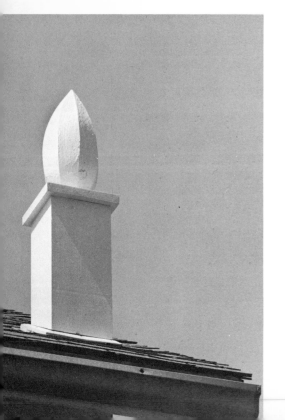

William Tyrell dated very few of the drawings which have come down to us bearing his signature, but some of them can be more easily related to existing buildings than the Robarts' Library chapel design. It may have been the drawing for the Ellis Chapel in Puslinch; it may equally have been intended for any one of a number of other places. The Ellis Methodist Chapel was certainly a diminutive building, and its flank wall is identical to that in the drawing, but it has a window on either side of the entrance doorway. In any case, the most distinctive feature of the Ellis chapel was internal – the eared Greek Revival trim which enframed a plaster panel – and, sabbatically, a minister – behind the pulpit (X-53).

Tyrell had emigrated from Kildare, Ireland, to Upper Canada in 1836 and had spent some time in trying to find his brother and a cousin who had preceded him to Canada. He finally located his brother, Edward, in Fredericksburg, and together they moved to Toronto where they opened a cabinetmaking shop. William Tyrell seems to have been either the more restless or the more ambitious of the two, as he soon forsook cabinetmaking for the building trade in Weston. In 1844 he built St. George's Anglican Church, Islington, in a manner so pleasing to its congregation that when they rebuilt it in brick in 1894, they reused the Tyrell belfry.

The vernacular box form, minus irrelevant belfries, could be converted to the Greek Revival style with astonishing ease. It was, in fact, hard to prevent such an occurrence, for the Greek temple – stripped of its columned portico – was nothing more nor less than a gable-roofed rectangular container. The Irish settlers along the Thames, in Middlesex, had a tendency to cloud the issue slightly by placing round-headed Tuscan windows in an otherwise basically Doric building (X-54), but on the whole the effect, as typified by Bethel Presbyterian Church – built midway between Arva and Birr in 1862 – was satisfying.

If it can be assumed that the style of most frequent occurrence among nineteenth-century churches in Ontario was the Gothic Revival, and if the gabled rectangular box represents the least common denominator of ecclesiastical form in that area, then it must follow that the archetypal vernacular church of Upper Canada and Canada West was a Gothic Revival gabled box building. A random choice of representative from a wide field of contenders could do no better than to cite St. Paul's Presbyterian, Nelson (X-55), in Halton County. Built in Confederation year and dedicated in the name of the apostle to the Gentiles, it has the proper basic shape. It was constructed in good sound brickwork, with well-cut stone quoins – for a reminiscent touch of Georgian building; good plain wooden Gothic mullions in its large, well-spaced windows; Regency wooden finials (X-56) to perk up the roof line. And, lest the true Goth feel slighted, it even boasts a buttress.

Brick was the common building medium for vernacular places of worship in the areas of older settlement when Canada West, née Upper Canada, entered Confederation as the Province of Ontario. But log was still the vernacular material in areas of later settlement (X-57), and would continue to be so for an appreciable time thereafter. Thus the story of ecclesiastical building in pre-Confederation Ontario ends where it began, with log construction in a different form but with identical purpose – to house the spiritual communion of a people with their God within simple hallowed walls.

*X-57: Madill Church.*

## Postlude

This last section attempts to add a graphic supplement to the text. The buildings built for worship in Ontario up to the mid-1880's are placed, by means of diagrams, in the stream of architectural history. Church design is subject to many influences which do not affect the design of houses, and some of these influences are shown graphically. There are also a few plans to show typical conditions, and some statistics.

We have spent six years in research. Our conjectures and conclusions are based on the evidence uncovered; later evidence may supplement our findings.

The purpose of this book is to induce readers to open their eyes and broaden their vision. If there are Anglican rectors in charge of early-nineteenth-century churches who do not believe their particular church ever had a central pulpit, let them lift the carpet and examine the floorboards. Perhaps it did. If there are Roman Catholic bishops ordering the destruction of high altars, let them pause; structures, as well as exhortation, have helped mankind toward that "peace of God, which passeth all understanding."

# A very brief story about church buildings

The plan for the early Christian church in Western Europe was taken from the ancient Roman *basilica* (1), a multi-purpose public building. This usually had a semicircular *apse* (A) in which stood a judge's chair and a symbolic altar upon which legal oaths were taken. There were several entrances to a basilica.

The Christian church used the apse for priest and altar (+), but elongated the plan (2) to give focus to the altar from an axial entrance. Additions were often made at the altar end where the action was. Churches requiring greater width than could be safely spanned by a wood truss (3) were divided into a central *nave* (N) and *side aisles* (S) by columns supporting arches which in turn supported a bearing wall for the roof. To light the nave, its roof could be raised to allow for an additional row of windows called a *clerestory* (C).

In the disturbed times of the early Middle Ages in Western Europe the great need was for fireproof masonry ceilings. These at first were stone-arched *barrel vaults* (4). Round-arched mediaeval styles are called *Romanesque*, as their inspiration was from Roman Imperial architecture.

In order to get more light *cross vaulting* (5) was developed. For ease of building such vaults in stone, the pointed arch was introduced and *ribs* (R) and transverse arches were erected as skeletons for the masonry infilling. Ribs and arches concentrated the weight of the stone vault and the wood roof, and tended to push walls outwards. To counteract this thrust *buttresses* (B) were built at right angles to the outer walls.

To carry the thrust downwards (6) the buttresses came to be heavily weighted at the roof line with stone *pinnacles* (P) and the buttresses were projected progressively outwards to contain this thrust.

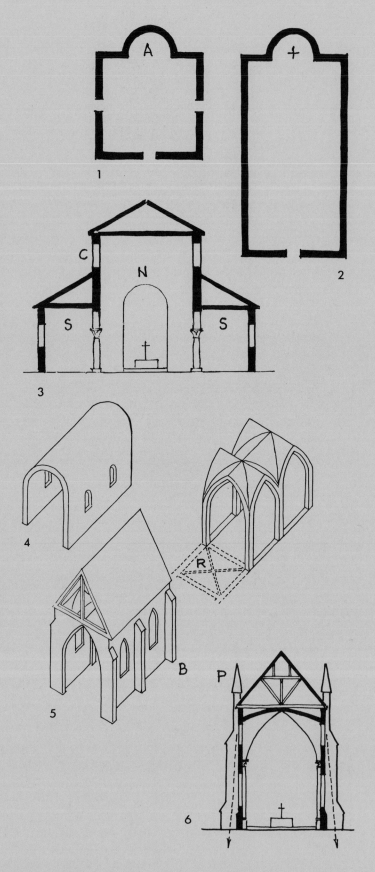

274

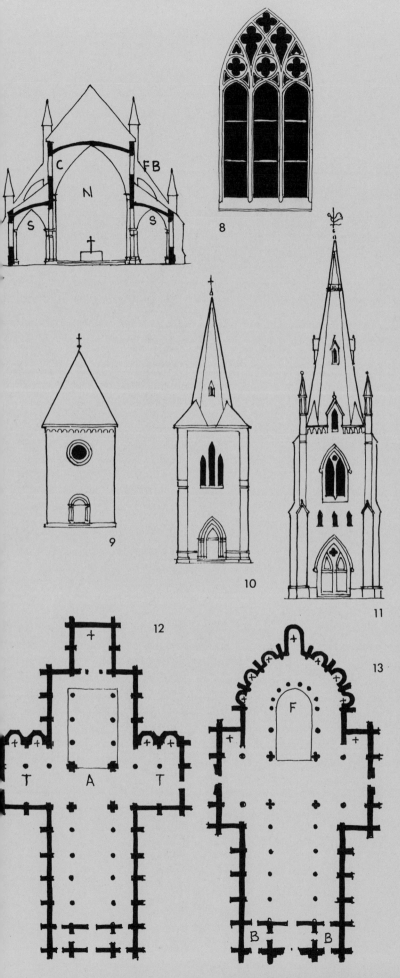

Churches requiring greater width than a stone-arched vault could span could also have nave (N) and aisles (S) and clerestories (C).

In such cases the thrust of the vaults was often carried on *flying buttresses* (FB). This pointed-arch system of engineering (6 and 7) eliminated the need for large areas of bearing walls, and immense glass windows could take their place.

Expanses of glass held together by lead *cames* needed a stone framework to hold them in place. This stonework eventually became a decorative *tracery* (8).

Towers in Romanesque churches were customary. They had little functional purpose except to hold bells. The earliest towers had pyramidal roofs.

With the lightness and height of the new style of pointed-arched churches, the pyramidal roofs of the Romanesque period became steeper (9). Then, to gain greater elegance, octagonal (10). Such roofs came to be called *spires* and in Western Europe were frequently built of stone and decorated with pinnacles and dormers (11). Tower walls were reinforced with buttresses. The pointed arch was never popular in Italy, however, and spires were unusual there.

The large mediaeval church plan of Western Europe became complex. Plans of a typical English great church (12) and a French great church (13) are shown.

In order to provide more space at the altar end and to give the plan the appearance of a cross, *transepts* (T) were added. In order to make better intercession with the saints, additional chapels with altars (+) dedicated to particular saints were added.

Towers were often at the crossing (A) or at the west end (B), while small spirelets or *flèches* above the high altar (F) were common in French churches.

275

## And a little about styles
## in Europe and Asia Minor

In Eastern Europe and Asia Minor the Christian church plan evolved from the architecture of Byzantium rather than from Rome. Hemispherical masonry domes were usual (1). At a later time bulbous-roofed towers became common in Eastern Europe (2), but the plan remained the same.

The pointed style of mediaeval Western Europe gradually disappeared in the social and political changes of the Renaissance, and came to be contemptuously termed *Gothic*. Renaissance society revived classical forms of architecture with round arches, Doric, Ionic and Corinthian columns, and ancient Roman moulding profiles.

The mediaeval church tower and spire were given classical form (3). The pointed arch was replaced with the round Roman arch. Geometry and proportionate relationship of spaces underlay design. The square, the circle and the *Golden Section* proportion ( − 5:8 − ) were regarded as the ideals.

Columns were applied flat to walls as *pilasters* (4) or free-standing as porticos (3). The Gothic basis of "decorated construction " in design was changed to "constructed decoration." Liveliness and curved lines were characteristic of churches built in the *rococo* style (5).

The basic church plan with the high altar (+) as the main focus and subsidiary altars (A) as lesser foci, was not greatly modified until the Reformation. Reformed churches gave pre-eminence to the pulpit (P) and avoided architecture which attempted to involve emotion. Many Reformed churches abolished altars altogether (6) and installed simple tables for the "Lord's Supper," or left space (S) for tables to be set up.

Upper Canada was opened for settlement in the late 1780's and the buildings of all denominations at this date were Classical in style. Differences in structure and in architectural feeling or style related to the differences in the liturgy of the denomination and the architectural tradition of the country of origin of the worshipper.

1. Cathedral at Bagarem, Armenia, 624
2. Church at Bogolyobo, Ukraine, 1614
3. St. Martin-in-the-Fields, London, 1722
4. Il Gesu, Rome, 1568
5. San Carlo alle Quattro Fontane, Rome, 1640
6. Scots' Kirk, Rotterdam, 1697

276

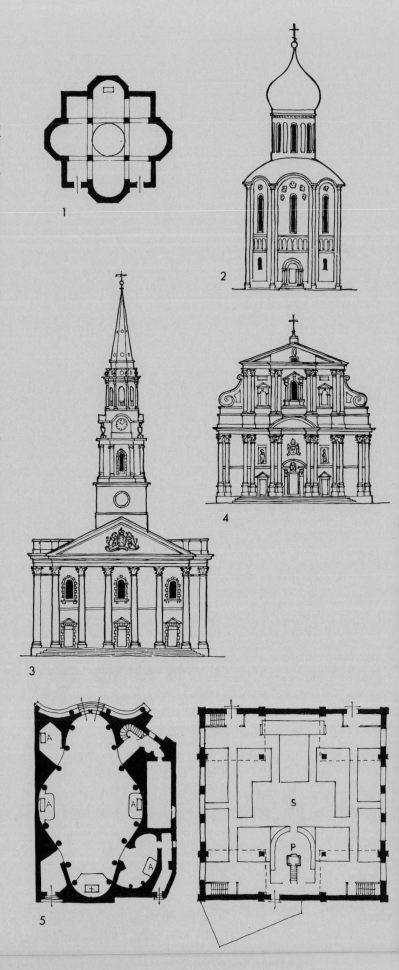

# Upper Canada begins

*Plans for the support
of the clergy in Upper Canada*

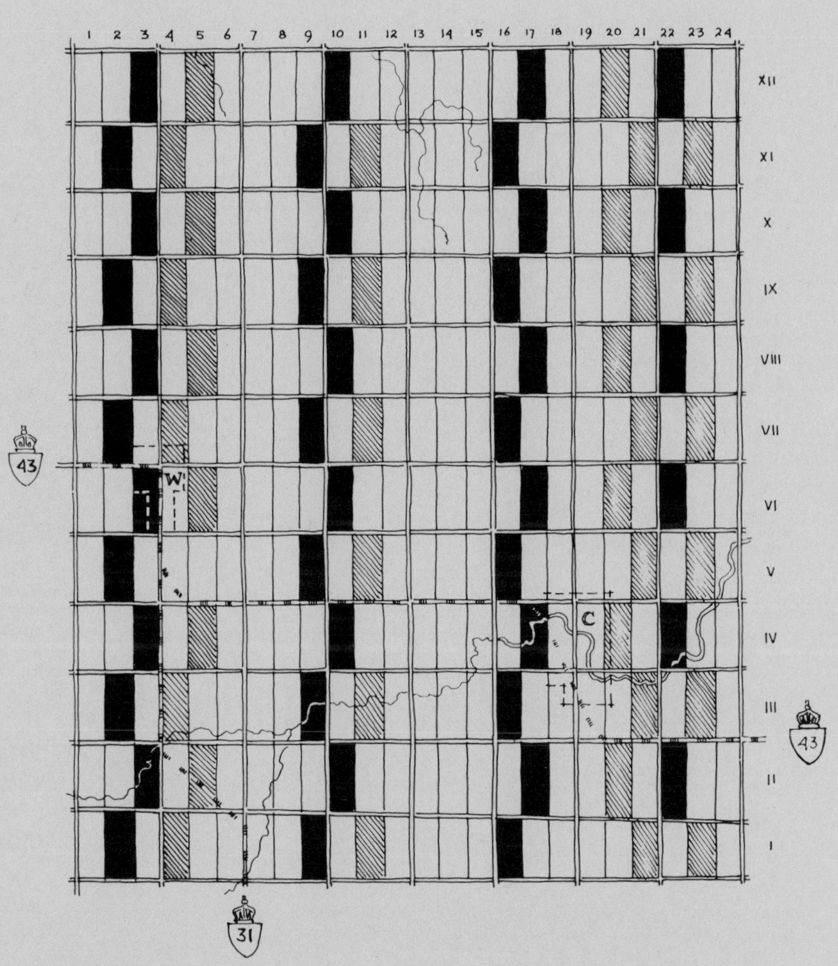

*Winchester Township 1800*

■ **CLERGY RESERVE**

▨ **CROWN RESERVE**

Upper Canada was laid out for settlement in conformity with a regional plan of development. Wilderness was surveyed into townships which were subdivided into bands or "concessions" which were cut at right angles by "lines." Between each concession and at each line was a 60-foot road allowance. Between the road allowances were lots for settlement. These lots were granted free by the Crown to those who would clear the roads of trees and start to develop the land.

Part of the government plan was to reserve lots until they could be sold or rented and so provide revenues to the Crown. One-seventh was reserved for "the support of a Protestant clergy," one-seventh for the Crown. Revenues did accrue; in

1832 sales brought in £15,132. But two million acres of undeveloped land inhibited settlement. There was also the problem of equitably distributing funds to "a Protestant clergy." In 1854 the scheme was abandoned.

The earliest "reserved" land was held in isolated blocks, but this system was superseded by chequerboard reservations of lots. The map shows Clergy and Crown Reserves in 1800 in the Township of Winchester, one township inland from the St. Lawrence River. (C) and (W) indicate the sites today of the town of Chesterville and the village of Winchester. The river is the South Nation. Today's highways are also shown.

277

## Upper Canada begins

*Influential buildings outside the province*

Without benefit of architects early buildings for worship were constructed by craftsmen (advised by laymen and clergy) in the traditions of the particular church to which they had belonged in their home country. Some buildings which may have influenced these craftsmen are shown.

The Church of Rome had the longest traditions in Western Europe but was a suppressed church in Britain where so many of its earliest Upper Canadian adherents came from. Therefore, the earliest influence on Roman Catholic church buildings came from Quebec. (1)

The United Church of England and Ireland (as it was called until 1871) had traditional church building styles in both British North America and in England. The only Anglican church of any stature actually seen by John Strachan before he became Archdeacon of York was the Cathedral at Quebec City, which echoed the Neo-Classic style in vogue in Britain. (2)

The Church of Scotland had several traditional plans which the Scots brought with them to North America. The focus of all plans, whether rectangular, T-shape, or square, was the pulpit. The earliest post-Reformation church in Scotland — at Burnt Island (3) — had a square plan and a private "laird's loft" with outside stair.

278

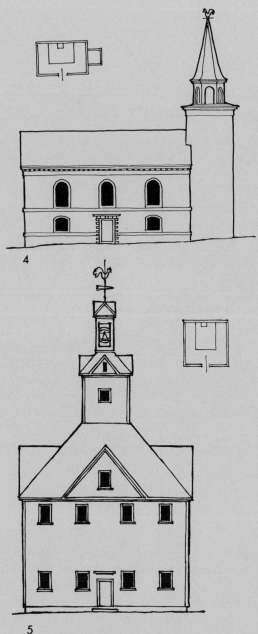

Loyalists from the Mohawk Valley in New York State would have remembered home churches, some of which had been burned in the Revolution. The plan for all Protestant congregations, English-, German-, and Mohawk-speaking, was similar — with a door on the long side of a rectangle opposite the pulpit. The Dutch Reform Church at Schoharie (4) was made of stone and fortified against Loyalists. After the war the names of Loyalist families which had helped to build it were chiselled off.

Congregationalists, the inheritors of the English Puritan tradition, remembered the meetinghouses (5) in the North American communities from whence they came.

Early Upper Canadian Methodist congregations could get inspiration from American meetinghouses (5), but British Methodists could refer more easily to John Wesley's church in London (6) which was copied in Montreal.

Baptists, Quakers, Mennonites and Dunkards had their own traditional attitudes toward the functional design of their places of worship in Upper Canada. Other denominations and other religions, negligibly represented among the population up till the date of Confederation, included the Greek Orthodox and Jewish faiths.

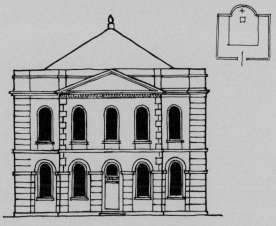

1. St. Laurent, Roman Catholic, Ile d'Orleans, Quebec, 1695
2. Anglican Cathedral, Quebec City, 1804
3. Burnt Island, Fife, Scotland, 1592, Belfry 1749
4. "Old Stone Fort," Schoharie, N.Y., 1772
5. West Springfield, Mass., 1702
6. John Wesley's Chapel, London, 1778

**The reason for the Oxford Movement
and the Methodists
and the Ecclesiologists
and the Gothic Revival**

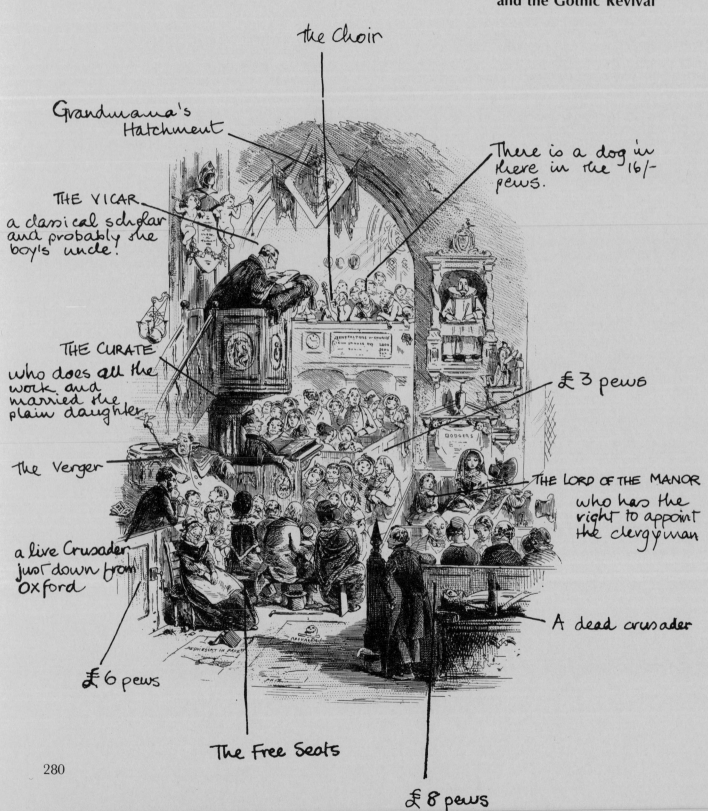

the Choir

Grandmama's Hatchment

There is a dog in there in the 16/- pews.

THE VICAR
a classical scholar and probably the boy's uncle!

THE CURATE
who does all the work and married the plain daughter

£ 3 pews

The Verger

THE LORD OF THE MANOR
who has the right to appoint the clergyman

a live Crusader just down from Oxford

£ 6 pews

A dead crusader

The Free Seats

£ 8 pews

An illustration from a Dickens' novel is used to illustrate an English Sunday morning church interior in 1830. The Protestant Reformation had brought the minister out from the chancel into the midst of his people. He had, however, by the eighteenth-century become separated from them by an immensely high pulpit, and, of course, by the class system. The altar in this illustration is of so little consequence that it is not shown.

In 1830 the Church of England was both lethargic and complacent; but Methodism was making serious inroads and the growing industrial cities lacked adequate church facilities. In the late 1830's a revitalization began that was to completely alter the scene portrayed. It was a revitalization that affected Upper Canada also.

The leaders in the nineteenth-century reformation of Church of England structures were the members of the Cambridge-based Ecclesiologist Society, which recommended the church at Long Stanton, Cambridgeshire (1250) as the ideal small rural parish church — a model for the North American builder. Prior to 1830 the chancel of the Long Stanton church had been curtained off and a fireplace installed so that the east end could be used as a school. The pulpit was located in the old nave as in the meetinghouse plan. (+) and (P) indicate the location of altar and pulpit before the Gothic Revival and + and P indicate their position after the change in the 1840's. Details derived from Long Stanton are found in many churches in Ontario.

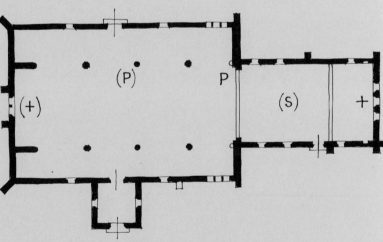

*"Do this in remembrance of me"*

## The Communion Place as a plan determinant

Some form of re-enactment of Christ's Last Supper has formed part of the liturgy of every Christian sect. The Protestant Reformation attempted to dispel the mystery which had come to surround the sacrifice of the mass, and the communal partaking of bread and wine was variously arranged by the Protestant denominations. The Reformation had also made the pulpit the focus in preference to the altar, and encouraged greater congregational participation. This altered the plan of non-Roman Catholic churches in Western Europe.

### For Anglican Churches

In Upper Canada during the nineteenth century the Lord's Supper was variously administered by different denominations, and within each denomination custom changed. With changed customs came changed plans. The greatest change in church architecture and in liturgical layout took place in the Church of England. It occurred as a result of the High Church movement, which succeeded in demoting the pulpit, in increasing the frequency of communion-taking, and also in introducing the Gothic Revival style. This evolution is illustrated by diagrams, in which P indicates the pulpit, D the desk or lectern, + the altar or communion table, V the passage to the vestry, and C the choir space.

Anglicans have always taken communion in two kinds, bread from a paten and wine from a chalice or cup served by a minister to communicants kneeling on a step in front of a rail. At St. George's Church, Saint Catharines (1819) the communion table was to one side. At Tyrconnel (1827) it was behind a central pulpit. At St. Paul's, Woodstock (1834) the table was given pride of place. In the modification (1835) of St. George's at St. Catharines, there was, for a time, a circular altar. At Christ Church, Vittoria, (1845) the plan is very similar to that of St. Paul's, Woodstock, except for the shape of the step.

At the early St. Paul's, Toronto (not shown) the pulpit was on rails and could be pushed to the side at communion times. At Trinity Church, Colborne (1845), a Regency Gothic church, the table, given a recess, became an undoubted altar, while the communion rail ran across the full width of the building.

At Christ Church, Tyendenaga (1843), a Gothic Revival church, the architect designed a raised chancel to hold an altar. The later St. Thomas' Church in St. Thomas (1870) had another form of raised chancel and the pulpit was relegated to a corner.

Until the late 1850's most Church of England choirs remained in the gallery at the back. Mediaeval churches did not, however, have rear galleries; therefore Gothic Revivalists deplored them. At St. George's, Guelph (1869), the choir (C) in this fully Gothic church was brought down and placed at the altar end.

The final Anglican solution, which remained almost unchanged for seventy-five years, is shown at St. James', Stratford (1869). Here a deep chancel with an altar placed in a sanctuary was constructed. This necessitated a divided choir. Gradually, improved forms of organs accompanied choirs wherever they were located.

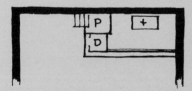

1819, St. George's, St. Catharines

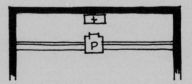

1827, St. Peter's, Tyrconnell

1834, St. Paul's, Woodstock

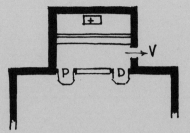

1843, Christ Church, Tyendenaga

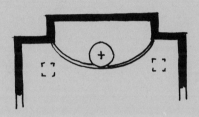

1835, St. George's, St. Catharines

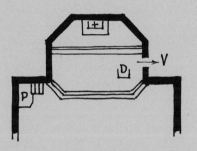

1870, St. Thomas' Church, St. Thomas

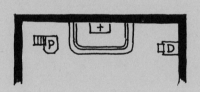

1845, Christ Church, Vittoria

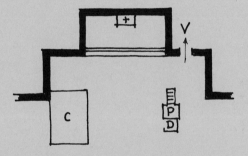

1869, St. George's, Guelph

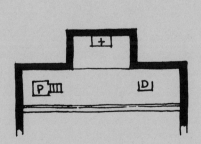

1845, Trinity Church, Colborne

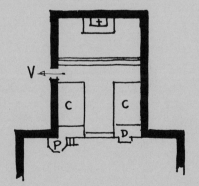

1869, St. James', Stratford

283

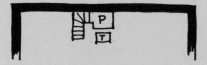

1809, Conger Meetinghouse

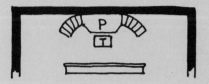

1832, Beaver Dams

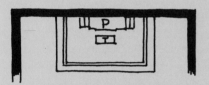

1867, Fitzroy Harbour

## For Methodist Churches

Until the 1870's, the Methodists took communion kneeling, as was done in the Church of England. During the nineteenth century the pulpit was always given pride of place. Diagrams illustrate the changes in the Methodist arrangement of pulpit (P), communion table (T), choir (C), and the kneeling step and rail.

In the Conger Meetinghouse (1809), no evidence is left of a kneeling step, and the pulpit is high. At Beaver Dams (1832) there was a kneeling step and rail. At Fitzroy Harbour (1867) there was the Methodist layout common in smaller churches during the 1850's and 1860's, with a wide pulpit on a raised platform and a table at a lower level in front— all within a railed step.

At Troy (1873) there was an apse with a large sofa on a raised pulpit platform. The choir at Troy was brought down and placed beside the step in the 1880's. The St. Paul Street Methodist Church, St. Catharines (c.1878) illustrates a very common late-nineteenth century arrangement: a centrally-placed choir above the pulpit platform with an ornamental organ (O) behind it. Communion rails were removed after congregations began taking communion while seated in their pews.

1873, Troy

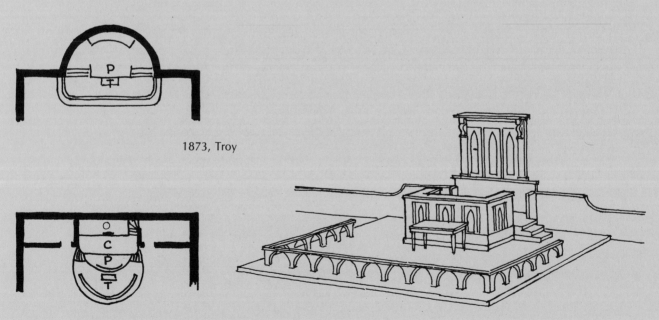

c.1878, St. Paul Street Methodist, St. Catharines

Fitzroy Harbour

## For Presbyterian Churches

The Presbyterian custom in Scotland, which was brought to Upper Canada, was to take communion seated at a table served by minister and elders. In early times or in primitive conditions, the table was set in the open air. Within a church a table (or tables) was set up in various ways as required. A common early plan was to rail off a space for the table in front of the central pulpit. Entry to this space was often controlled by gates, and persons whom the congregation felt had not led a disciplined life could be excluded. The space usually had a seat for the elders.

The Presbyterian Church was the Established Church in Scotland, and Scots ministers in Upper Canada tended to seek the privilege of a vestry with a private pulpit stair not visible to the congregation. In such plans access to the pulpit was from a door at the back.

A wide communion aisle was common in Scotland and Holland, but evidence of one in Upper Canada is at present lacking. These diagrams show Upper Canadian practice. P indicates pulpit, D the desk for precentor, or leader of the singing, G gates in the railed-off communion space, S the location of seats, V the vestry or minister's study.

Diagrams show the plans of communion places at Niagara-on-the-Lake (1831) where a private stair existed, and at Thorah (1840) where it did not. The communion space at Niagara was once larger than it is now. Both these buildings are Classical churches.

St. Paul's, Hamilton, (1854) is Gothic. There is no present evidence of the Hamilton communion space having been railed, but an extension was built behind the pulpit in 1909 and a centrally located choir installed behind the pulpit.

St. Andrew's, King Street, Toronto (1876) is Norman. Diagram shows original layout designed for the late-nineteenth-century practice of serving communion in individual cups to persons seated in their pews.

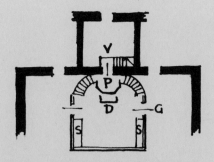

1831, Niagara-on-the-Lake

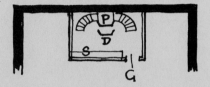

1840, Thorah

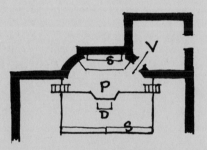

1854, St. Paul's, Hamilton

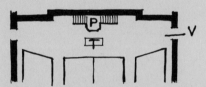

1876, St. Andrew's, King St., Toronto

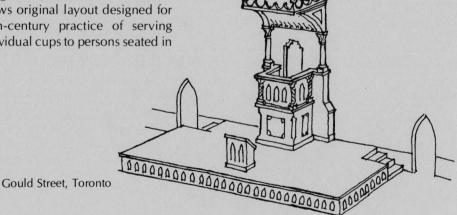

Gould Street, Toronto

285

*The Gothic Revival*
*English mediaeval periods with Ontario examples*

The style of architecture in which churches came to be built in Upper Canada followed trends in the English-speaking world. The most revolutionary architectural movement in any denomination was the revival of the Gothic styles of English mediaeval architecture. This revival of a "Christian style" began in the Church of England and was part of a nineteenth-century revitalization of that Church. The educated Anglican had a working knowledge of the four Gothic "periods."

Roman Catholic bishops supported the Gothic Revival, as pre-Reformation churches were obvi-

ously Roman, but the Ultramontanists of the late nineteenth century encouraged Roman Catholics to go back to the Roman basilicas for style inspiration. Methodists, Presbyterians and Baptists for a time succumbed to Gothic Revival fervour but eventually repudiated it and tried out other Revival styles. Mennonites, Quakers and other "plain people" scorned "steeple houses" as frivolous display.

Most small Ontario churches are vernacular and hard to classify stylistically, which is part of their charm.

## NORMAN ROMANESQUE PERIOD, 1066-1200

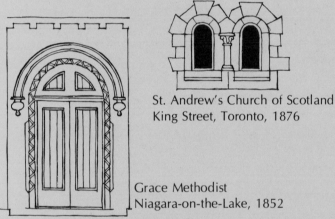

St. Andrew's Church of Scotland
King Street, Toronto, 1876

Grace Methodist
Niagara-on-the-Lake, 1852

## EARLY ENGLISH PERIOD, 1200-1300

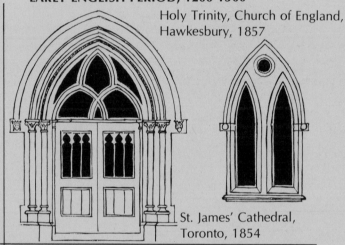

Holy Trinity, Church of England,
Hawkesbury, 1857

St. James' Cathedral,
Toronto, 1854

## DECORATED PERIOD, 1300-1400

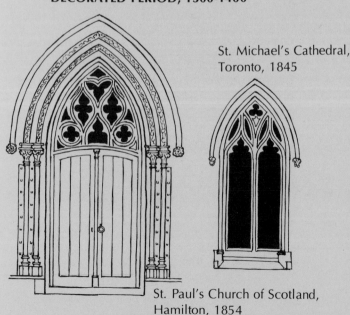

St. Michael's Cathedral,
Toronto, 1845

St. Paul's Church of Scotland,
Hamilton, 1854

## PERPENDICULAR PERIOD, 1400-1500

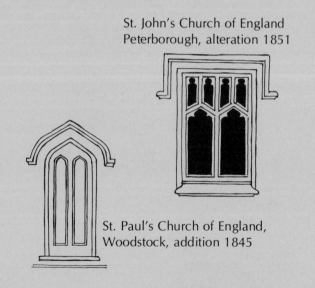

St. John's Church of England
Peterborough, alteration 1851

St. Paul's Church of England,
Woodstock, addition 1845

*Some examples of provincial styles in Upper Canada and Ontario*

## GEORGIAN

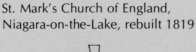

St. Mark's Church of England, Niagara-on-the-Lake, rebuilt 1819

St. Paul's Church of England, Woodstock, 1834

## NEO-CLASSIC

White's Methodist, Bayside, 1841

Christ Church, Church of England, Vittoria, 1845

## REGENCY GOTHIC

Church of England, St. Thomas, 1824

Trinity, Church of England, Colborne, 1845

## ITALIANATE

Baptist, Winchester, 1868

Wesleyan Methodist, Guelph, 1855

## GREEK REVIVAL

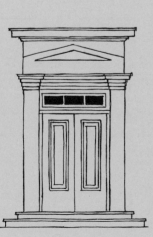

Bond St. Baptist, Toronto, 1848

Wesleyan Methodist, Vienna, 1845

## PAPAL BASILICAL

St. Simon & St. Jude Belle River, 1868 Roman Catholic,

St. Paul's Roman Catholic, Power St., Toronto, 1887

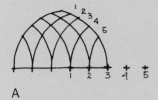

A

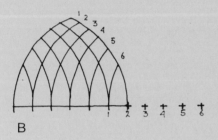

B

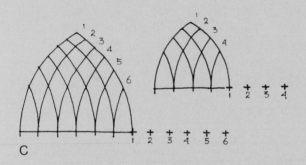

C

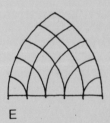

E

F

## The Interlace of glazing bars

The upper portion of a round-headed Georgian window had sash with radiating glazing bars. Panes below were rectangular.

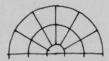

When the pointed arch became popular, the glazing bars in the head of the window were made to interlace, while the panes below remained rectangular. In Ontario interlacing glazing bars, introduced during what has been called the Regency period, became extremely popular, and were common from about 1830 to 1875 in vernacular churches of all denominations. In architect-designed churches the interlace was later discarded in favour of correct Gothic tracery, usually in wood, in the style of one of the periods of Gothic architecture shown on page 287.

The interlace may be categorized. In types A, B, C and D, the radius for the curved profile of the glazing bars remains the same, while the compass "centres" move outward along the line of the springing of the arch, in distances equal to the width of a pane. In type E the radius contracts and the centres remain at the edges of the sash. In Early or Regency Gothic style windows, two in type A and one in type B of the centres are located within the frame. This results in a lower pointed arched opening.

Type C is the most common in Ontario. Type F is occasionally seen in the cheaper carpenter's-Gothic chapels. Type G, common in Regency Britain and Ireland, was seen occasionally in Upper Canada, particularly in windows of the architect J. G. Howard. An example of his designs is shown in Type H. Many examples of interlacing bars in sash of varying widths exist. Identified with each diagram is a church in which a window of this particular type may be seen.

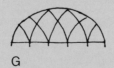

G

H

There exists in the archives of the Church of the Assumption in Windsor a glazing diagram and specifications for the glass panes for installation in the nave window sash, prepared by the architect in 1834. A facsimile of this diagram is shown to illustrate type D—a variant of type C.

In early windows the glazing bars were made as thin as possible for the sake of elegance in the interlace. Wide windows with thin glazing bars required for strength a wider central wooden mullion. This mullion bifurcated in the head of the sash, as shown. The lower portion of the sash could be raised for ventilation. It will be noted that there were eleven different-shaped panes with curved edges (A to K) cut from different-sized panes. The rectangular panes below were 8″×12″, although cheaper panes, 7″×9″, were more common at this date. (Larger pane sizes did not become readily available until later in the century.)

A double example of type E may be seen at Chippawa, designed by J. G. Howard.

All early glass was clear. As the century progressed, patterned, tinted and full-colour stained glass, with figures, came into fashion. In some churches the clear panes were whitewashed and a pattern scratched in the lime coating.

TYPE A— St. Thomas, Anglican, St. Thomas, 1824
TYPE B— St. Mary Magdalene, Anglican, Picton, 1834
TYPE C— St. Alexander, Roman Catholic, Lochiel, 1851
   — St. Paul, Lutheran, Erbsville, 1877
TYPE D— Church of the Assumption, Windsor, 1843
TYPE E— St. Andrew's Presbyterian, Lancaster, 1855
TYPE E'— Holy Trinity, Chippawa (1840)
TYPE F— Knox Presbyterian, Port Sydney, 1885
TYPE G— St. John's, Sandwich, 1819
TYPE H— Snake Island, 1842

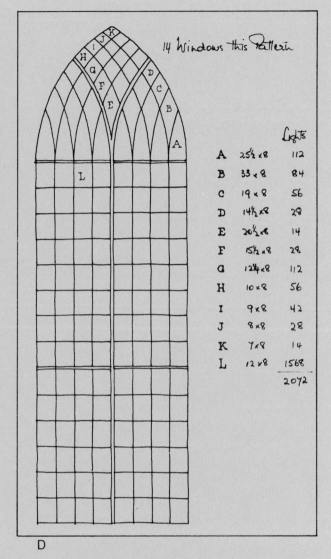

14 Windows this Pattern

| | | Lights |
|---|---|---|
| A | 25½ × 8 | 112 |
| B | 33 × 8 | 84 |
| C | 19 × 8 | 56 |
| D | 14½ × 8 | 28 |
| E | 20½ × 8 | 14 |
| F | 15½ × 8 | 28 |
| G | 12¼ × 8 | 112 |
| H | 10 × 8 | 56 |
| I | 9 × 8 | 42 |
| J | 8 × 8 | 28 |
| K | 7 × 8 | 14 |
| L | 12 × 8 | 1568 |
| | | 2072 |

D

E

289

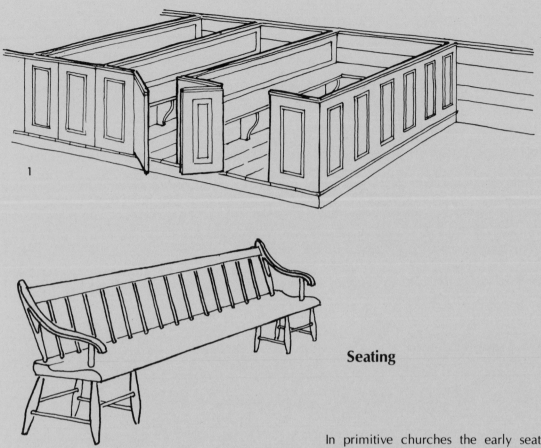

1

2

## Seating

In primitive churches the early seats were backless benches. As congregations became organized a maintenance budget became essential. To raise revenues most congregations of the major denominations arranged the construction of pews for sale or rent. Space for free seats was left at the back, in side galleries, or in a wide central passage.

The most desirable pews offered for sale were "box-pews," small wooden domains with seats on two, three or even four sides. These could be sufficiently large to hold tables, cushions and foot warmers, and all had doors. More convenient pews were slip pews, with or without doors, where worshippers faced in one direction. Most churches combined the two kinds. Pew plans carefully maintained in church records to show rents due are often the only evidence of original seating layouts.

Sketches show a small box pew and two slip pews somewhat in the manner of St. James', Maitland (1). Windsor benches, often referred to in the United States as deacons' benches, (2) were frequently used, and still exist as broken remnants in galleries and basements. In Holy Trinity, Toronto, where all seats were free, such benches were the first form of seating.

An undated pew plan (3) from Burritt's Rapids shows pews which were sold for a capital sum to help defray the cost of construction in 1831.

### Pew plan (3)

| Clergyman | | | £15 |
|---|---|---|---|
| £20 | | £20 | |
| £25 | | £16.10.0 | |
| £20 | | £16.10.0 | |
| £10 | | £18.5.0 | |
| £12 | | Reserve | |
| £11 | | £1.15.0 | |
| Free | | £1.15.0 | |
| £1.5.0 | | 16s | |
| Reserve | | 16s | |
| Vestry Rm | | Stairs | |

3

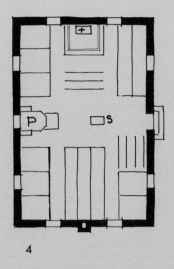

4

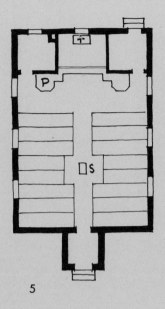

5

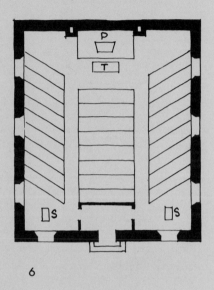

6

Some pre-1825 churches were almost square in plan and the seats were arranged as they best could be, to face toward the pulpit. An example of this is shown (4) — a conjectural diagram of the seating first set up in 1795 for St. John's Anglican, Bath. For churches with pulpits at the narrow end of a rectangular plan, the most common form of seating was parallel, as shown in the Ryerse Memorial Church at Port Ryerse (5).

With some denominations the seats at the side were built at an angle, so as to better face the minister. An example is the Presbyterian church at Camden East (6).

With the invention of wood lamination, curved seats became available in the late 1860's, and often replaced earlier pews, as at Grace Methodist, Niagara-on-the-Lake (7). The church which still contains the greatest number of box pews is probably the first St. Thomas' in St. Thomas, shown on page 117.

In the diagram 4 to 6, (P) indicates the location of a pulpit, (+) an altar, (T) a communion table, and (S) a stove.

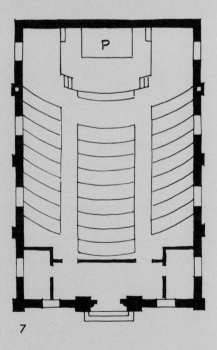

7

# Variety in pew ends

**Early or Primitive**

1
2
3
4
5
6

**1840-1860**

7
8
9
10

**1860-1880**

17
18
19
20

**1880-1890**

28
29
30
31
32

1. Providence Church, Upper Canada Village
2. River Brethren, South Easthope
3. African Episcopal, Edgar
4. Baptist, York Mills
5. Conger Meetinghouse, Picton (Methodist)
6. Quaker Meetinghouse, Newmarket
7. St. Alban's, Ottawa (Anglican)
8. St. James' Cathedral, Toronto (Anglican)
9. St. Alexander's, Lochiel (Roman Catholic)
10. St. Anthony of Padua, South Easthope
11. St. Peter's, Tyrconnell (Anglican)
12. Christ Church, Campbellford (Anglican)
13. St. Thomas', Shanty Bay (Anglican)
14. St. James-on-the-Lines, Penetanguishene (Anglican)
15. "Layer Cake" church, Bath (Presbyterian)
16. Holy Trinity, Hawkesbury, (Anglican)
17. Holy Trinity, Toronto (Anglican)
18. St. Paul's, Hamilton (Presbyterian)
19. Anglican Church, Dresden
20. St. John's, Jordan (Anglican)
21. St. Paul's Free Kirk, Bowmanville
22. St. Andrew's, King St., Toronto (Presbyterian)

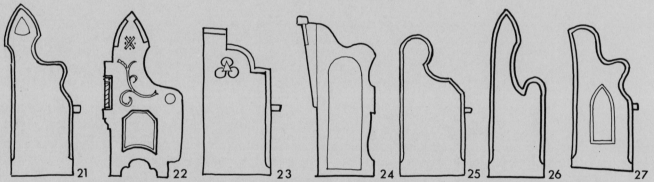

23. St. Bartholomew's, Ottawa (Anglican)
24. Zion Lutheran, Heidelberg
25. Baptist Church, Aylmer
26. Bishop Cronyn Memorial Church, London (Anglican)
27. Bible Christian, Lindsay
28. Church of Our Lady Cathedral, Guelph (Roman Catholic)
29. (metal) Knox Free Presbyterian, Perth
30. Catalogue of Rathbun Lumber Co.
31. Catalogue of Rathbun Lumber Co.
32. St. Mary's, Chesterville (Roman Catholic)

## Goths or Vandals

As the colony grew, all of its churches continually underwent extension, and most Georgian and Regency churches, if they were not either burned or pulled down, were Gothicized after 1850. To make a round-arched opening in a brick wall into a pointed opening left scars, and several Gothicized Georgian churches were therefore stuccoed. Round-arched Georgian window openings in stone churches were even harder to Gothicize, and a compromise was usually made by putting in "Venetian" or Italianate tracery to hold new stained-glass pictures. An example of extension and Gothicizing is shown in St. Paul's Anglican Church, Woodstock.

## Baptistries

The major denominations, with the exception of the Baptists, practised infant baptism by sprinkling water on the head of a child. Anglicans and Roman Catholics were encouraged to have fonts near the entrance of the church, signifying the entry of the child into the Church. Presbyterians were concerned with Congregational sponsorship, so children and adults were baptized from basins on or near the pulpit.

A major tenet of the Baptists, Anabaptists and Dunkards is the total immersion of adults at baptism in view of the congregation. In early times Baptists baptized in rivers or lakes, in the manner of John the Baptist, but later, especially in urban centres, a baptismal tank became the focal point of the interior, taking precedence even over the pulpit. A sketch shows the baptistry designed by Henry Langley for a church in Woodstock.

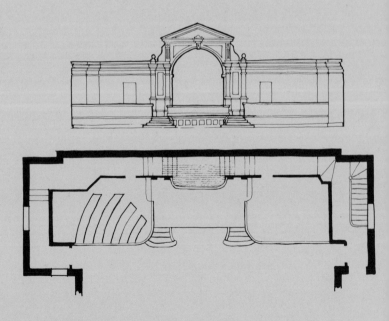

294

# The secular side

The single room of the North American meetinghouse was used for worship and education, and even for municipal administration. This Puritan system may have been brought to Upper Canada by Congregationalists and others but was certainly not general with Roman Catholics and Anglicans. Eventually additional space for Sunday Schools and for social occasions was universally required, and the secular side of the church found architectural expression. A great many small churches were raised and Sunday Schools were inserted in the basements. Some churches added school and social rooms at the back. The first synagogue in Ontario was built with school space on the lower floor. Many congregations, particularly the Anglicans, built parish halls. Some built a new church and used the old one as a parish hall. Some built a connecting link joining hall and church.

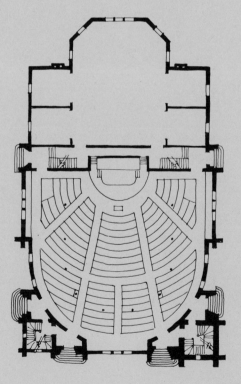

## The final solution

The final solution to the plan of a post-1870 church for Methodist, Presbyterian and Baptist was the Akron plan, which was first used for a church in Akron, Ohio. A typical Ontario example is shown in a plan prepared by Henry Langley for the Methodist Church at Woodstock. The Akron-plan church was usually dressed in Gothic garb, and accommodated much space for secular uses.

It was a plan not, however, used by Roman Catholic or Anglican congregations, whose final solution is shown on the following page.

The final nineteenth-century plan for a large Roman Catholic church is exemplified in that of St. Paul's Church, Power Street, Toronto. This was built in the Papal Basilical style with a central nave having arcades in the Ionic Order separating the nave from side aisles. Above the arcades were clerestories. The choir and organ were in a back gallery at the west. At the east end was a wide apse for the high altar and two side altars in small apses. Four confessionals were housed in projections off the nave. To the north of the west façade was a tall plain bell tower — the "campanile" of Italian architecture.

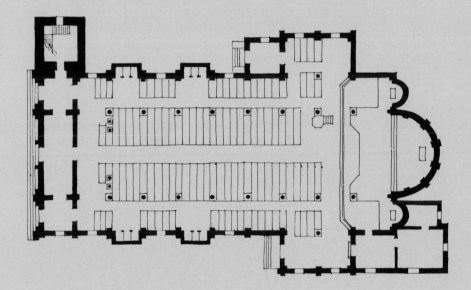

The final nineteenth-century plan for an Anglican church is exemplified in St. George's Church in Galt, also prepared by the architect Langley. It is the total Gothic Revival plan. There are side galleries and transepts. A chancel for the choir and clergy in front of the sanctury space for the altar. The west façade had a single Gothic tower.

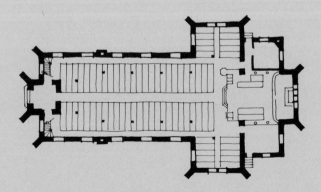

# Glossary

ALTAR TABERNACLE: a receptacle above the altar to contain the eucharistic Host

APSE: see page 297

ARCHITRAVE: lowest member of entablature

ARRIS: sharp edge formed by the meeting of two surfaces

ASHLAR MASONRY: squared stonework

ASTRAGAL: semicircular moulding

BARTIZANS: conical-roofed cylindrical turrets

BARREL VAULT: see page 274

BASILICA: see page 274

BATH STONE: yellow building stone found near Bath in Wiltshire

BATTLEMENT: a parapet with indentations

BELL-CAST: a curved roof profile flowing out at the eaves

BELL COTE: shelter for a bell

BELL LOFT: tower room containing bells

BLIND ARCADE, TRANSOM, ETC.: a line of arches, transom, etc. projecting slightly from a solid wall

BOSS: ornament at the intersection of ceiling ribs

BOX PEW: enclosed pew having seats on two or more sides

BROACH SPIRE: an octagonal spire rising without a parapet above a tower, with pyramidal forms at the angles of the tower

BUTTRESS: see page 274

CAMBER: flattened arch, usually segmental

CAMES: see page 275

CHAMFER: a bevelled corner

CHANCEL: the space reserved for clergy and choir

CHEVET: curved apse with radiating chapels

CLADDING: covering or surfacing

CLOCHER: belfry

CLERESTORY: upper stage in a building with windows above adjacent roofs; see page 274

COPING STONE: stone for protecting the top of a wall

CORBEL: masonry built out from a wall to support weight

CORBEL TABLE: plain piece of projecting wall supported by a range of corbels

CORNICE: the upper part of the entablature

CORONA: a crown, or the upper member of a cornice

CROCKET: a decorative carved floral ornament applied to steep gables in Gothic architecture

CROSS VAULTING: see page 274

CROW-STEPPED GABLE: stepped gable which affords perching place for birds

CUPOLA: a spherical roof covering a circular or polygonal form

CUSTODE: small cupboard in altar tabernacle

DRIP LABEL OR DRIP MOULD: moulding over heads of doors and windows to throw off rain

ENTABLATURE: the upper part of an Order of classical architecture comprising architrave, frieze and cornice

ENTASIS: a swelling or outward curve along the outline of a column shaft to counteract optical illusion

EPISTLE SIDE: side of chancel from which the Epistle is read

FENESTRATION: the architectural arrangement of windows and other openings in the walls of a building

FILLET: a small flat band

FINIAL: crowning detail of an architectural feature, particularly pinnacle, gable, etc.

FLECHE: a slender wooden spire arising from the roof

FLYING BUTTRESS: see page 275

FRIEZE: the middle part of the entablature

GABLE: the enclosing lines of a sloping roof

GOBLET PULPIT: polygonal pulpit on central support

"GROINING": in the context—vaulting

GOSPEL SIDE: side of chancel from which the Gospel is read

HARLED: roughcast

IN ANTIS: columns set between projecting walls finished with antas or pilasters

IN PLAN: shape or arrangement of horizontal plane

LABELS: see drip label

LITURGICALLY SITED: sited so that the congregation faces toward Jerusalem (usually east)

MULLIONS: vertical bars dividing windows into separate lights

MUNTINS: glazing bars

NARTHEX: entrance porch

NAVE: see page 274

NOGGING: a species of brickwork

OGEE ARCH: arch bounded by reversing curves

PARAPET: a low wall at the edge of a platform or above the roof-gutter

PATEN: a plate used for serving the bread or Host in a communion service

PEDIMENT: triangular piece of wall above entablature which fills in and supports a sloping roof

PILASTER: a column of rectangular section, engaged in the wall

PINNACLES: see page 274

PLINTH: stepped or moulded base of column or building

POPPYHEAD: ornamental finial

PORTICO: a colonnaded porch

PRESBYTERY: (arch.) the portion of the church reserved for the clergy or, (Ontario) priest's house

QUATREFOIL: panel divided by cusps (triangular projections) into four sections; see page 275, illus. 8

QUOIN: corner stone

RAKING CORNICE: cornice on the sloping side of a gable or pediment

REEDING: convex raised ornament, reverse of fluting

REREDOS: screen or ornamental work rising behind an altar

RETABLE: shelf or ledge behind altar for holding candles

RETURNED CORNICE: a short length of cornice perpendicular to an end of a longer cornice

RUBBLESTONE: walling stone not smoothed to give fine joints

SANCTUARY: the part of the church in which the altar is situated

SLIP PEW: a shallow enclosed pew having a single seat; see page 290

SOUNDING BOARD: structure over the pulpit to increase resonance

TEMPIETTA: small ornamental temple

TOISE: old French lineal measure, six French feet (6.395 English feet)

TRACERY: see page 275

TRANSEPT: see page 275

TRANSVERSE ARCH: see page 274

TRIFORUM: the space between the sloping roof over the aisle and the aisle vaulting

TUCK POINTING: filling masonry joints flush with mortar which is then grooved

TYMPANUM: the triangular space bounded by the cornice and raking cornices of the pediment

UMBRAGE: recessed sheltered space

VERGE BOARD OR BARGE BOARD: sloping board along edge of gable roof covering the roof timbers

VOUSSOIRS: truncated wedge-shaped blocks forming an arch

WEATHER BOARD OR CLAPBOARD: boards arranged to overlap horizontally on an exterior surface

# Acknowledgements

The authors and publisher are grateful to the following photographers and organizations for pictures reproduced in this work. Every effort has been made to ascertain the sources and to give due credit. Any oversight or error is inadvertent.

The Public Archives of Canada: II-4, VII-20, X-10, X-11

Archives of Ontario: IV-4, VIII-14, IX-6

The Archives of the United Church of Canada: III-20, VIII-11, X-41

Thomas Fisher Rare Book Library, University of Toronto: III-6, VIII-9

William L. Clements Library, Ann Arbor, Michigan: II-2

Collection of St. Andrew's Roman Catholic Church, St. Andrew's West, Ont: II-5

Royal Ontario Museum, Sigmund Samuel Canadiana Gallery: VIII-8

Metropolitan Toronto Library Board: I-13, IV-10, VI-30, VI-32, VI-33, VI-36, VII-13, VIII-10, IX-4, IX-5

Hiram Walker Museum, Windsor, Ontario: III-9, III-10

Archives of St. Paul's Presbyterian Church, Hamilton, Ontario: VI-5

Archives of St. James' Cathedral, Toronto: VIII-6, VIII-7

Collection of Marion MacRae: VI-34, VII-6

Photograph by Dorothy Taylor Studio: VI-26

Niagara-on-the-Lake Historical Society: VIII-2, VIII-4

Photographs by Philip Shackleton: I-11, III-25, III-25a, III-26, IV-20a, V-6, VI-18, VIII-21

Photographs by John A. Brebner: IV-15, IX-26

Photographs by John Willard: IX-11, IX-11a

Photograph by Anthony Adamson: I-1

Photograph by Marion MacRae: X-50

All other photographs by Page Toles

# Index

303